DOWN AND DIRTY
DOWN SOUTH

DOWN AND DIRTY
DOWN SOUTH

POLITICS AND THE ART OF REVENGE

Roger Glasgow

BUTLER CENTER BOOKS

LITTLE ROCK, ARKANSAS

The Butler Center for Arkansas Studies
Central Arkansas Library System
100 Rock Street
Little Rock, Arkansas 72201
www.butlercenter.org

First edition: March 2016

ISBN 978-1-935106-88-3 (hardcover)
ISBN 978-1-935106-89-0 (paperback)

Manager: Rod Lorenzen
Book and cover design: H. K. Stewart
Copyeditor/proofreader: Ali Welky

Library of Congress Cataloging-in-Publication Data

Names: Glasgow, Roger, author.
Title: Down and dirty down south : politics and the art of revenge / Roger Glasgow.
Description: Little Rock, Arkansas : Butler Center Books, 2016. | Includes bibliographical references.
Identifiers: LCCN 2015046454 (print) | LCCN 2016004950 (ebook) | ISBN 9781935106883 (hardcover : alk. paper) | ISBN 9781935106890 (pbk. : alk. paper) | ISBN 9781935106906 (e-book)
Subjects: LCSH: Glasgow, Roger. | Lawyers--Arkansas--Biography. | Political corruption--Arkansas--History--20th century. | Malicious accusation--Arkansas--History--20th century.
Classification: LCC KF373.G74 A3 2016 (print) | LCC KF373.G74 (ebook) | DDC 340.092--dc23

Printed in the United States of America
This book is printed on archival-quality paper that meets requirements of the American National Standard for Information Sciences, Permanence of Paper, Printed Library Materials, ANSI Z39.48-1984.

Butler Center Books, the publishing division of the Butler Center for Arkansas Studies, was made possible by the generosity of Dora Johnson Ragsdale and John G. Ragsdale Jr.

Her prophets are reckless, treacherous men.
Her priests have profaned the sanctuary.
They have done violence to the law.

Zephaniah 3:4

CONTENTS

PREFACE

The events set out in this memoir are true, and the people discussed are real. The account is based upon the author's recollections, notes, and memorabilia, as well as various newspaper articles, documents, and research.

The characters, times, happenings, and circumstances are accurate. However, as it is virtually impossible to recollect or reconstruct the actual words spoken long ago, much of the dialogue has been re-created to add interest as well as to help explain the actual events.

Roger Glasgow
2016

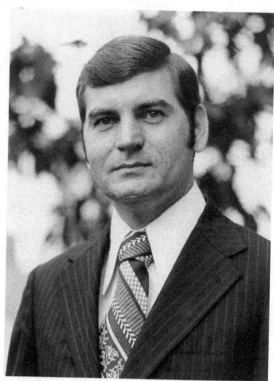

Roger Glasgow poses for a campaign photograph upon entering the race for Pulaski County prosecutor in 1972.

ACKNOWLEDGEMENTS

There are many people to thank for the realization of this work. First and foremost is my wonderful, beautiful, and exceedingly patient wife, Jennifer. This book would never have come together without the tireless hours she spent listening to my descriptions of events, ideas, and musings, plus her invaluable help in evaluating passages of writing and dialogue, as well as long periods devoted to correcting, editing, and organizing the material. Perhaps most of all I wish to express my gratitude for the generous lending of her skills to assist me in overcoming my grievous deficiencies with computers and other technical composition tools.

Also, I wish to thank my parents, Tom and Fern Glasgow, now deceased, and my seven siblings, who shared with me some of the joyous times recounted in this book, and unfailingly stood by me during the difficult ones.

Although my first wife, Jeannie, and I were divorced in the 1980s and she has since passed away, I would like to recognize the great debt I owe her for steadfastly standing by me during the ordeals recounted in this book.

In addition, I would like to express my deep gratitude to Ernie Dumas and Marvin Schwartz, without whose generous advice and assistance on all matters of format, style, editing, and illustrations, this work never would have made it to fruition.

The *Democrat-Gazette* generously allowed me to use photographs and other material from its archives. Ernie Dumas also allowed me use of George Fisher cartoons from his collection.

My ever dependable secretary, Kim Gaither, deserves a special note of thanks for sticking by me throughout this project, especially for her patient counsel and assistance concerning my sorely lacking skills with word-processing equipment.

I would also like to thank my publisher, Butler Center Books, especially Rod Lorenzen and David Stricklin, for their confidence in the project, Ali Welky for her excellent proofreading and editing, and H. K. Stewart for lending his expertise to the design of the book and cover.

I would be remiss not to remember my dog, Hershey, an eleven-year-old chocolate lab, who faithfully sat by my side during the considerable time I spent composing this story, except for those times when my papers got so spread out that it forced him off the couch. During those intervals, he removed himself to the floor or to a nearby easy chair and calmly endured until such time as I might interrupt my work and play "throw the stuffed duck" with him, or his favorite, "let's go out back and run around the house." Indubitably, a man's best friend.

People and Places

Roger Glasgow, author

Jeannie Glasgow, author's wife

Nashville, Arkansas

Tom Chesshir, author's friend and contemporary at
Southern Arkansas University (SAU)

Otis Eisenhower, city marshal

Tom and Fern Glasgow, author's parents

Fred Goacher, defendant in DWI case

Bobby Steel, circuit judge

Don Steel, author's former law partner

Royce Tallant, author's longtime friend

Lewis "Beef" Tollett, sheriff

Little Rock, Arkansas

Max Allison, political operative and author's campaign consultant

Sam Boyce, president of Arkansas Young Democrats and candidate for governor

Robert R. Brown, deputy prosecuting attorney and candidate for prosecuting attorney

Ben Combs, advertising executive

Judy Pryor Combs, TV personality with KATV, Channel 7

Allan Dishongh, lawyer and candidate for prosecuting attorney against Jim Guy Tucker

Phil Dixon, lawyer and head of "Attorneys for Glasgow"

Winslow Drummond, partner at Wright, Lindsey & Jennings law firm

John Fogleman, Arkansas Supreme Court associate justice

Dent Gitchel, lawyer and head of "Glasgow Defense Fund"

Harry Hastings Sr., businessman and reputed crime czar

Jim T. Hunter, owner of Delta Securities and author's political opponent

Robert Johnston, member of the Arkansas House of Representatives

Lee Munson, assistant attorney general and candidate for prosecuting attorney

Forrest Parkman, head of Little Rock Police Department (LRPD) Intelligence Unit

John Patterson, cab driver and police informant

Kenneth Pearson, head of the LRPD Vice Squad

W. R. "Witt" Stephens, Arkansas industrialist and banker

Tucker Steinmetz, reporter for the *Arkansas Gazette*

Ray Thornton, attorney general

Jim Guy Tucker, prosecuting attorney

Gale Weeks, chief of police

Mamie Ruth Williams, Ray Thornton's media director and author's campaign manager

George E. Wimberly, mayor and owner of Brice Drug Store

Edward L. Wright, senior partner at Wright, Lindsey & Jennings law firm

Magnolia, Arkansas (Southern Arkansas University–SAU)

Imon Bruce, president of SAU

William Nolan, professor at SAU and Arkansas Young Democrats faculty adviser

Fayetteville, Arkansas

Jim Hooper, author's law school classmate

Dean Grisso, administrative assistant to the law school dean

Robert A. Leflar, professor emeritus and former dean of the law school

Brownsville, Texas

Reynoldo Garza, U.S. district judge

Raul Gonzales, assistant U.S. attorney

Miriam Medley, U.S. customs agent

John Meharg, U.S. customs agent

Tom Sharp Jr., author's defense attorney

Earl Simmons, special investigator, U.S. Customs Service

John Vandiver, U.S. Customs Service investigator

Matamoros, Mexico

Juan Cortez, employee at Holiday Inn

Felipe Mayorquin, innkeeper at Holiday Inn

Political Figures

Dale Bumpers, Arkansas governor 1971–1975; U.S. senator 1975–1999

Bill Clinton, Arkansas attorney general 1977–1979; governor 1983–1992; U.S. president 1993–2001

Orval E. Faubus, Arkansas governor 1955–1967

J. William Fulbright, U.S. senator 1945–1974

Jim Johnson, Arkansas Supreme Court associate justice 1959–1966

Sid McMath, Arkansas governor 1949–1953

Wilbur D. Mills, U.S. congressman 1939–1977

David Pryor, Arkansas governor 1975–1979; U.S. senator 1979–1997

Joe Purcell, Arkansas attorney general 1967–1971

Winthrop Rockefeller, Arkansas governor 1967–1971

Part I

1. The Bridge

On the morning of August 25, 1972, my wife and I sat in our car as the line of traffic moved slowly forward toward the Gateway International Bridge at Matamoros, Mexico. Like many Americans coming back into the United States through that southern border crossing, we were looking forward to our return. A long drive across the flat plains of south Texas would bring us back to Little Rock. We were ready to put Mexico behind us, particularly after some disturbing events over the previous days at our Matamoros hotel.

The apprehension we felt was nothing I could specifically explain. But there was a gnawing discomfort in my neck and shoulders, as if I had been carrying a heavy backpack all day. I drummed my fingers on the Ford LTD's steering wheel as we inched forward, the traffic forming a single line as it approached the solo guard station in use that day. On the other side was Brownsville and the open road home.

As we drew closer, I could see a single U.S. customs official greeting every car with a series of questions. We were four or five cars back in the line, and I was impatiently estimating the time each car might need to get through the gate. I was really ready to get out of Mexico. The customs officer was a short, stocky woman whose brown uniform fit tightly on her barrel-shaped torso. She spoke the same words to each car, took their driver's identification, checked off a series of perfunctory questions, and sent each car through with an impersonal efficiency. I rolled down my side window, ready to slide through.

"Welcome to the United States," she said, stepping up to my open window. "Your driver's license, please."

I handed it to her and she examined it carefully.

"Why were you in Mexico?

"Vacation," I said, smiling.

"You are Mr. Glasgow?" she asked.

"Yes. I decided to take a vacation from shaving, too," I said, rubbing the scruffy new five-day beard I had grown. She didn't crack a smile, only looked at the license more intently, holding it in better light, adjusting her bifocals.

Finally, she said, "And this is Mrs. Glasgow?" pointing at Jeannie.

"Yes, it is," I said a little defensively.

"Where did you travel in Mexico?"

"We entered at Laredo, drove down to Monterrey, and back up to Matamoros," I said.

"Do you have anything to declare?" she asked.

"Some curios and souvenirs in the trunk, and two bottles of tequila, which we got in Matamoros," I answered.

"Have you been in contact with any animals, like out in a cow pasture or barn?"

"No."

"Any poultry, chickens, or the like?"

"Only to eat," I said, trying again to lighten the mood. She did not smile.

20

"Live poultry?" she emphasized with a stony look.

"No, sure haven't," I said.

"Do you have any fruits, vegetables, or other fresh produce?"

"No, we don't," I said, dropping all further attempts at humor.

"How long were you in Matamoros?" she asked.

"Two nights," I responded.

"What's in the ice chest?" she inquired, pointing toward the back seat.

"Ice," I said. Then, in response to her impassive glare, I added, "We're planning to get some sodas in Brownsville for the ride home."

"Pull over there," she said, pointing to a side ramp manned by another customs agent, a man with a no-nonsense expression.

I pulled over, and the agent asked me basically the same questions, leaving out the ones about animals and produce, but he also wanted to see my vehicle registration papers. I handed them to him, and he glanced at them briefly. Keeping the papers, he looked at me and said, "Would you both step out of the car, please?"

Unusual, I thought, but I knew it would not help matters to question his request. Jeannie and I got out of the car.

"Open your trunk," he commanded.

I complied, aware of the changed tone of his voice. The agent took a quick look around the inside of the trunk, which was crammed with our luggage and the numerous souvenirs we had bought, all wrapped in Mexican newspapers and taped up by the vendors who had sold them to us. Leaving the trunk open, the agent then walked over to a small building on the bridge that was part of the customs facility and summoned another male agent. They both came over to our car.

"Stand back, please," one of them said.

They opened the passenger-side door and pulled the seatback forward (our vehicle was a two-door hardtop). They removed the ice chest and began rummaging around the back seat.

In a moment, they had pulled the seat bottom loose from the floor attachments.

I could see through the opened door that they were pulling out an object from underneath the seat. The item was box-shaped and wrapped in newspapers. My attention was fixed on their actions and my mind was racing with silent questions. The wrapped item one of the agents now held in his hands was nothing I had ever seen before, a package I had neither bought nor placed under the car's rear seat.

The two agents looked grim, glanced at each other and nodded. A deep sense of dread came over me. I felt sure that something bad was about to happen.

The first agent walked over, gave me an icy stare, and said, "Mr. Glasgow, you are under arrest."

2. Freedom on the Line

The red-haired, fleshy woman in the tight-fitting customs agent uniform at the first booth, we later learned, was named Miriam C. Medley. In her testimony at the trial, Ms. Medley said she had decided our car deserved further attention, and based on that, she had directed us to the secondary inspection station. She said that some kind of "feeling" had come over her, specifying in particular the ice chest we had on the back seat ("strange for a nice car like that"), and she also mentioned the "McGovern for President" bumper sticker.

Without a doubt, the agents had been tipped off beforehand, not an infrequent occurrence at the border crossing. And a payoff was usually involved. The informers would usually be the same people who had placed the contraband in a car. Through this method, their cash profit would be gained in a far less risky manner than selling drugs on the street. These local entrepreneurs could work the system quite well. First, they would be helping some distant powerful friends by setting up the bust. Second, they would make the U.S. agents look good by delivering this easy score. Third, they would get paid for it. This was a sweet deal for everyone. Everyone except me, of course.

The whole episode, at the time, seemed surreal, like a slow-moving nightmare as I stood nearby, helpless. The two male agents at the secondary inspection station—John Meharg and his sidekick, Owen Crockett—wasted no time in locating the newspaper-wrapped package under the back seat. It was oblong, about the size of a brick, or perhaps a small loaf of bread, wrapped in Mexican newspapers and sealed with clear tape. They removed the whole seat bottom and flipped it upside down on a metal table. The entire cavity under the seat was crammed with similarly wrapped packages. Agent Meharg took a knife and sliced open the first package. It contained a greenish brown leafy substance. The distinct odor of marijuana was immediately present, the ripe smell overpowering the bridge's pervasive aroma of diesel exhaust.

Never in my life, before or since, have I been so abruptly stunned and dumbfounded. Something had gone terribly wrong. Someone had tampered with our car, and I felt quite certain it had something to do with the strange happenings at the Holiday Inn the day before. I knew we were in seriously deep trouble.

My lawyer instincts kicked in immediately, and I started re-questing, then insisting, that a fingerprint expert be brought in to see if the perpetrators' fingerprints could be lifted from the packaging. I further demanded that both Jeannie and I be allowed to submit to polygraph tests then and there, or anywhere else, to prove our innocence. I also fully realized the implication of what might happen if I was charged and convicted of drug smuggling. Everything that I was, everything I had striven for, everything I hoped to be, was on the line. Initially, I was of the opinion we were simply being used as couriers by unsavory drug smugglers in Mexico to transport their wares over the border without risk to themselves. They could retrieve the drugs from my car after it was safely across the border. From my participation in a drug policy conference two years earlier, I was aware that such things did happen.

Jeannie, surely the most innocent and unsuspecting soul of all time, was frantic with worry. She kept asking, "How did that stuff get in the car?" I kept telling her that someone must be using us to transport it across the border. I tried to reassure her that we could soon clear the whole thing up, but I was not sure at all that the matter would be dropped quickly. My instincts told me it was highly unlikely we would be allowed to just walk away. That assessment proved accurate, as the situation soon turned much more dire.

Agent Meharg directed his partner to remain with the evidence, then he barked at us, "Follow me!"

We were led into a square concrete-block building furnished with a few chairs and a metal table. "Wait here," Meharg said. "I need to call in my supervisor." After fifteen minutes or so, which felt like a lifetime, Inspector John Vandiver of the U.S. Customs Service arrived. He read me my Miranda rights, which made the arrest official.

I told Vandiver who I was and gave him my identification showing me to be Arkansas's deputy attorney general. He perused it briefly and went into an adjacent room, where I heard him making a telephone call. In the meantime, Agent Crockett was pulling the packages out of the seat cavity and placing them on the table. I noticed that his hands were all over the packages and plastic linings, and I cautioned him in a rather insistent tone to be more careful. He might be compromising evidence, I stated, by obscuring the original fingerprints.

Vandiver returned, and I requested that the packages not be handled further until they could be checked for fingerprints. I repeated my request that a fingerprint expert be brought in. And I repeatedly stated that we were innocent victims of smugglers who chose our vehicle to transport the drugs across the border. I volunteered once again that both Jeannie and I would be willing to take polygraph tests to verify our innocence.

Vandiver was having none of it. He said that he did not have the authority to authorize the polygraph, and he suggested rather cryptically that I request it from the U.S. magistrate, where I would soon be taken for formal charging. His attitude had turned hard and unyielding.

Shortly thereafter, Jeannie and I were driven to the federal courthouse in Brownsville, which was not far away. I was met by Assistant U.S. Attorney Raul Gonzales. He wasted no time.

"I have decided to charge you with transporting a controlled substance, marijuana, with intent to distribute," he said. "Being a lawyer, as I understand you are, you know this is a felony charge."

"I don't know anything about this," I said, still trying to be reasonable and point out the obvious. "I'm sure we are being used by drug smugglers as pigeons to get the stuff across the border. Why drag this out? We are both ready to take polygraph tests to prove our innocence."

Gonzales would have none of it. "The amount and the way it was concealed is not typical for planted drugs," he said. "I have decided that you will be charged."

I was fingerprinted and booked, then taken before U.S. Magistrate William Mallet, who set a $5,000 no-security bond and released me on my own recognizance. (Jeannie was not charged.) I again requested a polygraph, but Judge Mallet said that he lacked authority for that. I would have to take it up with U.S. District Judge Reynaldo Garza.

As soon as I was released, I called Mamie Ruth Williams for her advice on what I should do. Mamie Ruth was a media consultant and strategist in the Arkansas Attorney General's Office, where I worked at the time, and one of the most politically astute people

I have ever known. She was shocked, but she recovered quickly. Ever conscious of the press, Mamie Ruth cautioned that I needed to get my side of the story out as a part of the first wave of news stories. Otherwise, she said, only the arrest and charge would be reported, likely including statements from U.S. Customs and the U.S. Attorney. She emphasized that this would surely be a major headline story in Arkansas.

Desperately wanting to get out of Brownsville as soon as possible, I told her that Jeannie and I just needed to come home, where we could be among friends.

George Fisher cartoon of Mamie Ruth Williams.

"We are at our rope's end," I pleaded. "Jeannie is just about to come unglued, and I am not far behind."

"Listen to me," she said sharply. "This is very important. Get yourself together. You are now in the fight of your life. You need to understand that."

Backing off a little, Mamie Ruth explained her reasoning for why I needed to get my side of the story out as part of the

27

initial news coverage: "Roger, you need to remember that most members of the public make up their minds based on what they first read or hear. If you wait until later, the horse will already be out of the barn."

She asked if there were any members of the press at the courthouse. I told her of a conversation I had had with a reporter present at the magistrate appearance. The reporter had told me that stashing drugs in tourist vehicles to get them across the border happened all the time. He said it had happened to a friend of his not long ago.

"He seemed sympathetic," I said.

"Then by all means find him!" she exclaimed. "Tell him you would like to give him a statement, and relate everything that happened, especially the part about asking customs for the fingerprints and polygraph. His story is very likely to be picked up by the national wire services and get transmitted to outlets all across the country in time for tomorrow's newspapers. Now get cracking!"

"Okay," I said, duly chastised.

Mamie Ruth concluded by saying that she would find out the identity of the reporters who were assigned to this story by the *Arkansas Gazette* and *Democrat* papers and have them call me for a statement. Finally, she made it clear that this was going to be a very big story. Also, she said, I should call our boss, Ray Thornton, as soon as possible and tell him what had happened.

As I rapidly made my way down the federal courthouse corridors in search of the reporter, I began to realize the prescience of Mamie Ruth's advice. If I did not get my side of the story included in the first wave of coverage, my reputation would be ruined by the time the sun rose the next morning. At the same time, I suspected that my efforts would be futile. After all, there was no question that a very large amount of marijuana was found concealed in my car.

I found the local reporter walking out the front door of the courthouse. I ran to catch him, and, breathing hard, I asked if he would be writing a story about my case for the next day's Brownsville newspaper.

"Yes," he said, "your story is by far the most interesting of anything I've heard around here all day. Mind if I ask you a few questions?"

"That would be fine," I replied. "In fact, I've been looking for you. How about we start out with me giving you a statement?"

"Sure," he said, and he dutifully started taking notes on all I had to say.

When I was finished with the Brownsville reporter, I called Mamie Ruth again to tell her what had happened. She said that she had gotten the names and telephone numbers of the reporters assigned to the story for the Little Rock papers. I made contact and gave them a short statement. Finally, I got a call through to my boss, Arkansas Attorney General Ray Thornton, and apprised him of the situation.

3. Hope and Despair

While I was dealing with the press, Jeannie arranged our flight back to Little Rock later that day. We had to fly because the Customs Bureau had impounded our car. We caught a cab outside the federal courthouse and headed to the airport. On the flight home, we sat in anxious silence, dreading the days ahead, unable to think of anything but the worst outcomes awaiting us.

Mamie Ruth's prediction of the press response was accurate. The next morning, the front page of the *Arkansas Gazette* was dominated by the headline: "Official Seized on 'Pot' Count." The newspaper printed my photo, the worst image in their archive, I'm sure, for I looked like a mafia thug. A long news story followed. Before I could begin reading, my thoughts were racing. Conviction of a felony could carry a lengthy prison term and would automatically result in the loss of my law license. Life as I had known it would be over.

I steadied my nerves and began reading. Because of Mamie Ruth's advice, I did get the most salient parts of my own story included in the initial news coverage. The *Gazette* reported a portion of my statement, including the request for a polygraph test, along with a nice statement from Thornton:

> Customs agents said the marijuana was found wrapped in Mexican newspapers and stuffed between the springs of the back seat of Glasgow's car. Glasgow said he had not participated in any illegal activities. "My wife and I were taking a four-day vacation in Mexico," Glasgow said. "It was the first time we have been in Mexico. These developments are a terrible way to end a most pleasant trip. I have heard of this happening to other people, but you never expect it to happen to you. I am convinced that someone considered us likely prospects for the purpose of using us as couriers to smuggle illegal drugs across the border."
>
> Glasgow was taken before United States Magistrate William Mallet, who released him on his own recognizance after setting bond at $5,000. Glasgow asked to be given a lie-detector test, but Mallet refused to allow one.
>
> United States Attorney, J. B. Farris at Houston explained later that a decision on a polygraph test was up to the discretion of the magistrate. He said the matter of the polygraph test would probably be referred to federal Judge Reynaldo Gaza when a preliminary hearing is held...
>
> Thornton said Friday night that Glasgow had telephoned him during the afternoon to tell him what had happened. "He said he had absolutely no knowledge that the material was in his car, that he could only suppose that someone had put it there for some reason, perhaps planning to remove it after it had been carried across the line," Thornton said. "I have known Roger for many years and I have great confidence in his character, and naturally, I believe he's innocent," Thornton said. "I am confident that others who know him will share that belief."[1]

The *Arkansas Democrat* carried a similar story in the afternoon paper, quoting me, but also quoting Gonzales, the assistant U.S. attorney from Brownsville. Gonzales gave a markedly different statement from that given by Farris, the U.S. attorney in

Houston, regarding the issue of the polygraph test. Gonzales stated that the test was denied because polygraphs were "not admissible in court and could be rigged."[2]

The following day, Sunday, August 27, 1972, the *Gazette* and *Democrat* papers again carried front-page stories with more extensive quotes. The *Gazette* reported additional comments from me regarding the lie-detector request.

> "We're completely, totally innocent and have nothing to hide," Glasgow said. "We're most anxious to get this matter disposed of." The quickest way to do that, he said, would be to take a lie-detector test, and he said he tried to get one from the federal authorities in Texas, but they refused to give either of the Glasgows a test.
>
> "I immediately inquired about a polygraph [lie detector] test," he said. "I expressed not only a willingness but a desire, which finally turned into an insistence, that both my wife and I be administered polygraph tests."
>
> He said the authorities refused and said they did not have the facilities to give the tests.
>
> "But I will continue to insist upon either a polygraph test, truth serum or any other medically accepted test to determine truthfulness," he said. If the authorities won't give him one, he said, he would select a disinterested person to "administer one on our behalf."[3]

In addition to dealing with the media, I was working on two other immediate and critical issues: first, securing an attorney to defend me against the charges, and, second, contacting the Wright, Lindsey & Jennings law firm concerning my new job, which was scheduled to start on September 1, only four days later.

During that first weekend home, I met with Mamie Ruth and well-known Little Rock attorney Phillip Dixon, who had served as chair of the "Attorneys for Glasgow" committee during my campaign for prosecuting attorney. Dixon was a civil law attorney, but he knew some of the top criminal defense attorneys in Arkansas due to his service on several Arkansas Bar Association committees. He was sure some of them had connections with the Texas Criminal Defense Attorney Association and could provide us with some names.

We discussed, in general terms, whether we should go after a "big-name" attorney from a larger firm in one of the major metropolitan areas in Texas, such as Leon Jaworski of the Fulbright Jaworski firm in Houston, or whether we should use a local attorney in the Brownsville area. A big-name attorney would surely charge high fees. Further, an attorney not from Brownsville might lack knowledge of the attitudes and political leanings of the local population. We decided that our best choice was to find a good, competent attorney in Brownsville. Dixon said he would start searching immediately and keep me posted.

As to my job at Wright, Lindsey & Jennings, we all agreed I should avoid putting the firm on the spot by simply showing up for work on September 1. I called Ed Wright, the senior managing partner of the firm, at his home that afternoon. Wright was exceptionally gracious. He said he fully understood the manner in which I was handling things and even offered to help me find a good defense attorney. He was the immediate past president of the American Bar Association and had contacts with all sorts of lawyers nationwide.

I expressed my appreciation for his offer, then I told him I didn't see how I could immediately start a full-time position at the firm given the circumstances I was facing. Wright suggested I come to the firm's offices on Monday to discuss the situation. He also said he expected to have some information on possible defense attorney prospects by then. We made an appointment for 9 o'clock Monday morning.

I related the conversation to Mamie Ruth, "word for word" as she insisted. She thought for a while, and then said, "Sounds like they have already made up their minds. Ed just wants to go through the motions. But, I hope I am wrong."

I agreed. The outlook offered no positive outcome or glimmer of hope. I was charged with an unsavory felony, had no lawyer to represent me, had no money to hire one anyway, and now, seemingly, had no job. Bleak prospects, indeed.

A long, gloomy weekend lay ahead. Jeannie wanted to talk, but I put her off until Sunday morning. After breakfast, we reviewed our prospects. Declining to sugarcoat it, I told her I was meeting with members of the Wright firm the following day. Even if they still wanted me, I would not be able to start work until the criminal charge was settled. I had not yet located an attorney to represent me, and I didn't know if I could raise the money to retain one. Jeannie took it with amazing equanimity, which I credited to the fact that she was a product of her own tough upbringing.

"Don't worry," she said. "We'll get by somehow. We always have." At that moment, I appreciated her more than ever. She is a real jewel.

Just as we finished breakfast, the phone rang. It was an old law school classmate of mine, Dent Gitchel. Dent had been on the *Law Review* staff with me in school and had encouraged me to take the job at Wright, Lindsey & Jennings. I had always considered him to be a close friend.

"Roger, I want to tell you how sorry I am for the misfortune you and Jeannie had down in Mexico." He paused. "I guess 'misfortune' may not be the right word," he said, laughing thinly.

I laughed as well, the first time I had done so in three days. "Thanks," I said. "You can't imagine how much that means to me."

"It was such a shock," Dent said, "not only to me, but to everybody. Roger, I took the liberty of calling some of our classmates and mutual friends. We realize that you are going to have to hire a lawyer to get through this, a good lawyer at that, and we know that good lawyers don't come cheap. With your permission, I'd like to set up a little defense fund to help you out."

I couldn't say anything right away, for I was about to choke up. Finally, I managed to get out, "Thank you so much, Dent, that would be wonderful."

On Monday morning, promptly at 9:00, I stepped out of the elevator into the elegant walnut-paneled lobby of the Wright, Lindsey & Jennings firm on the twenty-second floor of the Worthen Bank Building. The receptionist noted my arrival, and Ed Wright soon emerged from one side of the front lobby and strode up to me. I had met him before, when he, Bob Lindsey, and their wives had invited Jeannie and me to dinner at the Little Rock Country Club shortly after I had accepted the job offer. I was struck anew by his elegant demeanor and fastidious dress.

"Roger, it's really good to see you again," he said warmly. "Please come on back."

He guided me to his office, the first one along a long hallway, which was a smaller version of the lobby, with dark walnut walls and an oriental rug on the floor. A stylish carved desk was situated in front of handsome bookcases filled with leather-bound law books.

"Have a seat, Roger," Wright said. "Would you care for some water or iced tea perhaps?"

"No, I guess not, but thank you," I replied, completing the niceties. All I could think of was the terrible news he was about to give me.

"We were all very dismayed at the terrible ordeal you had down in Brownsville," Wright said. "Of course, all I know of it is what I read in the papers, not always the most reliable source, and what you told me in our brief telephone conversation. Would you mind giving me a more thorough summary?"

I proceeded to tell him everything, in chronological order, as best I could. He listened intently, only occasionally breaking in to ask a question, usually to clarify something. When I was finished, he said, "That's a horrific experience for anyone. How do you plan to fight this thing?"

I told him about my quest to find the best lawyer for the job and mentioned Dent Gitchel's offer to set up a defense fund.

"I know Dent," he said, "a sterling young man and a fine lawyer."

Then I suddenly blurted out, involuntarily it seemed and totally without having even considered what I was about to say, "About the offer the firm has extended to me, and the start date, obviously I will be very busy and distracted

George Fisher cartoon of Edward L. Wright.

for the next few months, trying to deal with the legal process. I want you to know that I don't intend to hold the firm to the offer because I really won't be able to do much legal work for some indefinite amount of time. Under the circumstances, it would not be fair to either of us," I stammered, "and I'm really sorry for any embarrassment this has caused the firm."

I struggled to keep my composure, but I finally found it impossible to do so. I broke into deep sobs.

Wright sat silently for a while, saying nothing. Then, he sniffed a time or two, pulled a white handkerchief from the breast pocket of his black pinstriped suit jacket, and wiped his eyes.

"Roger, I have called a meeting of the firm partners for 10 o'clock this morning. This has to be a partnership decision, as I'm sure you appreciate. They all should be here by now. If you don't mind hanging around for a while longer, let us have our meeting, and I'll let you know."

"Of course," I said. Wright guided me back out to the lobby, where I sat for fifteen minutes or so. Thumbing idly through a magazine, I tried to appear busy and unconcerned, but I was waiting for the axe to fall. Wright returned after a while. He smiled and said, "Come on back, and I'll report on our meeting."

I went back to his office, where we were joined by Bob Lindsey and Dick Williams, senior partners in the firm, who had initially interviewed me for the job. Wright said, "I've invited Bob and Dick to join us to verify what I have to report, and correct any misstatements I might make. First, the partnership has voted unanimously that you should start work as scheduled, at full salary, with the understanding that you will not be able to devote yourself full time to your duties until you get this nasty business behind you."

He talked on about such things as the firm automobiles and the car-pool arrangement (who might pick me up in the mornings, and when, etc.), but I was so deliriously relieved that I barely heard another word.

4. FIND A LAWYER

Around midweek Phil Dixon provided me with the names and some information on possible defense attorneys in Texas. The most promising of them was Thomas Sharp Jr., who practiced in Brownsville. Sharp was in his early forties, and he had handled a good number of drug defense cases along the Rio Grande Valley. He was a University of Texas Law School graduate and had started a practice in Brownsville with his father, Tom Sharp Sr., who had passed away some ten years previous.

The father had been a highly successful and respected attorney in the valley and had had Reynaldo Garza as his partner for a number of years. Garza was now the U.S. district judge presiding over my case. Tom Sr. had been the first "Anglo" in the area to join forces with a Hispanic attorney, and they had done quite well in practice together. Judge Garza became the first Hispanic judge in the country chosen for the federal bench, appointed by President John F. Kennedy.

About this same time and before I officially started work at the firm, Ed Wright called me at home to say that he had gathered some information on defense attorney candidates. We met at his office that afternoon.

Once I had settled into the chair across from him, he asked, quite abruptly and in a very direct manner: "I don't mean to pry into your personal life, and I wouldn't ask this question except for the present circumstances. Have you ever smoked marijuana?"

The question was so unexpected that I did not have time to consider my answer, so I just blurted out the truth, "Yes, on two occasions."

"Just two occasions?" Wright said, raising an eyebrow slightly. "Tell me about it. You realize that your defense attorney will want to know the same thing."

"I know it sounds weird," I said, "like 'two beers' would sound to a traffic judge, but here's what happened. I had never experimented with marijuana in college, nor in law school for that matter. Then I wrote a *Law Review* article about marijuana laws being too harsh. I had done a good bit of medical research and found that marijuana was clearly much more benign than the hard narcotics. So I contended in the article that treating marijuana the same as the hard narcotics, in terms of punishment, was unconstitutional."[4]

Ed Wright smiled, rather wryly, and I thought I saw a slight twinkle in his otherwise inscrutable black eyes. "You won the Arkansas Bar Award for that article, if I remember correctly," he remarked.

"Yes, sir, I did," I said.

"And let me guess: You felt that you needed to verify your conclusion with some personal research, did you?"

"Yes, sir, that's about it," I said.

Wright seemed satisfied with my answers, and he moved on to a discussion of the potential defense attorneys for my case. I was pleased to learn that he had Tom Sharp Jr. on his list. We talked a little about what Sharp could bring to the table compared with the other candidates, and Wright commented that, if he were in my shoes, Sharp would probably be his top choice. I totally agreed, and we talked some more about topics I should cover with Tom when I called to discuss retaining him.

After a while, Wright paused, and said, "You know, I have had a decent amount of experience in hiring outside lawyers for specific work. Would you like for me to sit in on the call?"

"Yes, sir, that would be great," I said.

We made the call to Brownsville and got Sharp on the phone. Wright took the lead on the call, handled it thoroughly, incisively, and with great dexterity and amazing aplomb, far better than I could have done. He had obviously done his research, knew a lot about Tom, his father, Judge Garza, and a few of the other leading lawyers in the valley. He was able to drop names at appropriate moments, and he soon had Sharp eager to take the case on very reasonable terms. I owed Wright for another immense favor.

Sharp said that, as a first order of business, he would call Raul Gonzales to inform him of my new legal representation. Sharp wanted to feel out Gonzales's attitude and learn whatever he could. Sharp instructed me to immediately write out a detailed chronology of our travels in Mexico and gather up everything we had to document the trip. After that, he wanted us to come down to Brownsville for a face-to-face conference.

I started work at the Wright firm on Friday, September 1, 1972. Jeannie and I had just moved to a big rented house on Palm Street in the Colonial Court area of Little Rock, a couple of blocks off Markham Street. Promptly at 8 o'clock that morning, I walked out the front door to find a large blue Pontiac Bonneville parked in the front drive, with three men in suits and ties seated inside. This was one of the firm's five carpool vehicles, used to pick up and return home each day most of the firm's twenty lawyers (I was the twenty-first). My house was the last stop on the route driven by firm partner Jim Storey.

The car pool was an unexpected bonus and came in very handy at the time. Jeannie and I had jobs with different work schedules, and we were down to one car, the small 1966 Pontiac GTO she had owned since we were first married. The U.S. Customs Service had impounded my 1970 Ford LTD and was steadfastly refusing to release it.

5. DEFENSE STRATEGY

Tom Sharp's plan was to prove that the trip was no more than an innocent tourist vacation consisting of normal activities, places, times, and money spent. This would go a long way, he felt, in showing that we had no plan, reason, money, or opportunity to shop for marijuana.

At the time of our detention at the border, I had given Agent John Vandiver a detailed description of our itinerary while we were in Mexico, and I had agreed that he could record it, following my Miranda warnings, of course. The U.S. Customs Service investigation, assuming it conducted one, should coincide exactly with what I told him and prove that we had neither the desire nor means to smuggle marijuana into the United States. Unless the government concocted evidence out of thin air, or produced lying witnesses, the only thing it would be able to show was that the marijuana was in my car, which I had already admitted.

It took me several hours to dictate our travelogue into a small handheld recorder. I gave the tapes to Mamie Ruth Williams, who had a friend type up a transcript. Also, I gathered up the various corroborating documents: a stub from Jeannie's salary check of $50 that we cashed and the record of a withdrawal from our savings account of $170, from which we purchased $150 in travelers cheques and kept the remainder in cash, hardly an amount sufficient to purchase even a small amount of marijuana, much less the twenty-four pounds in the car.

We had receipts for most, if not all, of our payments for hotels, restaurants, gasoline, curios, and other small purchases along the way. In addition, we had the stubs from the travelers cheques showing when and where they had been cashed. Further, we had the AAA guidebook and the Mexico road map and travelogue for the trip. In this way, our every move while in Mexico could be tracked, checked, timed, and verified.

Within a couple of days after retaining Sharp to represent me, he called to inform me that Gonzales would soon be taking my case before a federal grand jury. This was routine, Sharp explained. Almost all criminal cases were presented to grand juries, and virtually all of them resulted in indictments. The grand jury routinely met once a month, and the prosecutors presented their cases in bulk, one after the other, usually doing no more than reading short synopses of the cases. The indictments were rubber-stamped by the grand jury. These proceedings were secret, and no one knew exactly what went on, except that a slew of indictments would be returned each month. The U.S. attorney would usually call a press conference on the more significant cases. Through this press attention, the prosecutors hoped to prejudice any potential trial jurors against the defendant.

I asked Sharp if I could appear and present evidence to the grand jury. Technically, he said, it was possible that a grand jury would allow a defendant to appear and present testimony, but he had never heard of that actually happening. If we were to ask, he was sure Gonzales would not agree, and that would probably be the end of it. I persisted, wondering what the harm would be in asking. Why give Gonzales a free platform to announce the indictment in a press conference? Wouldn't it be possible to blunt some of this by publicly requesting an opportunity to be heard by the grand jury? Sharp understood my point but said he wanted to give it some more thought.

Meanwhile, I finished the chronology and mailed it off. Sharp called and agreed that we had nothing to lose by making the grand jury appearance request. He said that he had mentioned it to Gonzales, who had laughed, stating that it was a defense tactic he hadn't heard before. Gonzales seemed surprisingly friendly, Sharp reported, much less adversarial than during their first phone conversation. If Gonzales was softening some, Sharp suggested that he might approach him again about setting up a polygraph test.

We spoke again a few days later. Gonzales had consented to the polygraph tests, Sharp explained, having cleared it with his superior, the U.S. attorney in Houston. They were now awaiting expected approval from the U.S. Department of Justice in Washington DC.

Sharp said that he and Gonzales discussed having the Texas State Police conduct the tests in Corpus Christi. The two attorneys would draw up an appropriate stipulation governing the process and stating how the results could be used. Sharp assured me that if the results turned out unambiguously in our favor, Gonzales would drop the case.

I was flooded with relief. "What great news!" I exclaimed. "When do you think it can happen? Jeannie and I will need some advance notice to take off work."

"Sometime in early October," he said. "We can schedule our personal conference down here to occur during the same trip. You'll need to come down to Brownsville the day before for our meeting, then I'll drive you up to Corpus Christi for the polygraph tests. You can fly home from there."

Lady Justice, it seemed, was finally ready to smile upon us.

Meanwhile, our news release setting out my request to be permitted to appear before the grand jury got a smattering of press coverage, but not much. Likewise, when the grand jury released the indictment a few days later, only a short squib about it appeared in the Arkansas papers. Gonzales did not call a press conference to announce the indictment or make any public statements. We felt that the lack of fuss about the indictment from Gonzales was good; apparently the plans for the polygraph tests and potential dismissal were going well.

During our telephone conversations, Sharp and I discussed our overall defense strategy. He advised a straightforward and simple approach with two prongs. First, we would trace our trip to Mexico—the planning, route, places stayed, purchases, etc.— and introduce all of the documentation I had gathered verifying all this. As the second prong of our defense strategy, Sharp thought we should call an array of the most high-caliber character witnesses we could get to testify at trial for me. In criminal cases, a defendant can produce witnesses to attest to good character and reputation. Likewise, the prosecution can counter that by evidence of poor reputation.

After the arrest, a large number of letters had been written on my behalf by high-profile and respected people, so we had a ready-made list of potential witnesses. Letters had been received, for example, from such notables as Robert R. Wright, dean of the University of Oklahoma School of Law, who was a professor at the University of Arkansas (UA) when I was in law school, and for whom I served as a research assistant; Robert A. Leflar, a celebrated longtime professor at the UA Law School and former dean there, who had also served as president of the Arkansas Constitutional

Convention when I was a delegate; Dale Bumpers, governor of Arkansas, with whom I had worked during legislative reapportionment and who had offered me the position of insurance commissioner; W. R. "Witt" Stephens, one of the most prominent and wealthy businessmen in Arkansas; U.S. District Judge G. Thomas Eisele, with whom I had previously served as a delegate to the Arkansas Constitutional Convention, and in whose court I had practiced; Bobby Steel, circuit judge in the judicial district that included my hometown of Nashville, Arkansas, before whom I had practiced law; David Pryor, U.S. congressman, who was a neighbor of mine and a personal friend; and J. William Fulbright, U.S. senator, who had come down to Southern State College to address the student body at my invitation when I was a student there. My letters also included one from Dwight Jones, superintendent of schools at Nashville and my old high school coach.

Sharp narrowed the list down, and we made our selection over the next few days of five character witnesses. They included Eisele, Steel, Wright, and Rev. A. D. Stuckey of Nashville. We also planned to call my mother, Fern Glasgow.

A few days later, eager to get our trip to Brownsville scheduled for the conference and the polygraph tests, I called Sharp. I could tell by the sound of his voice that something was wrong.

"Gonzales backed out on the polygraph tests," he said. He gave me a moment to digest this, then continued, "I really don't think there was anything Raul could do about it. He said the Justice Department in Washington had flat refused to go forward. The decision had been made at the very highest level."

"How can they back out?" I shouted angrily. "They had agreed!"

"Gonzales agreed to it," Sharp replied, a hint of resignation in his voice, "as did the U.S. attorney in Texas, but the Justice Department always has the final call."

"Those bastards don't care how innocent you are," I protested. "They just want another hide to nail to the wall."

"Raul said he pressed for it," Sharp replied, "and suggested in a sort of backhanded way that politics had perhaps played a role. I don't know."

"I guess it was the George McGovern bumper sticker on my car," I said bitterly.

"You know the U.S. attorney general is John Mitchell, Nixon's old campaign manager," Sharp said, searching for a little levity. "Maybe you are on the enemies list."

"Maybe I am," I replied. "Nixon hates all Democrats. It's all a part of his Southern Strategy."

"Well, we didn't lose any time over it," Sharp said. "We'll just proceed and get the case ready to go. If it's a trial they want, it's a trial they'll get."

We selected a date in early October for Jeannie and me to go to Brownsville. Sharp was exceptionally gracious—he would meet us at the airport, and he insisted we stay in a spare bedroom at his house.

A few days went by, during which I was busy with my work at Wright, Lindsey & Jennings. I was primarily doing legal research and reading abstracts for real-estate title opinions. I was grateful to have any work to do, for it kept me busy, brought in a steady paycheck, and, most of all, helped keep my mind off my troubles. I was painfully aware that the sword of Damocles was dangling above my head, and anything to divert my attention, even for a short while, was a godsend. In addition, a number of friends and well-wishers called to express their support. As in all challenging times, the concern of caring friends and acquaintances helped buoy my flagging spirits.

6. The Setup

One night in mid-September, Tom Sharp called. I could not recall him ever calling after work, so I took the phone with a fair amount of trepidation. The news, I thought, was either real good or real bad.

"Does the name John Patterson mean anything to you?" Sharp asked. "He is a cab driver in Little Rock."

"I don't know anybody who is a cab driver," I replied. "Why do you ask?"

"I just got a call from Raul. He said he had been contacted by the U.S. attorney in Little Rock, a guy named Sonny something," continued Sharp.

"Sonny Dillahunty. He's the U.S. attorney here," I said.

"Okay," Sharp went on. "It seems that Sonny got some information from a confidential informant up there, Patterson, this cab driver guy, who is considered reliable. The word is you were set up, that the marijuana was planted."

I was stunned and unable to speak for a moment. Then, recovering somewhat, I shouted to Jeannie, who was standing nearby, "Tom says somebody planted the marijuana on us. I was framed!"

"Well, Raul didn't go quite that far," Sharp continued, having no trouble hearing my shouting. "But, he felt he should tell me. Raul shoots pretty straight. He said he would check into it further and let me know. If the whole setup deal can be verified, he won't prosecute an innocent man."

"My God, Tom," I exulted. "That's the break we've been looking for!"

"Well, it's certainly something I thought you should know about right away," Sharp said. "But let's not get too excited just yet. Informant stories can be misleading. I should hear more tomorrow."

Sharp called the next day with more information. It seems that Patterson, who was a regular police informant in Little Rock, told of picking up a passenger named Jim Hunter at a house in North Little Rock. A party was under way, and Hunter, who had been drinking heavily, was in no position to drive himself home. In Patterson's cab, Hunter supposedly made some incriminating statements to the effect of, "How do you like the way we fixed up old Glasgow down on the border?"

Raul Gonzales had reported this to his superior, and they agreed to assign a couple of U.S. Customs Service special investigators to interview Patterson, and Hunter also, if he would consent. If the whole thing proved true, Gonzales would ask permission to *nolle prosequi* (voluntarily dismiss) the case, perhaps backed up with a polygraph from me.

"That would be a dandy way to dispose of it," I said.

"It may not be that simple," Sharp continued. "Patterson is an informant for the state prosecutor in Little Rock, not the feds, so we don't know how much credence he'll be given."

"Let me fill you in on the local politics," I said. "The prosecuting attorney here was Jim Guy Tucker, a friend of mine. When Tucker ran for state attorney general, I ran for his seat and lost to a guy named Lee Munson. Jim Hunter was one of Munson's biggest financial supporters. Munson was also supported by the Little Rock Police Department, particularly Police Chief Gale Weeks. They hate both Jim Guy and me. If the customs investigators get hooked up with any of them, you can bet they'll do everything they can to discredit the informant and turn the tables."

"There's not much we can do about that at this point," Sharp said, "but wait and see."

★ ★ ★

We heard nothing for the next few weeks. The longer the silence lasted, the worse I felt. I knew that if Lee Munson's people found out, they would do everything possible to interfere. Unable to stand it any longer, I called Tom Sharp and learned that the investigators had completed their interviews with John Patterson and Jim Hunter. Patterson had vaguely implicated Munson, so the investigators were arranging to interview him as well.

"I can't see anything good coming out of Munson getting involved," I said.

"I'll be getting copies of the statements from Patterson and Hunter," Sharp said, "plus the Munson statement and any others they take. We'll know more then."

A few days later, I received copies of the recorded statements of John Patterson and Jim T. Hunter.[5] I read each one a couple of times to be sure of what they said. I found myself shaking my head, dumbfounded at my own naiveté. I recalled a comment Mamie Ruth had once made about my being "a babe in the woods" about local politics. I had been clueless about the real nature of my political opponents. Now I was angry, but I was also embarrassed.

The details of what Hunter had told the cab driver and the casual brazenness with which it had all happened were startling. Patterson's story began on September 15, 1972, some three weeks after my arrest at the Mexican border. He had been called to a home in an exclusive area of North Little Rock to pick up a fare. He found three men in the driveway beside two automobiles, a Cadillac and a Lincoln Continental with a license plate reading "JTH." One of the men was Munson. Another was Hunter, who was drunk. Munson and the third man, whom Patterson did not know, were holding Hunter by the arm to keep him from getting into the Lincoln and driving home in his impaired condition. Patterson had driven Hunter in his cab before, and they recognized each other. On the way to Hunter's home, they began talking about the prosecuting attorney race. Patterson's interview contained the following exchange:

> And we got to talking about several different things, just common talk, and he asked me how I liked the way they fixed up Roger Glasgow down in Mexico. So I asked him at the time, "What do you mean, the way you fixed him up?" He said, "You didn't read that in the paper?" And I said, "Yes, I read it in the paper. Are you trying to tell me something about this?" And he said, "Well…" I said, "Everybody in town here thinks he is guilty." And he said, "Aw, bullshit. You know that man is not guilty of that." And I said, "Well, I don't know it for sure. Everybody I talked to thinks he's guilty." And he responded, "Well, he's not, believe me, he's not."
>
> So we got to talking a little bit more about different things and then I finally asked him. I said, "You mean you got enough power down there to do that?" And he said, "Well, let me tell you something, I'm not a millionaire, but I do have a little money." He said, "I do have influence across the border. I race horses down there in Mexico. I own a racing stable…and I go down there every year and race horses and I know a lot of people down there. I can get anything done in Mexico that I want.

From this and other statements made by Patterson, it was clear to me that Hunter and others had framed me. And it had been done with Munson's knowledge and approval. Before this,

I had never even imagined such a thing. But thinking back, plenty of clues were available if I had paid attention. I was aware of the widespread rumors that the bond business was heavily infiltrated by a group known as the Dixie Mafia, and I knew Hunter was the owner of a bond house, Delta Securities, and was one of Munson's chief supporters. I had seen him several times at campaign events in the company of Little Rock Police Department detectives, whom I also knew to be strong Munson supporters.

Patterson's transcript also revealed that Hunter's intent was more than punishment for my campaign activities. The plan was to permanently remove me from the political arena.

The transcript showed the following:

[Patterson:] When we rode on out and I finally asked him, "What does Lee Munson think about it?" And he said, "Aw, he knows all about it, he knows all about... It was done with his approval." And I said, "What was your purpose of doing this? He won the election." And he said, "Yes, but that no good rotten son of a bitch," he said.

Q. Referring to Glasgow?

A. Right. He said, "Did you see the dirt that he brought up during the campaign? He brought out more damn dirt. He really put it on us bad, and we figured that's the only way."

Q. What was he referring to when he said "dirt"? Was he referring to the racetrack business and the bookie business?

A. No, he was talking about the dirt that Roger Glasgow put on Mr. Lee Munson.

Q. Yes, but what type of dirt?

A. I don't know. He came out with some pretty bad stuff during the campaign on Lee Munson. He said, "We figure that he is the only one that can be able to run against Lee in the next election and we just fixed his wagon where he couldn't run at all."

Q. And this would be the day before he came back into the United States.

A. Yes, the night before.

Q. The night before. Was there any mention of how this was done physically? I mean did someone remove the back seat or did he make any indication how it was done physically?

A. The only thing he told me was that the night before while they were in the motel that they put it under their seat...

Q. Did he mention the motel?

A. No sir, he did not mention the name of the motel. He did mention the motel, but he didn't mention the name of the motel, but he did mention the motel.

Q. He said they put it under the seat?

A. Yes sir.

Patterson's statement also described an offer by Hunter to buy a list of other paid informants supplying confidential information to then-prosecuting attorney Jim Guy Tucker. At the time, Tucker's office was deep into an investigation into suspected corruption and racketeering by elements of the Little Rock Police Department, where Munson had strong support. As the newly elected prosecuting attorney, Munson would clearly be interested in a list of informants who might compromise his friends at the LRPD. Patterson stated that he was willing to obtain the list and supply it to Hunter, all the while realizing that Hunter intended to turn it over to Munson.

The transcript continued:

Q. Now, okay, you arrived at the residence of Jim T. Hunter, now what took place there?

A. We sat and talked for about 15 minutes I guess, and he was talking to me about different things and then he asked me if I thought I could do him a favor and I said, "Yeah, I probably could if everything…" He said, "Well I tell you what. I'll give you $100 now and I'll give you $100 when you get it." And I said, "Well what is it you want?" And he said, "Well, do you think you could get me a list of the paid informers from the prosecuting attorney's office?" I told him, "I don't know, that would be pretty hard to do, because you just don't get into Jim Guy Tucker's office like that, because he's got a tight office." And he said, "Well, do you know anybody up there?" And I responded, "I know some people up there." And he said, "Well if you can get me the list, I'll give you $100." And I said, "Well I'll try like hell to get it, but it's going to cost me something too." And he said, "At least whatever it is, I'll fix you up on it." And I said, "Okay."

Q. Did he indicate what he wanted the list for?

A. Yes, he said that Jim Guy Tucker wouldn't…leave them anything in the prosecuting attorney's office to work on after they took office the first of the year. And he said they needed the list in order so they could get work sooner. I agreed to get the list for them, if I could.

Q. At this point he gave you $10 for the cab and $100?

A. $100, yes.

Q. So he gave you a pretty good tip and put $100 on you?

A. Yes.

Q. Okay, then what happened? He gave you a phone number?

A. Yes sir, he gave me his home phone number.

Q. Now, after the conversation you had that night. Has he ever brought it up again?

A. Yes sir.

Q. He has brought it up again, and when was this?

A. It was on Sunday morning about 10 o'clock in the morning.

Q. This was last Sunday?

A. Yes. And we sat there and we had a long conversation. We talked for about an hour, I guess, and I asked him how this deal turned out down there in Mexico, because I had called his wife the day before trying to get in touch with him and she told me that he was in Texas.

Q. That would have been Saturday, right?

A. Yes sir, when I called her she told me that he would be back the next day; for me to call him then. I called him Sunday. It would have been Friday he was in Texas. He told me he had just got back from Juarez, Mexico, when I saw him that Sunday morning. I asked him, "Well, how did that deal turn out down there?" And he said, "Well, I bullshit a lot. You can't believe everything I say, because I am a liar." So then I asked him what type of business that he was in and he told me that he owned Delta Securities in the Worthen Bank building. I asked him what type of business that was and he said well, he said, he sells some securities. But, he said most of his money is made through the racetrack and his racehorses. The conversation got back on him and he was kinda reluctant to talk about it, he didn't want to talk about it too much.

Q. About the Glasgow affair?

A. Right. So then he kept asking me questions about myself and he kept turning a little switch on and off in the car, you could hear it clicking. When I asked him what the sound was, he told me it was the air conditioner, but the air conditioner wasn't blowing. So evidently he had a tape recorder in his car. That is what I believe it was, and so at the time I did sort of incriminate myself talking to him and the thing that I talked to him about, I was guilty of and so…

Q. So actually he's got a hammer of sorts on you at this stage of the game?

A. No sir, he don't have a hammer on me.

Q. Well he's got some information on you.

A. The prosecuting attorney already knows about it.

Q. Ok.

A. And there's no charges filed on it.

Q. Did you turn over a list?

A. Yes sir, I did.

In his statement, Jim Hunter admitted that he had been at the house in North Little Rock on the night in question, that John Patterson's cab had been hailed to drive him home because he had been drinking, and that a conversation occurred touching on the Mexico marijuana case. But Hunter claimed he was too drunk to remember exact detail. Interestingly, the content of Hunter's interview reveals that he had been told by the U.S. Customs Service investigators about the interview they had done with Patterson, including some of the statements Patterson had attributed to Hunter.

Q. Mr. Hunter, the allegation has been made concerning a statement made by you the night of September 15, 1972. Now we have previously discussed this allegation, have we not?

A. We have.

Q. Now, where were you the night of September 15, 1972?

A. The first part of the evening I was at the home of Ted Johnson in North Little Rock, Arkansas.

Q. How did you get home?

A. As the night wore on, I make a policy of not drinking and driving, and I rode home in a taxi.

Q. Did you know the cab driver?

A. I recognized him...he recognized me too.

Q. After getting into the cab with this driver did you have a conversation with him? …

A. Yes, we did have a conversation.

Q. Did the name of Roger Glasgow come up?

A. Yes it did. ...

Q. Did you at any time make the statement, to your recollection, to the effect that, we planted the marijuana or had it planted on Glasgow the night before he came back to the United States?

A. That's preposterous. I can't, no, I don't think so.

Q. Could you have?

A. I could've said anything but it's beyond my belief that I could have ever said those particular words.

Q. Did you discuss Lee Munson in any context during the cab drive?

A. I am sure Munson was discussed because he seemed to be impressed that I knew Lee Munson, and he already knew that I supported Munson.... The Glasgow affair (he was asking me questions) I say "affair," it was brought up. Was Glasgow guilty? Did I think he was guilty, you know. I of course, don't particularly care. I wasn't too much of a conversationalist; I actually don't remember all the details of the conversation.

Hunter also admitted later that he received the list of informants from Patterson, but he tried to make light of it. Finally, he conceded that Patterson had inquired again about the previous conversation of Hunter's role in the planting of the marijuana, but he passed that off as well, saying that the cab driver must have "misconstrued something."

The transcript continued:

Q. Did you subsequently have any contact with this cab driver?

A. Yes, I did.

Q. What was that occasion?

A. ...I got a phone call that woke me up from my sleep. I had been on the road, out of town, had gotten in late and was really tired; I asked him what he wanted and he said he would rather not talk about it on the phone. I didn't have any idea what he was talking about so I asked him to call me back in an hour so I could sleep just a bit longer. In an hour or so the phone rang again, it was this taxi driver.

Q. Did he give you anything at this meeting?

A. I did want to know what the big secret was that he didn't want to talk about over the phone. I was under the impression that he wanted to talk about me helping him in a business that was brought up, but he had a calling card with several names on it.

Q. Whose calling card? Do you recall?

A. I honestly do not; it was just a small card that had some names on it and he asked me if I wanted this list of names. I said what is it? He said, these are some of the informers in the prosecuting attorney's office. I said, not really, I don't like to get involved in things like that, but I did take the card and put it in my pocket.

Q. Did you have any other discussion with him at this time?

A. Yes, he brought up that Glasgow matter.

Q. Did he bring up the previous conversation concerning your having something to do with the plant in Mexico?

A. Yes he did.

Q. What did you say?

A. I said I didn't even know what he was talking about.

Q. Did he make any comment about your drinking?

A. I told him I was inebriated, but hell, he knew that. I looked at him like he was crazy. I told him he must have misconstrued something, but that conversation didn't last long at all.

After I had calmed down some from the shock of reading the transcripts, I called Tom Sharp. I was convinced that the details of the interviews would prove beyond any doubt what happened and why.

"I can't believe Gonzales would actually take this case to trial," I declared. "We'll make him look like a fool."

"It's not quite that simple, Roger," Sharp said. "Gonzales says there are discrepancies in what the cab driver said and the actual facts. For example, the driver claimed that the car was in a garage when the plant occurred, and there is no garage at the Holiday Inn."

"Oh hell," I said, "that's just a minor detail, and it's all hearsay. Hunter was telling the story and the driver was simply trying to recall it several weeks later. It's impossible to remember every detail perfectly. Besides I'm sure Hunter himself didn't personally do the dirty deed. He was probably some distance away and had his hired Mexican minions to do the actual plant. He likely didn't even know what kind of car it was or whether the car was outside or in a garage."

Sharp agreed but added, "There's still more to it than that. Gonzalez thinks Hunter was only guilty of drunk talk, and he says the cab driver has a lot of credibility problems, plus a fairly long rap sheet."

★ ★ ★

During the campaign I had an inside source at the Little Rock Police Department—for his protection, I'll just call him "Officer Jones"—who occasionally fed me information he regarded as important. He had been a sergeant in the detective division for several years but had been demoted back down to patrol by LRPD chief Gale Weeks. He was quite bitter at Weeks about that, but he had maintained a couple of good friends in the detective division who kept him abreast of various goings-on in the upper-officer ranks.

Officer Jones worked parttime as a security guard at Pfeifer-Blass, a downtown department store on Main Street. Jeannie also worked there in the cosmetics department at the time. Officer Jones learned that she was my wife and struck up a friendly relationship with her. At times, he would write her notes and provide other materials to deliver to me concerning the illegal happenings involving the upper echelon of the police department.

After I lost the election to Munson and took the ill-fated Mexico vacation trip, Officer Jones continued to pass information. One nugget of particular interest was a report, allegedly from a participant, of a big party at Buice Drug Store celebrating my arrest. The drugstore, owned by Little Rock mayor George Wimberly, was frequently used by police officers and city officials for back-room meetings. Once I heard about this, I arranged to meet with Jones at the Pfeifer-Blass store the next night. I wanted him to tell me the names of all who were there and as many details about the affair as he knew.

When we met, Jones told me that the party occurred two or three days after my arrest and was attended by many of the people who were involved in setting me up. Jones said Parkman had once laughingly told him that he and Hensley had been in Matamoros, Mexico, the same night the marijuana had been planted in my car. Hunter and some unidentified "federal agents" were also there, and several of them took advantage of the locale to consort with local prostitutes, no doubt while the dirty drugs deed was being done.

Jones told me how Parkman extravagantly related the setting at "boys town" on the south side of Matamoros where the prostitutes were. It was a kind of Old West replica, he said, with saloons lining both sides of a dirt street. The one they were in had a long bar along a back wall where the customers could order drinks, and a dance floor, complete with Mexican musicians. An array of couches surrounded the dance floor where the girls lounged, displayed their wares, and hustled. They all got roaring drunk and had a great time making their selections, dancing and lounging with the girls, groping and squeezing them.

Jones further identified the individuals in attendance at the late-night party at Buice Drug Store. In addition to the host Wimberly, the attendees included Munson, Pearson, Parkman, and Hensley. Jones did not know if Hunter was there, but he said he heard they all drank a lot of whiskey and vociferously celebrated a job well done.

Most of this information was of no particular surprise. From the Patterson and Hunter interviews, I already knew or strongly suspected that the individuals named were involved in my setup. But it was stunning nevertheless.

Later, I shared this information with Sharp, and I said that I wondered if we should subpoena Officer Jones, Wimberly, or Munson for trial.

"No," he said. "First off, what the source told you is all hearsay and therefore inadmissible in court. Secondly, you can be sure neither Munson nor Wimberly would admit anything. We would just muddy up the water and offer up free enemy witnesses. God only knows what they would say about you at trial."

"Yes," I agreed. "That's a can of worms we don't want to open up."

That ended the matter, but the image of that party, no doubt around the infamous table in the back of Wimberly's drugstore, stuck vividly in my mind. There was little left to do other than wait for the trial to begin.

Part II

7. AGE OF INNOCENCE

At the beginning of my ordeal, I considered my arrest at the Mexican border to be a stroke of bad luck. I believed Mexican drug dealers had chosen me as an unknowing "mule" to transport drugs across the border without risk to them. This was a fairly common occurrence along the border in those days. The package removed from beneath my car's rear seat was one of several hidden there. The stash contained nearly twenty-four pounds of marijuana, an amount with a street value of about $60,000 at the time. I was charged with drug smuggling, a federal offense the State of Texas took quite seriously. If convicted, as a first-time offender, I could receive a sentence of up to fifteen years in prison.

Over time, however, I began to suspect there was more to the situation than my random selection by unknown drug dealers. The strange course my prosecution took during the ensuing weeks convinced me that very sinister forces were at work.

I had just completed a hotly contested political race for prosecuting attorney for the sixth judicial district of Arkansas, which was primarily the Little Rock metropolitan area, plus rural Perry

County. I had narrowly lost the election in a runoff with the eventual winner, Lee Munson. There was some residual bad blood between our two camps, suggesting that his side might still be irritated. But he had won, and I had lost. Winners in political campaigns didn't usually go out of their way to destroy their opponents, particularly if it involved great political and legal risk to themselves. What reason would there be to engineer a set up of planting marijuana in my car? *No sane person would do such a thing out of pure pique*, I thought. It did not seem plausible.

Nothing in my past experience had engendered a suspicious mind. I had grown up near the town of Nashville in southwestern Arkansas in a tiny rural community called County Line. It was a very cloistered, parochial environment. Almost all of the white population was of Scots-Irish ancestry, and many were related to one another by blood or marriage. The Scots-Irish started moving to this part of Arkansas from the Appalachian hill country after the Civil War. My Arkansas heritage began with my great-grandfather, who came by wagon train from the piedmont of South Carolina when he was a young boy. His ancestors had sailed from the port of Larne, County Antrim, Northern Ireland, in the late 1700s. These people were a close-knit group, pious and hardworking. They were mostly small-acreage farmers and craftsmen who knew each other, attended the same church, and shared the same tightly held values. They were suspicious of outsiders and seldom married anyone other than their own kind.

I came about my naiveté honestly. I was the eldest of eight children born to Fern Carol Rosik Glasgow and Thomas Courtlyn Glasgow, and I was raised in a rural culture that demanded full effort to meet basic household needs. The conditions of my childhood home more closely resembled those from the previous century. There was no electricity; kerosene lamps provided the lighting, and heating came from a fireplace and wood stoves. With no indoor plumbing, water was obtained by bucket from a well, clothes were washed outside in a big iron pot heated by a wood fire, and an outhouse served as the toilet.

My parents met in 1939 while both were attending Chillicothe Business College just northeast of Kansas City, Missouri. They got married about a year later. Both were from rural, farm backgrounds and had not previously ventured far from home. I was born in St. Louis one month after the bombing of Pearl Harbor in December 1941, signaling the entry of the United States into World War II. Soon after the war started, my dad volunteered for the Army Air Corps, figuring he would get drafted anyway and harboring a dream of becoming a combat pilot. Within a year, he had completed basic training and was shipped off to the Pacific war theater.

Valentine's Day, 1941; St. Louis, Missouri, where the author's parents, Thomas Courtlyn Glasgow and Fern Carol Rosik, were married. World War II would soon intervene. The author's father would join the Army Air Corps, stationed in the Pacific, and the author and his mother would move in with his paternal grandparents in rural southwestern Arkansas for the duration of the war.

During the war years, my mother and I lived with my Glasgow grandparents in the County Line community in rural southwestern Arkansas, where my dad had been raised. The culture shock must have been enormous for her, as she was raised in a modern home on a flourishing corn farm in Iowa. Her childhood home had up-to-date amenities, such as electricity, inside hot and cold running water, a bathroom, and modern appliances. Until I was four years old, I had no relationship at all with my dad. He came home only once, granted leave for a week when my grandfather died. Until my dad returned from the war, I was raised by two women: my mother and my grandmother.

Before the death of my grandfather, things went relatively well for my mom and me at County Line. My grandfather was a kindly and gregarious man, and he took a

The author's grandparents, Urban and Grace Glasgow; 1944. The author was raised at their farm in Howard County, Arkansas, near Nashville, during the war years. His grandfather was to die suddenly within a year, leaving him with his mother and grandmother.

special liking to me. Sometimes when he was plowing his fields, he would let me ride on the mule's back or on a wooden box attached to the plow tongue. The box contained fascinating arrowheads and other Native American artifacts he had plowed up. To me, this was great fun.

After my grandfather's death, a serious strain soon developed between my mom and my grandmother, an old-fashioned woman who seemed hopelessly mired in the rituals of previous centuries. A clannish woman, she regarded my mother as an outsider, or worse still, as a "Yankee." The rift between the two women worked to my advantage, and I quickly discovered that I often had the run of the place and could go wherever I wanted, such as out exploring in the woods or over to a nearby neighbor's house. So I was "lost" a lot, and I kept both of them worried, out looking for me. Later in life I found a packet of "war letters" between my mother and father. After the exchange of endearments, many of these letters discussed my "running away" episodes. My mom blamed them on my grandmother, who she thought was spoiling me with her permissive ways and turning me into a "little hellion," whereas my dad usually dismissed them as the antics of a spirited and curious child.

By the time my father returned, I had become very independent minded and resistant to authority—"hardheaded" was the adjective most often used. My father started out as a strict disciplinarian and believer in corporal punishment. Most often, he used his belt, doubled back, to spank me, but I can remember occasions when he forced me to cut my own switches from a weeping willow tree beside my grandmother's house. My father softened his discipline methods over the years as seven additional children enlarged our family, but I was the first. I did not resent my dad's efforts to discipline me; I accepted that he was doing it for my betterment. But many times, due to his time away during the war years, and the fact that I didn't really get to know him, the punishment seemed illegitimate.

My traditional Arkansas rural childhood included many friends and playmates. Two sets of first cousins—children of my dad's older sisters, each with a boy just a year or two older than me—lived less than a mile away. As a child, I often played rough-and-tumble games with the boys, and later on, they would become my closest social friends. I liked them and, as an added bonus, they both had their own cars during their teenage years, whereas I didn't. Both often stopped off to pick me up to go to town for entertainment on weekends, and sometimes to double-date.

My father finally surrendered to my mother's wishes, and we moved away from my grandmother's place to a rental house in Bingen, another tiny community, about the same distance north of Nashville as County Line was to the west. We were all delighted with the house, an old plantation-style structure with lots of room and indoor plumbing. But we moved again within a short time when my dad bought a fifty-acre farm in the County Line area near his family. The location was perfect, but the old, run-down five-room farmhouse had no plumbing, and the well occasionally ran dry in the summers. Our toilet was an outhouse by the barn. It took my father three years to dig the well deeper, install a pump, plumb the house, and build a bathroom. During that time, I developed a special place in my heart for my mother, who was usually alone with a baby in her arms and a toddler hanging on her dress while my dad was at work at his job for the U.S. Soil Conservation Service and the older kids were in school. In addition to all the washing, cooking, and cleaning, she managed to hand-make most of our clothes at a sewing machine in the front room. These were the hardest three years I can remember.

These hard times, and the constant scarcity of money, had a lasting influence on me. I did everything I could to make money on my own. From the time I was eleven years old, I raised one of my dad's best beef calves each year as a 4H project, hand-feeding, training, and grooming it for showing at the county fair in the fall. At the close of the fair, there would always be an auction sale, attended by some of the wealthiest and most successful cattlemen in the county. As a reward to the youngsters who raised and trained the calves, the 4H members were allowed to lead their animals into the auction arena and stand to show them off, while the cattlemen bid on them. They always bid the animal to a premium price, at least half again what it would have brought at a regular sale. For my efforts, my dad gave me a small percentage of the proceeds.

Around age fifteen, I started working on a chicken-catching crew. The northern part of the county had long been prime peach-growing country, but it had begun to change over to the poultry business, a year-round enterprise immune to seasonal cold weather. A poultry company had built a hatchery in Nashville and contracted with farmers to build chicken houses. Farmers raised the birds in bulk from baby chicks to broiler size, a process that took about twelve weeks. Catching chickens was done by hand at night while the chickens were asleep. Loaded into crates, the birds were then trucked to the processing plant. This work would always take half the night, and sometimes all of it. The job was dirty, smelly, grueling, and boring. Except during the summers, I had to go to school the next morning. Sleep deprivation and weariness did not produce an alert, industrious student, and my grades suffered as a result, barely over a "C" average by the time I graduated.

I had a generally successful high school experience—aside from my grades, in which I had little interest. Fairly adept at sports, I ran track and played football both in junior high and high school. During my senior year, I was elected by my teammates as a captain of the football team, and was an all-district se-lection as well. The next fall, many of my teammates and other high school classmates who had done well, but no better than me, went on to college. I didn't. I was working as an announcer at a local radio station, KBHC. I got this job after the junior year school play, when my strong, melodious voice garnered me some attention. Our school vocational adviser knew the radio station was looking for a student intern and recommended me. I worked at the station off and on for the next couple of years for minimum wage. I had no vehicle, lived five miles out of town, and usually had to hitchhike back and forth to my job at the station.

I do not remember any African Americans living in our commu-nity when I was growing up, possibly because almost all of the original Scots-Irish settlers had only small land holdings and few, if any, owned slaves. However, I have two childhood memories involving African Americans, both reflecting the racial values of my white culture. In that pre–civil rights era, segregation was the norm, and with it came an attitude of white superiority.

Years before I was born, a black woman named Annie had worked for my grandparents. Characteristic of the time, only Annie's first name was used in our house. She was originally hired to help raise my dad as a baby when my grandmother became ill. Over the years, she would occasionally come by to visit. My dad thought a lot of her and she was very fond of him, calling him by his middle name, Courtlyn.

One day when I was about eight years old, while we were still living with my grandmother, Annie stopped by. She must have been in her eighties by that time. My dad greeted her warmly. Annie explained that she stopped by to share the news of the birth of her first great-grandchild. My dad asked the child's name.

"Oh, Mister Courtlyn," said Annie, beaming, "they gave him a biblical name, Haloid."

"Haloid?" queried my dad, raising his eyebrows. "Where does that name appear in the scripture, Annie? I don't believe I recall it."

"Oh, you know," she replied, "Our Father who art in heaven, Haloid be thy name."

My dad chuckled and then got a bit red faced, looking like he was about to burst out laughing. But he caught himself, congratulated Annie, and the visit continued for a bit longer. After she drove away and my dad was talking with my grandmother about the visit, I heard him say, "You will never guess what ole nigger Annie told me they had named her great-grandchild." My dad told her, and they both had a good laugh.

I recall feeling ill at ease. I knew my dad genuinely felt very kindly toward Annie and her family. But this was not the first time that I had heard him use the "N" word. The whole family regularly referred to Annie that way, as if it were just a part of her name. But there was something additionally discordant about this occasion. Annie had gone out of her way to proudly share personal news about her family, and my dad and his mother had made light of it.

Back then, use of the "N" word did not necessarily mean that the speaker was bigoted, but it did connote prejudice. In my grandmother's case, there was little question. I recall her complaints about the Civil War, which she somehow blamed on black people becoming "uppity." My dad was a product of the place and time in which he was raised, as was my mother. But in her Iowa childhood, the "N" word and the values it represented were shunned, and my mother often gently reprimanded my dad when he would slip.

The second incident occurred in 1958 when I was still in high school. Late one afternoon, my great-uncle, Kermit Glasgow, drove up our front driveway honking his truck horn furiously. Kermit brought news of a car accident a short distance up the road. A crashed vehicle was on fire, and its driver was trapped inside. Daddy and I immediately hopped into Kermit's truck, and we took off down the highway.

We found a car smashed against a giant oak, with a fire blazing under the hood. The driver's door was open, and a black man was half out of the car, his right leg still pinned underneath the steering wheel. Thick black smoke was pouring out from under the dash inside the car, and there was a strong smell of gasoline.

"Help me! Help me!" the man was screaming.

Daddy, Kermit, and I grabbed him and started pulling, but his foot was wedged underneath the brake pedal. I could see the fire was beginning to spread underneath the car, evidently going down the gas line. If it got to the gas tank, I realized, it could explode.

Now the man was screaming, "Cut it off! Cut it off! Oh God, I don't want to die." Then he began crying, seemingly accepting a bad fate. "I'm going to die," he blubbered.

Another vehicle pulled up, a pickup truck, and two white men jumped out to help. They had been fishing and had a cooler with fish and water in the back. They dumped the water, fish and all, onto the flaming car hood. They threw dirt on it, as well, and the flames momentarily subsided.

I was still twisting on his foot, and at the same time pulling up on the brake pedal. I could see the flames underneath. *Time's running out*, I thought. *I might die, too.*

Suddenly his foot came loose. My dad and I furiously dragged him away from the vehicle, our feet churning in the gravely soil. Just in time, too, for we heard a loud "Whoosh" and felt an explosion of searing hot air hit our faces and arms. The flames had reached the tank and engulfed the car, shooting up in a big fireball.

We had managed to drag the man a safe distance away to avoid him or us getting badly burned. The man had grown silent, staring at the fire, his eyes wide. "Thank you," he mumbled. We noticed for the first time that he had a strong odor of alcohol on his breath.

"Drunk," Daddy said.

"Lucky nigger," I heard one of the pickup men say. "Some people would have let him burn."

An ambulance and the sheriff soon arrived, and the crisis was over. Once Daddy and I got back home, and the adrenaline had slowed, I felt proud of what we had done. Knowing well the danger we faced, we had kept at it and saved a man's life. But the memory of the white man's crude remark stayed with me, and I realized the sad truth of what he had said.

8. The Abuse of Power

In the fall of 1958, I first became aware of pernicious politicians and the punitive actions that could be implemented by elected officials. The desegregation crisis at Little Rock Central High School had been headline news in Arkansas and throughout much of the nation the previous year. Nashville had its share of segregationists, as did most towns in the South, but it also had more than its fair share of level-headed and practical citizens in important spheres of public life. Local civic leaders realized President Dwight D. Eisenhower would enforce *Brown v. Board of Education* with the full strength of the federal government. We had no firebrand segregationists, or if we did, they kept quiet. There were no demonstrations or protests. Nashville integrated its public schools, slowly to be sure, but consistently and without incident.

Nashville is about 130 miles southwest of Little Rock. The distance at that time could be measured in more than miles. As a high school student in a small rural town, I had little awareness of the activities of state government. A year had passed, and Little Rock seemed to have addressed its problems. My teenaged world was busy with high school football, dating girls, and participation in the local 4H Club. On a trip to the State Fair and Livestock Show in Little Rock, however, I learned that the turmoil in Little Rock was continuing. Political maneuvers by Governor Orval Faubus and a group of reprehensible and complicit legislators had thwarted the federal enforcement effort. To my astonishment, I learned that public high schools had been closed. Little Rock students were experiencing what came to be known "The Lost Year."

George Fisher cartoon of Oval E. Faubus.

I was a member of our 4H Club county livestock judging team, and we had come to Little Rock because the team had scored well at a regional judging contest at Southern State College, now Southern Arkansas University (SAU), in Magnolia. The state contest was held in conjunction with the state fair. County extension agent Radus James, our team sponsor, took us up on a school day to participate.

We left early and arrived at Barton Coliseum and the fairgrounds late in the morning. To my eyes, the scene was stupendous—a giant lighted Ferris wheel was turning and there were rides of all kinds; row upon row of tents housing various games and prizes; carnival barkers calling out; food stands selling cotton candy, popcorn, peanuts, and such; a huge coliseum; and acres of animal show barns. I had never seen anything like it, and even at mid-day there were throngs of people. By comparison, the county fair at Nashville seemed paltry.

I saw a number of other high school students at the fair that day, particularly a few Central High School football players wearing their colorful letter jackets (yellow with black leather sleeves) festooned with yellow patches showing the years each player had lettered and the championships won during their careers. Most

Arkansans knew of the amazing football record compiled by Little Rock's Central High School—four state championships in a row and recognition as the number-one team in the nation. To me, and many other players at the smaller schools across the state, the Central players were demigods.

We chatted with some of these students, and it became clear that they were not part of the 4H livestock judging. They were able to be at the fair on a school day, we discovered, because their schools were closed for the year.

"Why?" I asked.

"You'll have to ask Governor Faubus," came the answer from one of the Central High guys. "He doesn't want us going to school with Negroes."

"I thought this was all over last year," I persisted. "What happened?"

"It's real weird," the Central student replied. "The teachers are at school, but they won't let the students in. And even though we're not going to school, the team still plays football. A lot of students have already transferred, including a lot of the cheerleaders and some of our best players. It's really frustrating."

"Sounds kind of crazy," I said.

"You're right," the boy said. "My dad says it's all about politics. Rotten is what it is."

I later learned just how pervasive the effort to stop integration of the public schools in Little Rock had been. Governor Faubus had been ably assisted by a group of reprehensible and complicit legislators, including Paul Van Dalsem, state representative from Perryville. He was also supported by Bruce Bennett, probably the most corrupt attorney general this state has had, at least in the post–World War II era. With this lineup of state officials, the blocking action against integration of the Little Rock schools proceeded posthaste.

Faubus was running for a third term as governor, seeking to protect his credentials as a committed segregationist. He called for a special session of the Arkansas legislature, presenting a series of sixteen bills through friendly legislators, including Representative Van Dalsem and Senator Joe Lee Anderson of Helena, designed to stop lawful integration. Among the laws passed was Act 4, which allowed the closure of any school in Arkansas that proceeded with integration, and Act 5, which provided state funding for any student who moved to another school to avoid integration, whether the school was publicly or privately funded.

The new laws closed all high schools in Little Rock, initiating the "Lost Year." This interrupted the education of some 4,000 students, locking them out of school and putting them, in effect, on their own. Parents, teachers, and administrators scrambled to find other schools for them, either by moving elsewhere or by enrolling them in private schools. Many students dropped out of school entirely. Others entered military service. Faubus, however, did not forget the most important thing: He decreed that the high school football games would continue as scheduled.[6]

But even more malevolent were the bills authored by Bennett designed to cripple civil rights groups that he considered to be "enemies of America." Most of these bills specifically targeted the National Association for the Advancement of Colored People (NAACP). These bills prevented the group from providing legal counsel or funding lawsuits in the state, kept NAACP members from becoming state employees, and opened NAACP membership rolls and personnel records to state scrutiny. Bennett publicly accused the NAACP of being associated with an international communist conspiracy. Demagogic U.S. senator Joe McCarthy, of the Senate's infamous communist-hunting Subcommittee on Investigations, who died in 1957, undoubtedly rejoiced from his grave.

In retrospect, the situation in Little Rock through the Lost Year was a continuing collision of politics and public sentiment. Public groups were formed to support either the closing or the re-opening of the schools. Forty-four Central High teachers were fired, and the superintendent and school board membership changed three times. By the end of the 1958–59 school year, a federal district court deemed unconstitutional the acts authorizing closure, the withholding of funds, and the firing of teachers for any schools. Finally, Little Rock's schools began to integrate, with the courts encouraging busing of students. Meanwhile, white flight to the suburbs began in earnest.[7] Overall, the reputation of Arkansas and its capital city suffered for a very long time. The stigma lingers to this day.

9. THE STING OF INJUSTICE

One additional episode in my youth provided a distinct Arkansas coming-of-age experience, rounding out my previous exposures to illicit sex, racism, and the wielding of political power. The incident gave insight into the attitudes of a few people in the criminal-justice system and their casual approach to denying citizens the rights of due process. Of all my childhood experiences, this one most presaged my dealings with the characters behind my arrest at the border twelve years later.

Like my high school peers in Little Rock, I, too, had lost a year. But my loss was due to my own lack of foresight and confidence. After graduating from high school in 1960, I had not applied for college. I believed my grades were too low. I also had no financial resources to pay for higher education. Instead, during that year, I knocked around the area, often with my longtime hometown buddy and former teammate Royce "Rat" Tallant. We moved from place to place and took odd jobs at low pay. The last, and worst, job was at a small machine shop in North Little Rock. Despite horrible working conditions—machine oil and metal shavings everywhere, the air filled with choking dust, and a near-constant harangue to work harder by a psychopathic boss—I had saved enough to make a down payment on a battered 1953 Chevy sedan, financed with a North Little Rock used-car dealer.

After a short time, Royce and I quit, each moving back to our parents' homes in Nashville. As there were no jobs there, my money soon ran out and I could not keep up the monthly payments on the old Chevy. When my dad found out about this, he told me that I had no choice but to take the car back to the dealer in North Little Rock and turn it in. I knew that he was right, so I set out on a journey that turned into one of the most frightening experiences of my young life.

Accompanied by my buddy Royce, I returned the car to the dealer. Now on foot, Royce and I would have to hitchhike back to Nashville. Royce contacted his uncle, Dewey Huggins, who lived in North Little Rock near the Missouri Pacific Railroad yard, and Dewey agreed to drive us out on the highway to start hitch-hiking home. Dewey drove a 1955 Ford Thunderbird, a sporty pink-and-gray hardtop convertible.

By midmorning, we were riding in the T-Bird out of Little Rock on the Benton highway. A highway police car from the Weights and Measures Division pulled up beside us, and the lone officer driving stared at us intently. Dewey waved at him, and the officer dropped back. He followed us awhile, then pulled his car back up beside us again and motioned for us to pull over. Dewey parked on the concrete shoulder. When the officer got out of his car and walked up to us, I noticed he was smiling and acting nonchalant.

Must not be anything to worry about, I thought.

The officer said that he had received a radio call from the State Police to be on the lookout for a car like ours, but he had no idea what it was about.

"I figured it had to be you," he said. "I doubt there are very many other pink T-Birds around here."

By this time, the three of us had stepped out of the car and were standing on the side of the highway with no reason to be concerned. Suddenly we heard the sound of a siren in the distance. Looking down the highway we could see a flashing red light approaching, then a blue-and-white state police cruiser materialized, hurtling toward us at high speed. The cruiser skidded and screeched to a stop beside us in the right travel lane. A uniformed state policeman was driving, with a plainclothes detective beside him. As soon as the vehicle came to a stop, the plainclothes guy jumped out, wielding a mean-looking pump shotgun, shouting, "Down! Get down on the ground, face first, all of you, right now!"

The uniformed officer was standing on the opposite side of the cruiser. His handgun was propped on the top of the car and pointed in our direction. Royce and I did as commanded, but Dewey continued to stand, holding his hands out in front of him. He said, "Wait, there must be some mistake…"

Plainclothes jammed his shotgun into Dewey's chest, saying, "You drop or I'll make you wish you had."

Dewey got down on his hands and knees, still pleading, "What is this all about?" before flattening out on his stomach. Then the Weights and Measures officer started protesting, "Hey, that is not necessary. These guys voluntarily stopped and waited."

"Shut up. This is none of your concern," growled Plainclothes. "They are under arrest. We'll take over from here. You go on about your business."

They cuffed us, roughly, then jerked us to our feet and crammed us in the back seat of the cruiser. The cruiser took off toward Little Rock. At the State Police headquarters building, we were fingerprinted and had our mugshots taken. My hands were shaking so badly that they had to redo my prints. Finally, we were split up and taken to separate interrogation rooms. The room I was led to looked like the ones you see in the movies—small and square with a darkened plate-glass window and a metal table with three chairs. The only illumination in the room was from a very bright, hooded "snake lamp" on the table.

I sat there alone for twenty minutes, shaking and trembling, my throat parched dry, badly needing a drink of water. In walked Plainclothes and pulled up a chair.

"Roger, I guess it's time that I introduced myself," he said. "I'm Detective Tracy."

He started out friendly, apologizing for the handcuffs and explaining that no charges would be filed if I cooperated.

"We didn't do anything," I said, screwing up my courage a notch. "Why did you pick us up?"

Tracy sat back in his chair and looked at me, his demeanor hardening. "Roger, I really don't have time to play games. You know very well why. Are you going to cooperate or not?"

"I am cooperating," I said, "but I don't know what you want."

At that, Tracy abruptly stood up. He told me to give my situation some serious thought and said that jail was a real option. Saying he would return in a few minutes, he left. About thirty minutes of silence and stillness followed as I sat alone in the bare room. Then the door opened again and Tracy walked in. He carried a rifle in one hand, what looked like a .22-caliber semi-automatic. He put the gun on the table between us.

"This yours?" he asked, watching me closely.

"No," I said firmly. "Where did it come from?"

He stood there awhile looking at me, then said, "It came from the trunk of your uncle's car."

"He's not my uncle," I said. "He's Royce Tallant's."

Tracy made no comment. Then he said, "When was the last time you were in the Safeway store at Asher and University?"

"I've never been in that store," I said quickly.

He did not respond but left the room again. Tracy came back in, this time with a chrome-colored revolver in his hand. He slammed it on the table. "What about this?"

"I don't know," I said. "You tell me."

"You shouldn't get smart. It's not good for your health."

"You should tell me what this is all about," I answered.

"That store was robbed about a week ago," Tracy said, "by two tall, young white men, one with a rifle and the other with a pistol. That's the description we got. These are the guns. You and your friend are the guys."

"Absolutely not," I insisted. "A week ago, we were at home with our parents in Nashville. You are barking up the wrong tree."

"I don't think so," Tracy said, getting up to leave. "If this doesn't check out, I'll see that the book is thrown at you."

When he returned, Tracy stood there staring at me. He seemed puzzled.

"You are free to go. Get out of here," he said, and opened the door. "Your friend is in the next room. He's being released also. I suggest that you guys go home to Nashville and stay there."

"What about Mr. Huggins?"

"We aren't through with him yet."

"How do you expect us to get home? We have no transportation."

"That's your problem."

"Well, can you at least take us back out on the highway where you got us?"

"We don't provide taxi service."

I had to grit my teeth to keep from losing my cool and saying more than I should. I left Tracy in the interrogation room and found Royce. Realizing there was nothing we could do about Dewey, we left the building and walked down Asher to University

Avenue and stood there with our thumbs out. It was late afternoon, about five o'clock, but our bad luck had finally turned. In a short time, we got a ride that took us back out to the Benton highway. There, we caught a ride with an eighteen-wheeler headed to Texarkana. We rode with him to Hope, where my dad came to pick us up.

On the ride back from Hope, we told my dad of the ordeal and how angry and bitter we felt. To my surprise, he seemed pretty upset about it, too. At first he wondered about the guns, but Royce explained that Dewey and his wife lived in a bad part of North Little Rock. She worked at the Timex factory at night, and Dewey kept guns for protection. He had always carried the .22 rifle in the trunk of his car and the .32 revolver under the seat.

The next day, my dad told me he was going to call Bobby Steel, the circuit judge, and have Royce and me talk with him about what had happened. He called and briefly gave Judge Steel a rundown of the facts. Steel said he could see us that afternoon.

Royce and I met Steel in his office at the courthouse in Nashville. He seemed to already know a good deal about the situation from what my dad had told him. We suspected he had already called someone in Little Rock, possibly somebody higher up in the State Police (his brother George "Jetty" Steel was on the State Police Commission). He asked us a few questions about what had happened, then picked up the phone and dialed a number.

"I'd like to speak with Detective John Tracy, please," Steel said.

There was a short wait, and then Steel continued. "Detective Tracy, this is Bobby Steel. I'm the circuit judge for the Ninth Judicial District, which includes Nashville. I have a couple of young men in my office and understand that you picked them up and took them in for questioning yesterday?"

A pause. "What was the reason you picked them up?" A longer pause.

"Queer bait?" Steel exploded. "What the hell are you talking about? These boys are well-respected members of this community. They are football players, for Christ's sake!" Another pause. "Listen, for future reference, any time you decide to pick up and question a young man from down here, you call me first. Is that clear?" The silence was deafening in the judge's office after his outburst. He listened on the phone a moment longer. "Okay, good, make sure you do," Steel said, and he hung up the phone.

"What did he say?" I asked.

"He made up a story about homosexuals picking up and molesting young men. He thought you were involved in that because the car matched a report."

"That's just stupid," I protested. "Besides, he told us we were picked up because of a Safeway store robbery."

Steel looked at us and grinned. "He wasn't going to repeat that obvious lie with me. But his ass is in the wringer now. He'll think twice before doing that again."

Royce and I thanked him profusely for standing up for us, and we left feeling a little better. It was another maturing moment for me, but one that left me feeling very disillusioned. My initial understanding concerned the abuse of power by those in the criminal-justice system. That was a revelation in itself. Even more disturbing was the realization that bullying and intimidating behavior by the State Police was commonplace.

10. A College Education

A year had passed since high school graduation, and I had gone nowhere, still with no car, no money, no hope for a better future. Slowly, inexorably it seemed, without even realizing it, I had given up. I often found myself hanging around the pool hall in Nashville with other pitiful losers.

Then one day in the summer of 1961, I got a break. Two former high school buddies and sports teammates, Bobby Feemster and Thomas Chesshir, invited me to ride with them to Southern State College at Magnolia (now Southern Arkansas University—SAU), about seventy-five miles away. The previous year, they had been on partial sports scholarships at North Texas State College in Commerce, Texas. Now, both had transferred to Southern State, and they were driving down that day to enroll for the fall semester.

The idea was for me to just ride along and keep them company. But a chance meeting on campus changed the course of my life and put me on the career track that I have continued on to this day.

On campus, my friends went to check on their enrollment, and I found myself standing in front of the administration building with nothing to do. I went inside to escape the heat of the day. As I was loitering, dumbly gazing at a hallway bulletin board, someone walked up behind me. I turned around to see a tall, lanky, balding man with a long, angular face. The man carried himself with a stately bearing and had a serious expression.

"Hello," he said. "I'm Imon Bruce." The name meant nothing to me. "Are you joining us for school this fall?"

"Er, no, I'm not," I stammered. "I just came down with a couple of friends who are enrolling here."

"If you don't mind my asking," Bruce ventured, "are you going to college somewhere else?"

"No, sir. I would like to go to college, but I just haven't managed to work it out yet," I said. In truth, I had thought many times during the past year of going to college, but I had no money and no options for earning anything other than minimum wage.

"Well, I do not know your personal situation, and do not want to intrude," he said, "but we have a wide range of financial-assistance packages available for our students."

"Yes, sir," I said. "I noticed that, but, see, I am the oldest of eight children and my parents just cannot afford to help out much, and I've got nothing saved up."

By this time, I felt pretty worthless, and the only thing I wanted was to get away and save what little was left of my fragile dignity. But Bruce persisted. I still had no idea exactly who he was, other than obviously an important person at the college. In a calm and soothing manner, he said, "If you truly want to go to college, I believe that we can make it happen. Come with me down to my office and let's talk." After a short walk down the hall, Bruce ushered me through a door with a big window that had stenciled on it, "College President."

I went home that afternoon with a package of materials for student aid through the National Defense Student Loan (NDSL) program (back then, a college education was considered a matter of national defense), which also included applications for on-campus jobs and an enrollment application. Bruce also sent me off that day with the statement, made with calm assurance, that he would see me in the fall.

Later that summer, when I went out to our mailbox on the highway, as I had every day for several weeks, I found an official-looking envelope from the NDSL program, addressed to me. I knew at that moment that the contents of this envelope would dictate the course of the rest of my life. I went back to my bedroom—rather "our" bedroom, as there were three of us boys sleeping in a small bedroom at the back of the old farmhouse—and with clammy, sweating fingers, I opened the envelope, took out the letter, and read, "Your application for a student loan in the sum of $350 has been approved for the fall semester 1961."

The fates had turned my way. I was off to college!

★ ★ ★

Political views were abundant at Southern State College (which became SAU in 1976). This was during the early years of the civil rights movement and the Vietnam War. There was profound social and political tumult everywhere, and the student body was a hotbed of political activism.

For a small college in the Deep South, SAU had a surprising number of progressive, even liberal, students; a roughly equal number held very conservative views. Fascinated by this mixing bowl of differing political opinions, I changed my major after one semester from general studies to history, with a minor in political science. I frequented the college library to read about American history, particularly regarding the South. I remember being quite surprised, and shocked, when I read about Jim Crow laws.

Like many others who had grown up in the South, I had observed the effects of these laws without considering their inherent flaws. I recall having some puzzlement over a few things I saw, such as why black people had a separate entry to the movie theater in Nashville and had to sit in the balcony, and why there were "white only" signs on public drinking fountains. But these practices seemed to be the natural order of things. I didn't pay them much mind.

After I started going to the library, I learned that segregation and Jim Crow laws were not limited to drinking fountains and theaters. They covered all manner of things, from voting, holding public office, and serving on juries, to cross dating and interracial sex and marriage. The laws prohibited any activity that smacked of black people "mixing" with the white population in any way. Beyond the prohibitions in areas such as public schools, transportation, hospitals, housing, and prisons, these laws even extended beyond life, to burial plots and cemeteries. The more I read about it, the more I recognized how the laws were specifically and blatantly designed to thwart the exercise by African Americans of their civil rights.

True, I had gone to school in a segregated system in Nashville. I knew that blacks lived in a separate part of town that had dirt streets, broken-down houses, and shabby schools. And I often heard blacks ridiculed by whites. I had also seen televised news of the civil rights movement, including the demonstrations in Birmingham, Alabama, and the use of fire hoses and attack dogs against non-violent protestors. But I had no real appreciation of the vicious ways that racism could show itself in everyday life. That changed one night in Magnolia in 1963.

While at SAU, my friendship continued with Tom Chesshir, who had a part-time job as a night radio operator for the Magnolia Police Department. Chesshir had developed a friendly relationship with one of the officers, a wiry white guy in his late thirties named Jimmy. One Saturday night, Jimmy invited Chesshir and me to accompany him in his police car as he made his rounds and responded to radio calls. A ten-year veteran of the department, Jimmy wore highly polished black cowboy boots, nicely pressed standard-issue trousers, and a crisp ironed white shirt with a shiny badge attached. Jimmy's attitude of self pride, I soon learned, was accompanied by a swaggering and menacing racism.

On the night we joined him, Jimmy got a radio call about a suspected burglary in a black neighborhood on the south side of town.

"This should be fun," he said, turning on his flashing red light and siren, flying down the highway at high speed until we reached the area, then barreling down narrow city streets with water-filled ditches on both sides. It was common in those days in the black sections of town, particularly on a Saturday night, for a sizable number of pedestrians, men and women, young and old, to be out walking in the streets. Jimmy took great delight in forcing them off the street into the ditches.

"Watch this—I'll make them jump," he would say while careening down the streets, laughing gleefully. He sped up and down, scattering people like flapping chickens, but he never bothered to stop at a house or conduct any investigation.

Later we drove out on the highway toward El Dorado and came up behind a ragged-looking pickup truck driving slowly with no taillights. "Uh oh," said Jimmy. "Looky here. This'll be a good'un."

In the next ten minutes, Jimmy behaved in the most despicable manner, abusing his position as a public servant and demonstrating a deep-rooted bigotry and the essential cowardice that lies at the heart of most bullying. The driver of the truck was an elderly black man, with short gray hair and a whitish goatee. Chesshir and I watched incredulously as Jimmy stuck his pistol in the man's face, smacked him hard on the back of his neck with it, and generally terrified him, before writing a basic citation and turning him loose. As the shaken man drove away, Jimmy laughed and said, "Crazy ole nigger ought not be allowed on the highway."

The experience was one that I would never forget. Racism was endemic in many parts of the South, I realized, and flourished especially in local law enforcement circles. Arkansas was no exception. Most white people gave law enforcement the benefit of the doubt in any dispute over alleged heavy-handed tactics against black people. From that point on, I didn't. I also remembered my frightening encounter with the Arkansas State Police a couple of years earlier. It wasn't just black people who got harassed.

In my freshman year I joined the Young Democrats Club, and, by my sophomore year, I had been elected president. By that time, I had developed a cadre of friends who knew of my interest in politics, and they thought, I guess, that I had some talents to offer. With their encouragement, I ran for vice president of the student body during my junior year, and I was elected from a three-person field of candidates. I held both of these positions until college graduation.

I had the good fortune to get both U.S. senator J. William Fulbright and David Pryor, then in the state House of Representatives, to come down to Magnolia to address student gatherings. Pryor, then in his late twenties, was from nearby Camden. He was one of the leaders of a progressive-minded "Young Turk" group of state representatives. During the height of the Orval Faubus era, this group often found itself on the opposite side of Faubus's old guard cronies. Pryor had generated a good bit of statewide publicity and was in demand as a guest speaker. He would be up for reelection in the next cycle, so he was eager to make as many events as he could. When I called in the early spring of 1963, he readily agreed to come down and meet with the Young Democrats Club.

At the suggestion of our faculty sponsor, political science professor William Nolan, we also invited the student senate members, as well as students from Nolan's political science classes. In all, we rounded up about fifty students and met with Pryor in the college cafeteria for a meal, followed by his presentation. The whole affair was quite informal, and Pryor generally avoided controversial topics, primarily giving an inspirational talk about the value of public service. He was friendly and lik-

George Fisher cartoon of David Pryor.

able, and everyone seemed impressed. Fulbright's appearance, however, was in a whole different category.

It was the fall of 1964, and I had just spent the summer working as an intern in the newly formed press office of the Smithsonian Institution in Washington DC. Fulbright served as a regent for the Smithsonian. Through his patronage—and helped considerably by the efforts of his administrative assistant, Parker Westbrook, who was originally from my hometown of Nashville—I landed this plum job. While in Washington that summer, I had met Senator Fulbright at an event on the National Mall celebrating the opening of the Museum of American History.

Returning to SAU for the fall semester, I got the idea that we should invite Senator Fulbright to address the student body. I knew it was a longshot, for it was not an election year for him, and I had no illusions that my influence would carry any weight. But I called Parker Westbrook to feel out the possibilities, and he suggested that I write the senator an invitation letter. Parker said that Fulbright would be making a few trips back home to Arkansas that fall, and the SAU visit might fit his schedule. I wrote the letter and, to my amazement, he agreed.

I informed Professor Nolan, who was simply agog, and he quickly notified the college president, Dr. Imon Bruce, who was equally excited. Never in recent memory, it seemed, had the campus been fortunate enough to land such an illustrious speaker, one of worldwide reputation and fame. The whole student body, the faculty, and the community at large were quite excited once the word got out.

Fulbright spoke at the open-air Greek amphitheatre on the southeast edge of the campus. The weather turned out to be perfect when the appointed day arrived, and all went according to plan. I escorted Senator Fulbright to the theatre for his 7 p.m. program and was amazed at the large crowd that had turned out. The concrete steps of the theatre were packed, and several additional rows of metal folding chairs were filled. In addition, many people were standing behind those seated.

I noticed that a good number of the attendees, particularly those who were standing, were not students, but older adults, presumably from Magnolia and surrounding areas. Some of the townsfolk were rather rough looking, wearing overalls and straw hats. Senator Fulbright was one of the more moderate senators in the

George Fisher cartoon of J. William Fulbright.

South at that time. The John Birch Society was in full swing, and Ku Klux Klan recruiting posters were still seen nailed to trees and posts across the countryside. Professor Nolan had forewarned me that some of these elements might be there.

I made some short introductory remarks, emphasizing Senator Fulbright's deep Arkansas roots. He was a graduate of the University of Arkansas with a BA in political science in 1925, where he had been president of the student body, captain of the tennis team, and a four-year star running back for the Razorback football team. He had also won a Rhodes scholarship to Oxford, where he got two more degrees, and then graduated from law school at George Washington in DC and returned home to teach at the law school in Fayetteville. To cap it off, at the age of thirty-nine, he became president of the University of Arkansas—the youngest president of a major university in the country.

I deliberately left out some of his political and legislative accomplishments, which I figured most intelligent people already knew, such as his long service as chairman of the Senate Foreign Relations Committee; his efforts in establishing the United Nations; his fight against McCarthyism, including his lone vote against the appropriations bill to fund Joe McCarthy's Special Investigative Committee; his sponsorship of the McCarthy censure resolution; and his founding of the Fulbright Scholarship and Foreign Student Exchange Program. I didn't figure the guys in the overalls and straw hats standing at the back needed to be reminded of all that.

Senator Fulbright, on the other hand, didn't hold back. He spoke eloquently of the importance of the UN, the need for multilateralism in international affairs, and the dangers of the "arrogance of power" (he was soon to author a book by that title). The student body and the faculty listened attentively and politely, occasionally breaking into brief rounds of restrained applause. But I was still worried about the overalls guys. They stood stone still and silent. Soon it happened: off in a dark corner came the loud, throaty taunt, "Communist!" That was immediately followed by another gruff shout, "We don't need no socialism around here!"

Senator Fulbright immediately stepped forward a few feet away from the microphone in the direction from which the taunts came, and said, in a deep, forceful, melodious voice:

"You know, I think the greatest of our Constitution's Bill of Rights is freedom of speech, as embodied in the First Amendment. This does not mean freedom to speak your mind just in your own home, or church, or among likeminded people. It means public discourse. The Constitution says that there shall be no abridgement of the freedom of speech, or interference with the right to peaceably assemble." He went on, "So long as you behave yourself, and do not interfere with the work of the government, you can go to any town square and say just about anything you want, or engage in discourse with others with whom you disagree until you are blue in the face. So far as I know we are the only country on earth that allows the unfettered expression of opinion, and I think it's one of our greatest strengths."

Directly addressing the hecklers, he continued, "Those of you who spoke up against communism and socialism just now, I invite you to step up and have a discussion about whatever is on your mind. I am vehemently opposed to both of those philosophies, and I would be glad to discuss them with you, if you are willing, out here in the open." Then he concluded, with his stentorian voice ringing, "But not with some ignoramus hiding in the dark!"

It was dead quiet for a second or two. Nobody moved. Then a thunderous applause erupted from all around that lasted, it seemed, for several minutes. I could see some vague dark figures slinking away from the back of the crowd. Never, to this day, have I seen such masterful crowd control. Fulbright was fifty-nine years of age, yet he moved lithely, still the athlete, and gracefully delivered the most eloquent yet devastating salvo of words I have ever heard.

★ ★ ★

By my junior year, I had been recruited to serve on a state panel of "Student Leaders for Faubus," consisting of several student body presidents from other colleges and universities across the state. While not enamored of Governor Oval Faubus, I thought this would be an excellent opportunity to get to know some notable people who were likely to become future leaders.

I met with this panel and with Faubus in Little Rock a couple of times. We were introduced to some of his media people, and we cut some television ads extolling the virtues of the Faubus administration. This was quite heady for a country boy like me, of course, but the more I learned about Faubus and the policies of his administration, the less I thought of him.

At a state convention of Young Democrats held during my senior year in college, there was an anti-Faubus slate of candidates seeking elected positions within the state organization, as well as a pro-Faubus group. Normally, the Young Democrats Club comprised college students, not older adult politicians, but these were not normal times.

Faubus had served five consecutive two-year terms as governor and had developed opposition among the more progressive-minded members of the Democratic Party after the 1957 Little Rock school desegregation crisis. Most of this opposition was centered in the larger urban areas, such as Little Rock. However, Faubus remained strong in the rural areas, where most of the state's population was located at that time, so he had never been seriously challenged.

This was about to change, and the Young Democrats Club would prove to be the determinative vehicle. At the state convention, I sided strongly with the anti-Faubus group, who would prove to be exceedingly daring. The convention was held at the Marion Hotel, the premier gathering place for all Arkansas politicians great and small.

Members of the pro-Faubus group, feeling totally confident of victory, had ensconced themselves on the upper, more desirable floors of the hotel, and they then repaired to the "Gar Hole" bar in the basement, where they imbibed until the wee hours. The starting time for the convention was nine o'clock the next morning.

The opposition members, led by Sam Boyce, a practicing lawyer in his mid-thirties from Newport, were staying on a lower floor. Although it was against their nature, they avoided the alcohol (for the most part), kept their wits about them, prepared a plan for the next morning, and went to bed early.

Confident that the pro-Faubus forces would be hung over and stumbling in late for the convention, the anti-Faubus forces disabled the elevators (trapping the president, Faubus aide John Browning, and their candidate for president of the Young Democrats, Sheffield Nelson, inside one). The plot to disable the elevators had been hatched the previous evening. Someone in our crowd knew someone who worked in hotel maintenance— reportedly my future friend and mentor R. M. "Max" Allison— and had agreed to throw the electrical switch that controlled the elevators at a certain time the next morning. I had attended the plotting meeting, and I got down to the convention floor early, eagerly watching, and voting, as the scheme we had put together quickly moved forward.

We gathered in the ballroom well ahead of time, and we had the vice president of the Young Democrats, Roy Lee Hight, gavel the convention to order at exactly nine o'clock. The first order of business was the election of our next president. As was planned, Sam Boyce was the only one nominated, since the leaders of the Faubus forces were stuck upstairs.

Roy Lee intoned, "Do I hear any other nominations?" then went on very quickly: "Hearing no further nominations, is there a motion for the election of Mr. Sam Boyce by acclamation?" The motion was stated, and Boyce was quickly elected by acclamation. Somebody estimated that this clever maneuver took less than three minutes.

By this time, the pro-Faubus forces had made their way into the room by way of the stairs, but it was too late. They later appealed to the national organization of Young Democrats, but they were denied. Governor Faubus had suffered his first significant defeat, and I had been an integral part of it.

Governor Faubus was furious, as this was the first chink in his armor. Until that time, he had seemed unstoppable, and he had a reputation for making enemies pay a price for opposing him. One would think that he would not go so far as to cause trouble for a relatively insignificant student at a small college in southern Arkansas. But he did.

Somehow, the Faubus people found out that I had been associated with the events at the convention. Shortly after I arrived back on campus, I was asked to meet Dr. Bruce in his office. At the meeting, Bruce told me he had received a call from Governor Faubus's office.

"I cannot imagine why Governor Faubus would be interested in anything I did," I said.

"Apparently they are quite displeased with what happened up there, with the Young Democrats' convention and all, and they evidently think that you are a part of it in some way," he explained. "I thought that you might be able to shed some light on the subject."

"All I did was cast a vote," I said, choosing not to mention the elevator plot.

"You know, as a public college, we get a lot of our funding through the state legislature, and the governor's office has a big role in that, so I thought it was important to have you over," Bruce explained.

So I told him the gist of the story, leaving out some of the more colorful parts, such as the stuck elevators. I told him that the convention started at the appointed time, but the Faubus folks were upset that the convention didn't wait on them to get there before starting.

"They brought it on themselves," Bruce said. "You can't hold up the service waiting on the choir to arrive."

"That's what I thought," I said. "I was committed to vote for Boyce anyway."

Bruce and I talked a bit longer, but he dismissed the incident as inconsequential. Reflecting back on the elevator stunt in later years, I had some misgivings. True, it was for a noble cause, to deliver a body blow to Orval Faubus, then at the height of his powers, but it was also a low blow. What if the shoe had been on the other foot, and the Faubus people at the convention had pulled the stunt on us? We would have been awfully mad, but we would not have been surprised. That was the difference. The Faubus folks had been stunned, and I had to admit it felt mighty good.

11. Opportunities Open Up

During the spring semester of 1965, I started giving serious thought to what I should do after graduation, scheduled for December of that year. I was working toward a BS degree with a major in history and a minor in political science. A visit with the SAU career counselor quickly revealed that my higher education had not prepared me for high wages.

His first suggestion was that I pursue a master's degree in history and seek a college teaching position. At my request, he identified the average starting salary for a college history instructor in Arkansas as about $8,000 a year. I had been able to earn close to that amount catching chickens.

"Any other suggestions?" I asked.

"You could consider law school," he said.

The earning potential for lawyers was a bit more rewarding. The counselor told me that the salary range for beginning attorneys at larger urban-area firms was $10,000 to $16,000 a year. After ten years in practice, the median pay was around $50,000 at a big-city firm.

"What does it take to get admitted to law school?" I asked.

He reviewed the grades on my transcript and my GED scores. All were high enough, I was informed, to take the LSAT (law school aptitude test). I left the meeting with information on how to obtain the admission application and other paperwork for the law school at the University of Arkansas in Fayetteville. I walked back across the SAU campus to my dorm room, talking to myself and weighing my options. My college summers had been spent digging ditches in silver mines in Idaho, before landing the job at the Smithsonian. I sure didn't want to make a career of mining, or any other kind of manual labor.

"I really don't have much choice," I concluded. "I've got to go to law school, but how in the hell can I afford that?"

A few months later, in January 1966, I left my parents' farmhouse outside Nashville and headed up State Highway 71 toward Fayetteville. Although I had graduated from college and been admitted to law school, I had no money or savings other than the $50 my mother had squirreled away for me. That winter day in 1966, however, I headed north to the UA campus, knowing that registration fees and numerous other costs awaited me. I had only a vague hope of obtaining some type of student loan or financing.

I was driving a 1955 Oldsmobile, a car I bought after working at the Smithsonian in DC the previous two summers. Saving money for the car was possible only because I had free lodging with my aunt, Donna Mitchell, who at the time ran the DC office of Governor Nelson Rockefeller of New York and later followed him to the Old Executive Office Building next to the White House when he became vice president. Aunt Donna had no children, but she doted on me and my seven younger brothers and sisters. She was of major assistance in enabling all eight of us to graduate from college and several of us to get graduate degrees. She was an incomparable treasure, and all of us owed her a lot.

The cold and overcast weather that January day offered bleak prospects. Just north of De Queen, I encountered a snowstorm that increased in intensity throughout my 180-mile trek to the university campus. State Police had put up barricades to prevent traffic from attempting the steep and twisted route of Highway 71, at the time the primary road to Fayetteville. After much pleading with them, I was warned that no rescue units would be available if my old, heavy car slid off the mountain highway. I was allowed to go on.

By the time I reached Fayetteville late that afternoon, nearly a foot of snow was on the ground and more was falling. I got a room in an inexpensive motel near campus, and I watched in dismay as another foot of snow fell during the night, resulting in the largest snowfall for the Fayetteville area in recent history. When I went out to get in my car the next morning, nothing was moving, so I decided to walk to campus. It was not easy going, for the snow was deep and there were several sizable hills to negotiate. But I made it, getting there about nine o'clock with my shoes, socks, and pant legs soaked.

The campus was blanketed by snow, and no one was walking about. I walked up to the door of the law school building, following a single set of footprints. I expected that the door would be locked, but I pulled on the handle and it opened. I went inside, noticing that the light was on in the dean's office. The law school dean at that time was Ralph Barnhart, and I would get to know him well over the next three years. I got to know even better his secretary, known to all as Mrs. Grisso, or privately among the law students as Dean Grisso, for she was the one to see if you needed to get something done.

Mrs. Grisso was standing behind the counter outside the dean's office. When I walked up to her, she told me that the entire university, including the law school, was closed because of the

104

weather. But in her characteristic style, she asked if she could help me with anything.

"I hope so," I said, feeling anxious. "See, I'm from Nashville, and I am a new student hoping to enter law school up here, and I drove up yesterday not expecting all this snow, and I understood that registration was scheduled for today, but I couldn't drive my car in the snow, so I walked."

Mrs. Grisso responded sympathetically, showing little apparent concern for the prospects of a law school student who could barely piece together a rational sentence. She drew me out for more detail and quickly recognized I was in need of some financial assistance. She pulled my file from the office cabinets and perused my academic records.

"You have a pretty good scholastic record," she said. "I think there may be some additional financial help we can line up."

With her knowledge of the university system and the law school enrollment process, she was able to get me preregistered and cleared to attend classes. She guided my applications for a national defense loan and a Meriwether scholarship (named in honor of the previous law school dean). The only cost she was unable to defray was the price of my textbooks. She urged me to purchase them right away. "You'll sure need those," she chuckled.

I preregistered the next day and then applied for and started classes. The aid was approved. I got some books, and, eventually, some part-time work. In all, it was barely enough to scrape by, but I was used to that.

The important thing was, I was going to law school.

12. HOT SPRINGS GAMING AND POLITICS

When I first entered law school in Fayetteville in January 1966, my earliest friends and roommates were Mike Ellis, from Hot Springs, and Mike Horn, from San Angelo, Texas. Both were from prominent, wealthy families, and both seemed to be attending law school more for the purpose of entering into the family businesses than to become practicing lawyers. We rented a house on North College Street about three blocks from the law school.

The two Mikes were rather indifferent "straight C" type students, preferring the nightlife to striving much in their law courses. I was a bit more ambitious, enjoying the bars but managing to keep a B grade point average, even though I was somewhat slack in class attendance. Mike Ellis and I were greatly interested in Arkansas politics and had many lively discussions. His father was Leonard Ellis, sheriff of Garland County from 1955 to 1960, and county clerk for almost two decades before that. The elder Ellis was closely tied in with the Hot Springs illegal gambling and racketeering establishment that was prevalent at the time.

One weekend in mid-spring, Mike invited me down to spend the weekend with him at his parents' home in Hot Springs. Mike's family lived in an older neighborhood off Park Avenue, not far from the downtown business district and Central Avenue, which was home to Bathhouse Row, the Arlington Hotel, the Southern Club, and a number of other smaller clubs/casinos. The top casino/night club in town was the new, luxurious Vapors Club, just west on Park Avenue, which had opened in 1960. The Vapors was owned by Dane Harris, one of Leonard Ellis's best longtime friends.

Leonard Ellis was a handsome man in his early fifties, with a square face and jaw, black hair liberally speckled with gray, and a friendly expression. I liked him immediately. That evening, he took us to dinner at the Velda Rose Hotel, where he was the manager. We talked about law school and Razorback football for most of the evening, until Ellis finally broached the subject of the upcoming election and its possible effect on the Hot Springs economy.

"You know, Hot Springs has more riding on this election than most towns," he said. "Our economy is almost totally based on the hospitality industry. Tourism is all we've ever had."

Mike and I nodded in agreement but didn't say anything. Ellis clearly had more he wanted to get off his chest.

"Dane Harris," he continued, "an old army buddy of mine, has sunk hundreds of thousands of dollars into the Vapors, one of the finest nightclubs anywhere. He brings in top talent—Tony Bennett, the McGuire Sisters, the Smothers Brothers, Phyllis Diller. There is no other place in Arkansas, or even in the surrounding states, that can attract that kind of talent. And the shows are always filled. If we lose that caliber of entertainment, our economy will dry up."

I knew that the economy of Hot Springs depended upon tourism, and I also knew that the main driver of the tourist industry was gambling. By the time of my visit in 1966, the town's famous bathhouses had lost much of their allure. A good number of people still frequented Bathhouse Row, but usually that was not their primary reason for coming—gambling was. While Hot Springs and the surrounding mountains were certainly beautiful, the region had minimal manufacturing and agricultural enterprises. Illegal gambling was the main thing that kept the local economy alive, and the pay-offs to the politicians to keep it going got expensive.

Continuing our conversation, Leonard Ellis spoke of the importance of the casinos. He said his friend Dane Harris's Vapors night club and several additional casinos brought significant business to local restaurants, hotels, and downtown shops.

"That's what gets the people with money to come here all year long," Ellis said. "The horse racing at Oaklawn only lasts for seven weeks in the spring. We can't survive on that."

The Oaklawn Park was Arkansas's only legal horseracing venue, a status established by the legislature in 1929 when a bill was passed allowing pari-mutuel wagering there. Ellis strongly believed that casino gaming needed to be legalized, as well.

"Gaming is gaming," Ellis insisted, "whether at the track or at a casino."

I noticed that Leonard Ellis always used the term "gaming" instead of "gambling," because he thought it sounded better, I suppose. And he never said "illegal." Leonard then took the dinner conversation to its most contentious topic.

"Roger, Mike tells me that you have an interest in politics. Is this so?" he inquired.

"Well, I keep up with politics generally, but I doubt that I would ever become a candidate myself," I replied.

"Nor would I," Leonard said, smiling, "not anymore anyway—serving twenty-five years as county clerk and sheriff was quite enough for me. But I'm curious about this election that's coming up. Rockefeller almost beat Faubus two years ago, and he has already announced he will run again. I'm not sure any of the Democrats whose names I've heard thrown around can beat him. What do you think?"

Arkansas politics was buzzing with speculation in 1966. After serving six straight terms, Orval Faubus had announced that he would not run again for governor. Faubus had always been a dependable friend of Hot Springs' illegal gambling industry, allowing it to flourish in the open during his time in office, and he had been rewarded handsomely for it. But now, Ellis and others were concerned that Winthrop Rockefeller, the transplanted millionaire from New York and a leading Arkansas gubernatorial candidate, would not be as supportive.

"Rockefeller has more money than God, but he has no connections to Hot Springs," Ellis said. "He doesn't even know us. Why would he be interested in helping us out?"

Our conversation turned to the several candidates in the Democratic primary for governor. Of those who had announced, none seemed willing to maintain the same kind of support for the Hot Springs gambling houses they had enjoyed under Faubus.

"It doesn't look like a particularly strong field," I said, trying to sound sagacious. "I imagine Frank Holt will be the favorite."

"Yes, I guess that he'll be seen as the establishment candidate," Leonard said thoughtfully. "He was a decent enough Supreme Court judge, but he has less personality than a toad frog." Mike and I both laughed while Leonard smiled, his dark eyes twinkling. *A man with a sense of humor*, I thought. *I like that.*

"Mike told me that you might do some work for Sam Boyce this summer," Leonard continued.

My friendship with Boyce began during my college years when I was president of the Young Democrats Club. Boyce, president of the statewide Young Democrats organization, had already announced his intention to run in the Democratic gubernatorial primary that summer.

"Yes, maybe," I said, "although I don't think he has much of a chance to win, and I doubt that he thinks so either. I think he just hopes to do well enough to get known around the state and perhaps position himself for a run at attorney general or even governor in the future."

"It would be an interesting summer job anyway," Leonard allowed.

"That was my thinking," I said, unaware that I was already attracted by the complex and secretive world of Arkansas politics. "I would get to rub shoulders with a lot of people out on the campaign trail."

★ ★ ★

The next day, Mike gave me the grand tour of all the hot spots in the Spa City, as Hot Springs was called. We went by the Southern Club, which was already open and busy in the early afternoon on a Saturday. Its escalator, reportedly the first in Arkansas, was just inside the ornate marble-floored lobby, accessed through brass-plated double doors from street level. The escalator whisked patrons up to the casino on the second floor, where two burly, uniformed guards stood eyeing the people who stepped off. They knew Mike, and they ushered us in with a flourish.

The escalator was a tourist attraction in itself. People came from miles around with their kids just for the experience of riding on the thing. I had never been in a casino and was flabbergasted at the lavish décor and the multitude of clanging slot machines, as well as the card tables with uniformed croupiers. I was equally impressed by the skimpily dressed young women selling cocktails and cigarettes.

After we left the Southern Club, Mike gave me a drive-by of the "mansion," the most famous whorehouse in Hot Springs, run by madam Maxine Jones. It was a two-story, red-brick, over-elaborate building on a side street close to the downtown business district, with Maxine's name emblazoned across the front. It was still a little early in the afternoon for a tour, so we passed on that. Jones would later write *Call Me Madam*, a tell-all book that identified the mobsters and prominent underworld figures from the East and West Coasts who were among her clientele.[8]

Jones's book did not offer details on the business relationships between these men and local Hot Springs civic leaders. But over time, those friendships became known. Among the most prominent of the Hot Springs underworld figures was Owen Vincent "Owney" Madden, who had been a mob boss and hit man in New York City in the 1930s. He had moved to Hot Springs in 1933, a time when other mafia bosses were also spending time there. Madden partnered with Leonard Ellis's friend Dane Harris to build the Vapors in 1960. He was also known to have owned a major stake in the Southern Club and the Belvedere Country Club.

In New York, Madden had been a professional gunman and killer and was wounded many times. He was sentenced to the infamous Sing Sing prison for manslaughter, paroled eight years later, and sent back to Sing Sing again for parole violations in 1932. He was released again and, in his forties, supposedly in chronic ill health because of his old bullet wounds, started looking for a new life and a new career. He found it in Hot Springs, getting married to a local gift-shop clerk, Agnes Demby, and striking up a decades-long business relationship with Hot Springs mayor Leo McLaughlin.[9]

Widely recognized as the public face of the Hot Springs crime syndicate that managed gambling, prostitution, book making, and other illegal activities, McLaughlin had been the most powerful politician in Garland County for many years. He and

Madden were made for each other. After obtaining a controlling interest in the Southern Club, across the street from the Arlington Hotel, Madden was frequently seen out on the veranda, nattily dressed in a white suit, red tie, and straw fedora, entertaining his old mobster friends: a Who's Who register of gangland chiefs, including Frank Costello, Meyer Lansky, Lucky Luciano, and Al Capone. Despite his many gunshot wounds, Madden lived an active life in Hot Springs until his death in 1965 at age seventy-four.

Leonard Ellis stoutly contended that the casinos were locally owned and locally run by Hot Springs residents. He never mentioned that Dane Harris had been in partnership with Madden, and he denied that there was any mob influence in Hot Springs at all. Such influence may have waned by the time Mike Ellis invited me down for the weekend that spring in 1966, but it was generally acknowledged that the mob was still alive and well in the town.

A decade earlier, the Hot Springs gambling industry encountered political opposition during the "GI Revolt" that swept Hot Springs resident Sidney McMath into the governor's office for two terms beginning in 1949. McMath was friends with fellow Hot Springs GIs Dane Harris and Leonard Ellis, along with others. They supported him in his race for governor, as well as in a previous race for prosecuting attorney for the 18th Judicial District (Garland and Montgomery Counties), to which he was elected in 1947.

McMath despised Mayor Leo McLaughlin, his corrupt political machine, and his control of

George Fisher cartoon of Sid McMath.

the illegal gambling and vice enterprises in Hot Springs. In particular, he bridled against the stealing of elections that had kept the McLaughlin machine in power for over two decades. McMath prosecuted McLaughlin twice for multiple illegal activities, sending some of his cronies to jail, but McLaughlin escaped punishment both times.

McMath ran for governor on a reform "throw the rascals out" agenda. This included shutting down the illegal activities in Hot Springs. McMath's friends, such as Harris and Ellis, were disappointed, but they understood. They were prepared to lie low until things blew over, hoping that, over time, McMath would loosen up. He never really did, but after two terms, and an intervening term by superconservative Francis Cherry, he was succeeded by a governor who would prove much more pliant, Orval Faubus.

In his incisive biography of Faubus, noted Arkansas author Roy Reed described the effect that the Faubus succession as governor had on illegal gambling in Hot Springs:

> The McLaughlin machine stayed in office twenty years, partly by stealing votes with casual brazenness. Because cooperation from the state capitol was necessary, the gambling interests tried to buy friendship there. It is said that the standard campaign contribution to a friendly governor in those days was $50,000. The returning World War II veterans led by McMath finally overthrew the machine and temporarily ended the gambling and its attendant corruption....Then Faubus became governor. He quickly sent a signal: gambling was a local affair for Hot Springs, and he did not intend to interfere unless the people there wanted him to. Since most leading businessmen of the town wanted gambling, that meant there would be no police raids from Little Rock. Casinos quickly sprang to life again.
>
> Faubus's good friend, traveling companion and hunting buddy, Harry Hastings Sr., quietly insinuated himself into the action. He had served jail time during prohibition, but had survived to become Arkansas's biggest wholesaler of

liquor. At Hot Springs, he became a silent partner of his boyhood friend, Dane Harris, who would become the dominant public figure of the gambling industry.[10]

There was much speculation during this period as to how much Hot Springs gambling money was getting into Faubus's pockets. Most everyone who knew anything about it figured it was a lot. Leonard Ellis indicated as much during our dinner chat, but gave no numbers. Probably he had no idea as to the exact figure. Apparently, no single bagman transported the money to Faubus. He seemingly had many sources.

Reed addressed this subject also:

Clay White, an FBI agent who investigated Hot Springs gambling and later became sheriff of Garland County, came to believe, based on his inside contacts, that the gamblers sent money to Faubus in two ways. First, the election year contributions amounted to at least $50,000, he said, and up to $25,000 more if it was needed to pay for last minute advertising. The routine pay-off month by month ran to about $75,000 a year, he said—a bargain, he noted, considering the high revenues that the casinos took in. White's investigation showed that the money was stowed in a black bag and delivered to Little Rock every Saturday night by a high state official.[11]

Other than the occasional campaign contribution from Hot Springs businessmen, Faubus, of course, never admitted receiving the bags of money. He always maintained that the Hot Springs contributions were insignificant. Toward the end of his tenure as governor, Faubus granted an interview to a reporter for the *Washington Post*. Reed described the event, saying, "Faubus maintained a kind of amazed innocence. [The *Post* reporter] interviewed Faubus at the Arlington Hotel and was assured that no gambling was going on anywhere in town. The reporter walked across the street to the Southern Club and found its casino operating with a house full of players."[12]

As Leonard Ellis had feared, Winthrop Rockefeller won the 1966 governor's race, handily beating the Democratic nominee, arch segregationist "Justice Jim" Johnson, who was a former Supreme Court justice. After Rockefeller took office in 1967, the State Police, under newly appointed director Lynn Davis (a former FBI agent), conducted a final raid of the gambling establishments in Hot Springs. Plans for the raid were kept secret, and most of the gambling houses were raided simultaneously. It was a great success, resulting in virtually all the pieces of gambling apparatus—such as slot machines and roulette, black jack, and dice tables—being confiscated, dumped, and burned. The raid signaled the end of the illegal gambling industry in Hot Springs.

While this was going on, Faubus was finishing up his version of the Taj Mahal, a monument to himself atop a mountain overlooking his old hometown of Huntsville in Madison County. The grand edifice, designed by renowned architect E. Fay Jones of Fayetteville, was 214 feet wide and built of cedar, glass, and native stone. It was estimated to cost $200,000 to $300,000, a very substantial sum back then. Faubus earned $10,000 a year as governor. When asked where he got the money to pay for such a house, he replied that he was very frugal and "had saved it." In fact, he owed a considerable mortgage.

13. RASCALS

In those days, Fourth of July social celebrations were held atop two of the highest mountains along the south side of the Arkansas River: Petit Jean Mountain near Morrilton and Mount Nebo near Russellville. Families attended these gatherings, setting up tents, spreading picnic meals on the ground, and, at the end of the day, setting off fireworks. During an election year, candidates for various political offices would mount a platform, usually a flatbed trailer with a sound system, and orate to the crowds.

The 1966 Democratic gubernatorial primary race attracted a field of seven candidates, including Sam Boyce and two Supreme Court justices, Frank Holt and Jim Johnson. In the Democratic primary for attorney general, incumbent Bruce Bennett was opposed by Joe Purcell, a rather obscure municipal judge from Benton. Over the Fourth of July weekend in 1966, these candidates and many others were scrambling to cover various political events.

It was virtually impossible for the candidates to speak at every event, so Sam Boyce decided he would speak at the Petit

Jean event and have me cover the Mount Nebo event on his behalf. With Boyce's campaign strategist Jim McDougal in the car, we drove to Mount Nebo, where I was to be dropped off and picked up after Boyce had spoken at Petit Jean.

We drove out Arkansas Highway 10 on a hot and sunny July day. As our car rounded a curve heading up the mountain, we saw a white Cadillac on the side of the road. We slowed down and noticed a big man with whitish hair on the other side of the road, tugging mightily to remove a Joe Purcell sign that was securely nailed to a tree.

"That's Bruce Bennett!" yelled Sam. "Stop. Back up!" Our driver did, and Sam, who was in the front passenger seat, rolled down his window, cupped his hands as if holding a camera, and shouted, "Hey Bruce, smile! You're on *Candid Camera!*"

Bennett saw who it was and started walking toward our car with a stricken look on his face, his hands held out in apparent supplication. "Take off!" Sam commanded our driver, gleefully calling back to Bennett, "See ya, Bruce!"

McDougal, laughing so hard tears were coming to his eyes, commented: "Sure wish we had a camera. Imagine what Joe Purcell would have given for the picture."

"Bruce must be getting mighty desperate," said Sam. "I think Joe just might win the thing."

Purcell did win, beating Bennett handily in the primary, then defeating a Republican challenger, Jerry Thomasson of Arkadelphia, in the fall general election to become Arkansas attorney general.

Bruce Bennett, together with several other Faubus legislative cronies, had earned the enmity of Arkansas voters. Led by an irate group based in central Arkansas, voters took their ire out on several old-guard, pro-Faubus types. In addition to Bennett, these included longtime legislative leaders such as Paul Van

Dalsem of Perryville; Glen F. Walther Jr., former speaker of the House from Little Rock; and J. H. Cottrell of Little Rock, the then-reigning speaker.[13]

The anti-Faubus "Rascals" movement had gotten huge impetus from ignorant and offensive comments made by Van Dalsem concerning women's rights and participation in government. In a speech given to the Little Rock Optimist Club in 1963, Van Dalsem had stated: "We don't have any of these university women in Perry County, but I'll tell you what we do up there when one of our women starts poking around in something she doesn't know anything about. We get her an extra milk cow. If that don't work, we give her a little more garden to tend to. And then, if that's not enough, we get her pregnant and keep her barefoot."

These remarks were reported by Roy Reed in the *Arkansas Gazette*, and a firestorm of epic proportions erupted, just in time for the "Rascals" group to get organized and field candidates for the 1966 elections. And most of the old-guard politicians *were* thrown out—Bennett, Van Dalsem, Walther, and Cottrell all lost to Rascal-supported candidates.

Lurking just under the surface and not well known to many Arkansans at the time was one of the biggest and most scandalous financial frauds ever to hit the state. In the center of this scandal was Attorney General Bruce Bennett.

An amorphous, hybrid financial institution—immune from oversight or regulation by the state—was created by Bennett and a twenty-five-year-old used-car dealer named Ernest A. Bartlett Jr. and assisted by a number of Faubus chums. From the organization of Arkansas Loan and Thrift Corporation (AL&T) in December 1964 until it was placed in receivership in March 1968, this strange company bilked more than 2,000 people and churches out of more than three million dollars. Its actions wiped out the life savings of many and greatly enriched Bennett and his cohorts.

Shady deals were part of AL&T from the start. Bennett had the incorporation papers prepared in the Attorney General's Office by an assistant, who was given a block of shares in the new company for his trouble. AL&T then joined with a defunct company, United Loan and Investment, which held a charter from 1937 as an industrial loan company. That gave AL&T the authority to take deposits.

Meanwhile, Paul Van Dalsem, Faubus's floor leader in the state House of Representatives, arranged for Bennett to buy an active insurance company from House Speaker J. H. Cottrell. Bennett immediately sold the inactive United Loan and Investment to AL&T at a large profit. He renamed the insurance company Savings Guaranty Corporation (Savings for short). Though it was a shell company with no assets (other than worthless stock in AL&T), Bennett advertised that it would "insure people's deposits in AL&T."

To get the transaction past the state insurance examiner, such that he could certify that Savings had the necessary capital to "insure the deposits," AL&T wrote a check on its own account for $580,000 to Savings Guaranty, which sent the money back to AL&T in return for a worthless IOU as soon as a state insurance examiner had examined the books.

AL&T opened its headquarters in Van Buren and had branches in seven other Arkansas cities. It advertised profusely in newspapers, television, and other media that it would pay a 5.75% interest rate for deposits, a higher rate than allowed by law to banks and savings & loans. It also said that the deposits would be safer than if the FDIC (Federal Insurance Corporation) insured them.

To avoid any oversight or regulation by the state, Bennett issued five official attorney general opinions (none of them ever made public) to Van Dalsem and state regulatory agencies. The opinions stated that AL&T operated under an old industrial loan charter, rather than bank or savings & loan charters. No one had any authority to regulate its activities or those of Savings. With legislative acquiescence and the benign approval of the Faubus administration, AL&T ran free, completely unchecked by anyone.[14]

Like most scams and Ponzi schemes, AL&T eventually began to unravel as the money disappeared into the pockets of Bennett, his friends, and their confederates. Rumors of impending bankruptcy or receivership began to fly. Frightened depositors began to rush to withdraw their money, many finding that for one reason or another, it was not immediately available.

After Joe Purcell defeated Bennett for attorney general, he quickly moved to shutter AL&T by filing a lawsuit in Pulaski County Chancery Court. Former Faubus aides quickly came to the rescue, and the case was assigned to Chancellor Kay L. Matthews, a former Faubus aide. AL&T's CEO, Ernest Bartlett, hired lawyer Claude Carpenter Jr., another former Faubus aide and Matthews's law and business partner. Carpenter was paid a substantial retainer to represent the company.

Matthews never brought the case to trial, instead granting delay after delay, until he finally disqualified himself from the case more than two years later. As AL&T's lawyer, Carpenter never had to do any actual work. Later named as a co-conspirator in a federal grand jury indictment, he testified at Bartlett's trial in 1969 that he did nothing for the fees except travel with Bartlett in his private plane to gamble in Las Vegas and talk about Razorback football with him when Bartlett dropped by his office in Little Rock.

Things finally began to move after Judge Matthews disqualified himself. The next week, on March 13, 1968, acting on a motion by the federal Securities and Exchange Commission, U.S. District Judge John E. Miller of Fort Smith closed AL&T and put it into receivership. The receiver eventually recovered about one-fourth of the $4.2 million deposited.

A federal grand jury indicted Bennett, Bartlett, and brothers Afton and Hoyt Borum (two AL&T officers from Booneville) for securities violations, postal fraud, and wire fraud. Bartlett was convicted and received a prison term of five years and a fine of $5,000. The Borum brothers were also convicted but were punished even less.

Bennett, however, was never even brought to trial. U.S. District Judge Oren Harris, an old buddy of Bennett's from El Dorado, severed his case from those of the other defendants, then gave him a continuance based upon Bennett's claim that he had throat cancer. His case never went to trial. Bennett died on August 26, 1979, over ten years later, never having given any recompense for his crimes.

The scope and extent of the graft, fraud, and corruption practiced by Governor Orval Faubus, Attorney General Bruce Bennett, and their respective minions throughout their public careers were truly breathtaking. Corruption at the highest levels of government inevitably breeds similar practices at lower levels.

As I would later discover in a very painful way, such corruption had gained hardy roots in Little Rock.

14. Affinity for the Stump

My assistance to Sam Boyce's campaign was in full swing in the summer of 1966. Sam had his central campaign office at the Sam Peck Hotel in Little Rock, and several young people were on his staff. The campaign rented rooms at the hotel, and some of us bunked there when we were not traveling around the state on the campaign trail. In those days, the principal way for candidates to meet and greet the voters was the old-fashioned "stump" rallies held at courthouse squares. Sam was an astute political strategist and loved backroom maneuvering, but he was not particularly fond of speaking from the stump.

Often, several of these events would be going on at the same time in different towns. When this occurred, Sam would pick out the events he thought were the most important, select one where he would speak, and send one or two surrogates to cover the other locations. Right away, he started calling on me to act as a surrogate speaker on his behalf. I enjoyed this role, sitting up on a platform or a flatbed truck on the courthouse square at some rural county seat, usually in the early evening, taking my turn to address the assembled crowd on behalf of the Sam Boyce for Governor campaign.

In political terminology, I had "an affinity for the stump." As the summer went on, Sam called upon me more and more to make these speeches for him. At some point in the campaign, people became confused, apparently thinking that I actually was Sam Boyce. Often somebody from the audience would come up to me after an event had concluded and say: "Mr. Boyce, it sure is a pleasure to meet you. That was a real fine speech you made."

I got to meet people from all over the state, including the important local politicians who always attended these events and were frequently running for some political office themselves, as well as the candidates who were running for governor and other statewide offices. On the day of the Democratic primary, Sam finished fourth in the seven-man field, but he had provided me with a great opportunity to appear on stage and rub shoulders with a lot of important Arkansans who would later prove valuable in my career.

The summer of 1966 and the months that followed during my senior year in law school provided three additional milestones in my life—one personal, one professional, and one political.

The personal milestone involved meeting the young woman who was to become my wife. In a scenario typical to a college town at that time, two cars pulled into a drive-in diner in Fayetteville and parked side by side. The two men in the first car smiled at the two attractive women in the other. A conversation began, and names and phone numbers were exchanged. I was interested in the girl with big hazel eyes and blond hair styled in a perky cut. Jeannie was about three years my senior, drove a nice car, and had a good job as a salesperson with a women's clothing store in Fayetteville. She was a graduate of Fayetteville High School and still lived with her parents, who were retired.

We continued seeing each other over the next few months, and I grew fond of her. I liked her parents, as well. They were "hill folks" who had lived in the area for generations. No one in her family had gone to college, but they all had a lot of native sense and were exceptionally kind and generous. That winter I caught a very harsh strain of influenza, called the "Hong Kong flu." Jeannie started bringing me hot chicken soup her mother had made. When Jeannie caught the bug as well, we were both so sick we could hardly move. Her parents invited me to their house so they could care for us both at the same time. They put a set of twin beds in the living room and nursed us back to health over the next few days. I was eternally grateful. Our shared illness and recuperation was a bonding experience for us. Also, I was spending additional time with Jeannie because I had lost my car and she still had the new Pontiac GTO that originally brought her to the drive-in diner.

My 1955 Oldsmobile was a casualty of a brief episode that reflects the larger environment of people and politics I was entering at the time. The setting was the law school fraternity's annual beer bust, attended by fraternity members, the *Law Review* staff, and many of the law professors. It was held in a pasture on the banks of a local creek. I drove out in my Olds with one of my best friends in law school, Jim Hooper. Over the course of the afternoon, we consumed more beer than was prudent. After the party, one of the other law students, Guy "Mutt" Jones Jr., son of a somewhat notorious state senator, got in his new Corvette and started spinning donuts around us as we were trying to leave, throwing up dirt, rocks, and clouds of dust. Guy raced his car out onto the two-lane blacktop highway bordering the pasture, sliding sideways and squealing his tires the whole time. He then sped off down the road in a cloud of smoke.

Demonstrating the clear-headedness that follows an afternoon of beer drinking, Jim Hooper and I raced out onto the highway in my thirteen-year-old Oldsmobile and attempted to catch up with Guy's new Corvette. A sharp turn across a one-lane bridge brought the chase to an end. Guy's car made the turn in style; mine crashed into the embankment. In a stroke of good luck, neither Jim nor I were hurt beyond some bumps and bruises, but my vehicle was totaled. Even worse, we were now sitting in the middle of a fairly well-traveled roadway, not far from the city limits of Springdale, which was known for its no-nonsense police force.

We needed to do something quickly about my car, at that point inoperable and immovable, as well as avoid getting arrested for driving under the influence. Fortunately, Jim worked parttime for a bail bondsman in Springdale. He went to a nearby house, borrowed the phone, and called his boss to explain the situation. Jim's boss called the Springdale police to report a minor single-vehicle accident with no personal injuries. He also arranged for a wrecker to remove the vehicle. The police were satisfied that there was nothing to investigate. Jim and I were spared the legal consequences of our actions because, much like in politics, we had a friend who knew how to manipulate the system.

My new status as a pedestrian gave occasion for Jeannie and me to spend more time together, and by the end of the year, we were going steady. I started thinking of the challenges of marriage. Jeannie's formal education was limited and she had no interest (or means at the time) of going back to school. She was naturally shy, especially around strangers, and lacked confidence in social situations. I was set upon a career in law and politics, and I appreciated the kind of social skills that a spouse would need to help propel that kind of life. But I truly loved her, owed her and her family a lot, and felt that we could make a go of it if that was the course we set upon.

At the time, I was financing law school, with its mounting student loan debts, by holding down three part-time jobs. I worked as a night clerk at a liquor store, in the law library during the day, and doing research and editing for Professor Robert Wright for the law textbook he was writing. Through it all, my grades remained good, and I made the *Law Review* and the dean's list. Jeannie and I were already engaged, in a sort of informal way, since I could not afford a ring. We decided it would be prudent to move up our wedding date. We could move into the campus married-student housing units, which were within easy walking distance of the law school, and we could use her car to shuttle each other back and forth to our jobs.

We got married in the summer of 1967 in a quiet ceremony held at the home of Jeannie's twin sister, "Bert" Moore, who lived next door to their parents. Jeannie continued working at the clothing store, and I began getting more serious about my classes and my future career as a lawyer.

The author and his first wife, Jeannie Glasgow, shortly after their marriage in Fayetteville, Arkansas, in 1967.

Sadly, Jeannie's mother passed away the very next summer, and her father followed about two years later. Jeannie had lost both her parents in a short period after we were married, and I was now without two wonderful in-laws, who had been loyal friends and dependable supporters.

★ ★ ★

The second milestone of this period, the professional one, involved the announcement of a state constitutional convention to be held in Little Rock. The convention, scheduled for the summer of 1969, would be attended by delegates elected by popular vote from existing legislative districts during the fall general election of 1968. I got it in my head that I could run for a delegate position.

After all, I would have graduated from law school by the time the convention was to start, and presumably I would have passed the state bar exam and been admitted to practice in Arkansas as a new lawyer. The convention was to focus on modernizing the state's antiquated 1874 constitution. Constitutional law was one of my favorite subjects, and I had just written the top paper in my constitutional law class. I should be a natural!

My best approach would be to run from my home legislative district in southwestern Arkansas, which consisted of both Howard and Sevier Counties, Nashville and De Queen being the respective county seats. Who else down there would want to run for such a position? Nobody came to mind. It might even be possible, I thought, to make my plans known early enough to preempt any others who might be considering the race.

I drove down to Nashville, planning to combine visits with my parents and some of the important movers and shakers in the district, as well as the few practicing lawyers there, to feel them out about my prospects. I received much encouragement, even overt enthusiasm, from a good number of key people. All of the lawyers in the district and the newspaper editors at both the Nashville and De Queen papers expressed support.

More importantly, I received positive support from Bobby Steel, the circuit judge who lived in Nashville and had both of these counties in his judicial district. From his office at the courthouse in Nashville, Judge Steel had gained astute knowledge of local political matters, and he knew who in the district might be considering a run for some political office. He told me that he had not heard of anyone else expressing interest in the constitutional convention delegate position.

Steel seemed surprised that I was interested. He asked if I had already lined up a position with a law firm or made any other plans for what I would do after graduation. I got the impression he was wondering if I might be planning to come back to Nashville to practice law. For many years, he and his two brothers had monopolized the law practice there, and I figured they were not disposed to encourage competition. I had best be noncommittal on that point, I figured.

"Passing the bar exam would be the first thing," I said. "But, I would like to get into private law practice, if I can."

"Are you thinking big city, small town, or something in between?"

"I'm not sure," I said. "The market's tough right now. I've talked to some firms but haven't nailed anything down yet."

"You should be a natural for one of the big Little Rock firms," he said. "They are always on the lookout for smart young lawyers. I bet that you are already on their radar."

"Nobody's beating down my door yet," I said. "But I'm thinking this delegate position would give me something to do in Little Rock while searching for a permanent position, if I don't have something nailed down by then."

Judge Steel looked at me as if he had more on his mind, but he had apparently decided to let it go, saying instead: "Well, you go ahead and get elected to this constitutional delegate position. You'll do a fine job and also make a lot of really good contacts from all over the state. Something will come up, I'm sure of that."

Then, unexpectedly, after I had taken a step or two toward the door, he added, "Roger, I think you should go ahead and publicly announce for the position. I'll bet you will be unopposed."

It came to pass just like that. I announced and the papers printed the announcement, with Louis "Swampy" Graves, owner and editor of the *Nashville News*—a family friend who had followed my career all the way through high school sports, college, and law school—adding a gratuitous and flattering sketch of my past accomplishments.

I anxiously awaited the filing deadline for the election, hoping no one else would file for the delegate position. The deadline passed and no one did. So I was in, unopposed.

The third milestone, the political one, provided an introduction to some of the leading public figures in Arkansas at the time.

Frank Holt, one of the seven gubernatorial primary candidates in 1966, was from a prominent Little Rock political family. He had served one term as attorney general in 1958, and he was considered the top "establishment" candidate in the crowded 1966 field. Frank had a troop of young supporters who followed him around to the various political events in the state, all wearing ties and matching blue blazers, not typical attire in rural Arkansas in the heat of summer.

One young supporter stood out in particular, a tall, somewhat scraggly looking young man with a full head of fuzzy reddish-brown hair. His name was Bill Clinton. I was not very impressed with him then. My opinion changed a few years later when he was campaigning for attorney general. At an early fundraising event, Clinton told a story about the 1966 campaign trail. It seems he was in the audience one evening at a rally held on the front steps of the courthouse in Hope, his hometown. I had spoken at the rally on behalf of Sam Boyce, and Clinton remembered it, telling the gathered supporters, "This guy gave the best political stump speech I've ever heard." I became a good bit more impressed with him after that.

George Fisher cartoon of Bill Clinton.

During those few years—the late 1960s to early '70s—Arkansas was undergoing a sea change in politics. A brand-new breed of younger, more progressive, and public-spirited politicians was coming to the forefront. Senator J. William Fulbright had stood at the vanguard of this more moderate political climate in Arkansas, mostly alone, for years. But now he influenced a new generation of politicians opposed to racial prejudice and the "good-old-boy" networks practicing the "states' rights" style of confrontational politics. In much of the South in the early '60s, Southern governors such as George Wallace of Alabama, Lester Maddox of Georgia, and our own Orval Faubus held sway. In 1966 in Arkansas, the dam finally burst, and I was right in the middle of the deluge.

The winner of the Democratic primary for governor that year was Jim Johnson, a segregationist who enjoyed the sobriquet "Justice Jim" because he had served seven years on the state Supreme Court. Opposing him was the Republican Winthrop Rockefeller, a member of the famous New York Rockefeller family. He had moved to Arkansas in 1953, established his home atop Petit Jean Mountain, and started a cattle-farming operation. Rockefeller had served as head of the Arkansas Industrial Development

Commission under Faubus, where he became interested in moving the state forward, or at least into the twentieth century.

Many moderate Democrats, including myself, joined a "Democrats for Rockefeller" group and actively supported him in the election. He won and served two terms until he was defeated for a third term by Dale Bumpers, then a little known but progressive Democrat from the tiny town of Charleston in Franklin County. Bumpers was an articulate campaigner with a bright smile and fresh vitality. He, too, was to play a large role in my future fortunes.

Bumpers was sworn in as governor and Ray Thornton as attorney general on the same day in January 1971. The Attorney General's Office proved to be a stepping stone for many aspiring politicians of the era. Thornton went on to serve in Congress, an initial three terms from a southern Arkansas district and later three additional terms from the central Arkansas district. Thornton was then elected to the Arkansas Supreme Court. Clinton served one term as attorney general, then was elected governor, and then was elected president of the United States, where he served two terms, the only Arkansan ever to reach the presidency. Jim Guy Tucker, a prosecuting attorney in Pulaski County, also served two terms as attorney general prior to his election to the U.S. Congress and then becoming lieutenant governor and governor.

Though neither Bumpers nor Pryor served as attorney general, both were U.S. senators for many years. I knew all of these politicians quite well and had many occasions to interact with them on various matters over the years. They all stood by me when things got tough.

15. Small-Town Law Practice

Not long after the filing deadline had passed and my unopposed election to the delegate position was assured, I learned that an established attorney in Nashville had inquired about me. Don Steel, who was Judge Bobby Steel's younger brother, was considering adding another lawyer to his solo practice. Clearly, my conversation with Judge Steel the past summer had been brought to his attention. The potential job fit directly into my plans of moving back to Nashville.

Don Steel mainly had a "walk-in" plaintiff practice, with some divorce and other types of domestic-relations cases, a few criminal-defense cases, and an occasional descendant's estate. His professional reputation was based on his skill at trying jury cases. He was in his forties, with prematurely graying hair, pale blue eyes, and a spare medium build. While not a robust man, Don seemed healthy enough. I was soon to find out differently.

At our meeting in Nashville, Don laid out an intriguing proposition, revealing another behind-the-scenes scenario of local politics and payment for legal services.

The author and law partner Don Steel when the author joined the law practice in Nashville, Arkansas, in 1969.

First, Don explained that in addition to his private practice, he also served as deputy prosecuting attorney for two counties in the six-county judicial district that covered southwestern Arkansas. Based on the existing "cash fee system" by which deputy prosecutors were compensated, this provided a steady, dependable income. A gentlemen's agreement existed among the lawyers in the district that the prosecuting attorney position would "rotate." While it was an elective office, each significant lawyer (meaning a member of the informal "gentlemen's club"), when he reached a certain age and number of years in practice, was entitled to two or three unopposed terms as prosecuting attorney. Now it was Don's turn. He had received assurance from every lawyer in the district that, if he announced for the position, he would be unopposed. So it seemed a cinch that Don would become the prosecuting attorney in January 1970.

In addition, the local attorneys had an understanding beforehand as to which lawyer would serve as deputy prosecutor in which county. Normally, the district prosecuting attorney could select the deputy for his home county and one or perhaps two of the other smaller counties where there was no lawyer, or at least not a "significant" one.

The prosecuting attorney himself was paid a decent salary by the state and usually personally handled all of the major felony trials, often with the assistance of the deputy from the county where the case was filed. The deputies handled all of the lesser "misdemeanor" cases, such as DWI and other automobile infractions, most game and fish violations, simple assault and battery, and public drunkenness.

Upon being charged with a misdemeanor, a defendant was required to post a cash bond to avoid being kept in jail until trial, which could be months away. At that time, the defendant was also responsible for hiring his or her own attorney. Few defendants could afford both bail and an attorney. All defendants were charged and given an opportunity to enter a plea of either guilty, not guilty, or *nolo contendere*.

If a not-guilty plea was entered, the case went to the trial docket and later was set for trial. For guilty or *nolo* pleas, sentencing usually occurred immediately, most often in the form of a fine in the amount of the cash bond, and sometimes an additional amount for more serious offenses.

What made it lucrative for the deputy prosecuting attorneys was that the bond forfeiture and/or additional fine was always cash, which was split 50/50 between the county and the deputy. In the bigger counties, where a larger number of misdemeanor cases were filed, this resulted in a nice payday for the deputy, usually for very little work. Don told me that he would appoint me as the deputy for Howard County, which had a sizable criminal case load, and possibly also for one or two of the smaller counties in the district.

Second, Don proposed a true partnership, to be named Steel & Glasgow, in which all fees earned by either of us would go into the kitty, and a certain amount, thirty percent, would go to Don for overhead, including secretarial help and other office expenses, and the remainder would be split between us 65/35.

Based on his salary as prosecuting attorney and the cash fees that I would bring in as a deputy, we estimated that my monthly share would be between $1,000 and $1,500 a month. That, I knew, was more than the large firms in Little Rock were paying to starting associates. I was pleased.

Finally, we discussed my duties at the Arkansas Constitutional Convention. We figured this would take two or three months at most. My pay there would be less than what I could make at the firm, but the convention would not be in session every day, so I could still get some law work done. We agreed that I would receive a third of my pay from the firm while attending the convention.

I would assume my duties at Steel & Glasgow as soon as I passed the bar examination and was sworn in and licensed by the Arkansas Supreme Court. The exam was scheduled in March. It would take the board of bar examiners about a month to get the papers graded and announce the results, another few weeks to get sworn in, and a little longer to find a place for Jeannie and me to live. Also, we needed to find Jeannie a job. I figured we could get started around June.

Luckily, everything proceeded as scheduled. I passed the bar, Jeannie got a job as a sales clerk at a women's clothing shop on Main Street, and we rented a small duplex apartment in town. The law office location was convenient to both the duplex and Jeannie's work.

My first couple of months as a Nashville lawyer were slow. I did a little legal research and helped Don with his cases. We played golf at the Nashville country club most Friday afternoons with Don's business friends. Don was a fair golfer, but he was fidgety and easily upset when he would hit a bad shot or miss a putt. I noticed that his hands and arms would jerk slightly on these occasions, like a nervous tic. Sometimes he would try to cover this with a wan smile, or a nervous laugh, only to be betrayed by a quiver in his lower lip. One of Don's friends told me privately that I needn't worry about Don's nervous tics, as he had had a drinking problem years ago when he was in the state Senate but had been sober for several years.

My world began to get more interesting with the start of the Arkansas Constitutional Convention of 1969. One hundred delegates met in the chambers of the Arkansas House of Representatives at the Arkansas State Capitol. When I found the way to my assigned seat on the back row, I was pleased to discover that I was seated next to Ray H. Thornton Jr.

Ray, who represented Grant County in central Arkansas, was a member of the Stephens family, one of the wealthiest and most politically prominent families in Arkansas. Though fourteen years older than me, Ray was friendly and outgoing. He had a ready laugh and was a hard worker. Ray was also rather vain, I discovered, and sensitive about the large bald spot expanding on the top of his head; he covered it with a bad-looking comb-over. More importantly, I took note of his political style. He was very cautious in making decisions on many of the important issues addressed by the convention, often being the last to vote.

The convention got under way, and I became a leader in a faction of "Young Turks," which generally favored progressive ideas. Ray was a leader of a more moderate, loosely knit, business-oriented group. Our interests frequently overlapped, and we found ourselves rounding up votes for each other and speaking out for each other's positions. As our friendship developed, Ray Thornton confided in me that he was planning to enter the race for attorney general in the 1970 election and would be pleased to have my support in his campaign.

All in all, by the time summer had ended, the convention had completed its main plenary session and I had returned to full-time law practice. Things were looking pretty good. Jeannie and I had managed to buy a new car and new furniture for our apartment. I had joined the country club and begun to enjoy the Nashville social scene. Small-town law practice, it seemed, offered a comfortable and stable life.

★ ★ ★

The bottom fell out one Saturday morning when I got a call at home from a good friend, Ray Blakely, a former teammate on the 1959 Nashville Scrapper high school football team.

"Have you been listening to the radio this morning?" Ray asked.

"No," I said. "Why?"

"Your law partner just went on the air and announced that he was withdrawing his candidacy for prosecuting attorney."

Ray described the radio announcement as best he could reconstruct it. He said Don's statement was confusing and shrill. Don talked about how his brothers (a third Steel brother was also a practicing attorney in Nashville) were against him and never wanted him to have the job. Though he made little sense overall, Don clearly stated several times that he was pulling out of the race, Ray said.

I stood with the telephone receiver in my hand for a long moment, trying to digest what I had just heard. When I told Jeannie that Don had apparently had a nervous breakdown, we immediately recognized that our success in Nashville was in jeopardy. Struggling to determine what our next step should be, we decided to visit with my parents at the family farm.

I always felt better after going home when something serious came up. Both of my parents were as solid as boulders in a crisis, of which there had been many over the years involving one family member or another. We called on that Saturday afternoon and talked briefly with my mom, explaining the situation. She said we should come over after church the next day. She would fix my favorite Sunday meal: pan-fried chicken with mashed potatoes and gravy, purple-hull peas, fried okra, fresh tomatoes, and cornbread. And after dinner settled, we would have some hand-cranked ice cream with fresh peaches for dessert, a Sunday afternoon staple for which our family was justifiably famous. It would be the perfect medicine she was sure, and then we could talk.

At home on the farm, we had a big, round oak table, surrounded by eight straight-backed, cane-bottomed chairs, all of which had been handed down for generations. The table was in the kitchen, which was a large room. After the Sunday noon meal, it was customary to clear the dishes and flatware, store the remaining food in the refrigerator, and sit around the table to discuss the topics of the day.

My mom already knew about Don's announcement on the radio the previous morning. Though she was not listening at the time, news travels fast in a small community. I filled everyone in on the details, as best I knew them, and we discussed various alternatives that might be open to me. My mom thought I should withdraw from the law firm as soon as reasonably possible and strike out on my own, perhaps even consider running for prosecuting attorney myself. I knew, however, that Don's withdrawal from the race would attract other lawyers in the district eager for the job. If I ran, I would be facing a contested race with several opponents, all of whom would be more experienced and have

138

more resources than I had. Daddy, always more conservative, felt I should stay with Don for the time being but keep an eye out for other opportunities.

Don soon took another bad turn. He showed up at the office on Monday, but he kept his door closed through the day and left early. I did not have an opportunity to talk with him. The following day, he did not show up at all. Nor did his wife, Darlene, who was our secretary.

Around midmorning I got a call from Sheriff Lewis "Beef" Tollett, a burly, muscular man who always wore cowboy boots and a white Western hat. I had developed a good relationship with Tollett since returning to Nashville to practice law.

"Can you meet me at Don's house?" he asked. "I may need some help."

"What's happened?" I asked.

Tollett did not answer my question but only urged me to come quickly.

Don's house was only a few minutes away. The sheriff's car was already there, and Darlene met me at the door.

"They're in the bedroom," she said, looking panicked.

I found Don on the bed in his pajamas, being held down by Beef. Don's face was flushed and he was struggling, alternatively shouting incoherent words and moaning piteously. When Don saw me, he calmed down some and tried to control himself.

Beef said that Don had suffered a nervous breakdown and we should take him to the mental health ward at Baptist Hospital in Little Rock. Don started protesting, saying he was all right and did not need to go to the hospital. Beef, Darlene, and I finally persuaded him to go, and the three of us drove him to Little Rock in the back of Beef's sheriff car. Don slept much of the way, and Beef explained to me that this was not the first time an episode like this had happened; in fact, it had occurred several times in past years and was related to excessive drinking. In recent times, those who knew him thought Don had quit drinking and had overcome his problem with alcohol. I didn't say anything, just shook my head sympathetically, but I had the nagging feeling that Don's problem wasn't solely due to drinking.

We got Don admitted to hospital, and Beef and I returned to Nashville. My mind was racing, turning over anew every scenario for an alternative career path. It was obvious to me that Don would be out of commission for quite a while, and it was possible that he might never fully recover.

I discussed with Beef the chances of running for the prosecuting attorney position. He was sympathetic but pointed out the obvious challenges of organizing and financing such a race on short notice. Beef suggested that I hold on to Don's practice until he was able to return, and maybe we could build back to the point that it would be profitable enough to support us both. I knew this would no longer be possible and that I was without any good choices. Beef must have sensed my train of thought, for he suddenly said: "You are a smart guy, Roger, and a good lawyer. You can make it."

I didn't share his optimism. I felt even less secure two days later when Fred Pickens, a lawyer from Ashdown who was considered next in line under the gentlemen's agreement, announced he was running for prosecuting attorney.

16. Small-Town Justice

Following Don's collapse, my professional prospects seemed bleak. In addition, there were payments due on a new car and our furniture. Jeannie was growing increasingly nervous about our personal finances and our ability to earn enough to get by.

Fortunately, I had developed strong friendships with Nashville city fathers and other prominent citizens who wanted me to stay in town. Over the next couple of months, I was elected president of the Rotary club, Nashville's premier civic organization, and I was offered the opportunity to become city attorney. Although city attorney was an elected position, the city fathers convinced the incumbent attorney, an older lawyer whom everyone called Judge Carmichael, to retire. The City Council would then appoint me as his replacement. Plus, the City Council authorized a modest increase in pay, from $150 per month to $250.

During the early fall of 1969, Don returned from his stay in the hospital. He eventually started coming to the office, but he wasn't able to do much. There wasn't much for Don or me to do anyway because most private clients had been scared away. But I struggled on, covering the criminal dockets in the two counties where Don was the deputy prosecuting attorney and working on what little existing private practice we still had.

One case from the period offered insight into the state's antiquated judicial system and its potential for manipulation by local enforcement agencies. Back then, the old 1874 state constitution provided for a system of lesser courts to try misdemeanor cases in front of people who were not lawyers and had no legal training whatsoever. This allowed local justices of the peace and city mayors to serve as the "judges" in a mayor's court. If a defendant lost his or her case in one of these lesser courts, which was a virtual certainty, then a *de novo* appeal could be brought to the circuit court, and the case would be tried anew before a jury.

My client was a local man named Fred Goacher. He appeared in my office on a Monday morning looking red-eyed and disheveled, having just spent the night in the county jail. Goacher said he had been arrested on speeding and DWI charges the previous morning. He said he was not guilty, and he needed a lawyer to fight the charge. The incident began, Goacher said, when he was driving to a service station in town to get a flat tire fixed and was stopped by a Nashville police officer.

"Who was this cop?" I inquired.

"He was a city cop, I think. I don't know his name," he said. He pulled a crumpled piece of paper from his jeans pocket and handed it to me. "Here, I still have the ticket. His name should be on there."

I unfolded the paper and read the name on the bottom: "Otis Eisenhower."

Eisenhower was the city marshal then. He was a big man, with a thick frame and muscular arms. He attended our church, Emmanuel Baptist in Nashville, and was notorious for sleeping during the sermons. One Sunday, the pastor decided to put on a short play in which two or three actors traveled from church to church, enacting a scene of Jesus Christ being taken by the Roman guards. Eisenhower, of course, was asleep, but when he heard the shouting and scuffling from the stage, he woke up, thought it was real, and got up with his gun drawn to save the day. Fortunately, the pastor was able to assure Eisenhower that it was just a play, and he returned to his seat, quite embarrassed.

I asked Goacher a few more questions, learning that Eisenhower told Goacher that he had crossed the center line of the road and had been speeding around a curve. Goacher told me, however, that he was on a dirt road with no center line and the curve was far too sharp for any excessive speed. Eisenhower then asked where Goacher was going. Told about the flat tire, Eisenhower asked to Goacher to open the trunk of his car. In the trunk was a cooler with both unopened and empty beer cans and melted ice water. Goacher explained that this was the residue of a lake outing on Saturday afternoon, the previous day, and that no alcohol had been consumed on Saturday evening or Sunday morning. When Eisenhower saw the cooler and its contents, he arrested Goacher for DWI.

Knowing Eisenhower, I was convinced that Goacher's story was true. I told him I would try to help him and explained the long process that lay ahead. Because the charge had been filed in mayor's court, we would have to deal with it there first. I had never heard of anyone beating a charge in mayor's court. We would surely lose there, but by taking an appeal to the circuit court, we could get a new trial in front of a jury. We might have a chance of winning the case there.

Not wanting to lose the business, I quoted Goacher a ridiculously low fee of $500. He agreed, stating, "This is just not right, and I want to fight it to the end."

On the appointed date for the case to be tried in mayor's court, I showed up with my secretary—Don's wife, Darlene—to record the proceedings in shorthand. Eisenhower was there with the beer cooler, along with the mayor, Bill Holliday. Mayor Holliday was in his forties, ran a small grocery store, and had no more than a high school education. Holliday and Eisenhower had been friends since high school. The pair had years of experience charging and convicting people of various misdemeanors.

But Mayor Holliday had never had a trial in his court before, and he had no idea what to do or how to proceed. I had to explain to him that he was to serve as the judge and decide whether my client was guilty or innocent of the charge.

"Well, that's easy," he said. "Otis has the evidence and he's guilty."

"No," I explained, "you might end up finding him guilty, but we have to have a trial first."

I detailed the whole process to Holliday and Eisenhower, going so far as to rearrange the courtroom furniture, pulling out a desk to serve as the trial bench and instructing Holliday to sit in a chair behind the desk as the judge to hear the testimony. I set up another chair beside the desk for the witness to sit in while testifying. Then I noticed that there was no one present to represent the prosecution. I inquired if Judge Carmichael, the city attorney, was expected to be there.

"Nobody has contacted him," Holliday said. "I didn't know he was supposed to be here."

We called Carmichael's office and asked him to come over. He arrived, all flustered and confused, fussing that this was very unprecedented and highly irregular. But, after some explaining, he agreed to prompt Eisenhower enough to get his testimony out.

I instructed the mayor on how to administer the oath to Eisenhower, who was sworn in. With the beer cooler situated on the desk as evidence—still full of the water, beers, and empty cans—Eisenhower recounted the events of that Sunday morning, asserting that my client was stopped because he was over the center line and speeding. Eisenhower said that despite Goacher's claim that he was on his way to get a flat tire fixed, he did not see a flat tire in the trunk. He did affirm seeing the beer cooler and said that Goacher had bloodshot eyes and reeked of alcohol.

"Did you clock him, to know how fast he was going?" I asked.

"No," he admitted.

"This was that narrow dirt road coming down from Sand Hill, in a curve, where you saw him?"

"Yes, it was," he replied.

"Did the cooler have three cans of beer in it, together with the two empties, just as it does now?" I asked. "And was there the same amount of water in it?"

"Yes, I believe so. I haven't changed anything," he said.

"There was no ice in the chest, and the water was warm, just as it is now," I pressed.

"Ah, yes," he answered, hesitating.

"Did you see him drinking any beer?" I continued.

"No," he said.

"So your basis for believing he had been drinking was that he had bloodshot eyes and smelled of alcohol?"

"Yes, that's right," Eisenhower replied, looking confident.

"A person can have bloodshot eyes for reasons other than alcohol consumption," I said. "For example, your eyes might be bloodshot because you didn't get enough sleep, or because they were irritated for some reason."

"Yes, I suppose so," he said.

"Did Mr. Goacher breathe on you, get up in your face?" I pushed.

"No, he didn't get in my face," Eisenhower replied.

"Did you get up in his?" I asked.

"No, I didn't," he said indignantly.

"Was Mr. Goacher slurring his speech or stumbling around, unsteady on his feet?" I asked, pushing harder.

"No, I wouldn't say that," Eisenhower admitted.

"Someone could have the smell of alcohol about their person, without necessarily drinking it—actually taking it in their mouth and swallowing it. For example, it could have been spilled on his clothes, correct?" I asked, still pressing hard.

"Well, I suppose it could happen."

"So you really don't have any personal knowledge that Mr. Goacher had been drinking that Sunday morning, do you?" I said, going in for the kill.

"Yes, he was," said Eisenhower, raising his voice. "I'm sure of it."

"Is there anything else you would like to add?" I asked. "Have you told us everything you know about it?"

"Yes, I have," said Eisenhower.

At that point I had gotten everything out of Eisenhower I wanted, and Darlene had taken it all down in shorthand, which would later be typed up in a transcript to be filed as the record on appeal to the circuit court. I did not call my client or any other witnesses to the stand.

I was pleased. I had nailed down the exact testimony of the state's principal, and possibly only, witness; gotten some important concessions from him; and revealed nothing of our case. The transcript of Eisenhower's testimony would come in handy at trial.

"What now?" asked Mayor Holliday. "Is that it?"

"Yes," I said. "It's time for you to announce your decision. Do you find him guilty or innocent?"

"Guilty," he said, looking triumphant.

The appeal was duly lodged, and Circuit Judge Bobby Steel set the case for jury trial about three weeks distant. To my surprise, I had set off something of a firestorm among the law-enforcement community in the district. No attorney in memory had appealed a misdemeanor case from a lesser court to the circuit court, and asked for a jury trial to boot. Holliday and Eisenhower were upset, and they shared their grievances with others in the law-enforcement community, including the State Police, the sheriff, and the prosecuting attorney for the entire judicial district, a lawyer named Joe Hardigree from Mena.

When the list of witnesses was exchanged before trial, I noticed that the prosecution had listed Sheriff Lewis Tollett. I was somewhat surprised by this, so I dropped by the sheriff's office for a visit. Beef Tollett told me that he had put Goacher in jail that Sunday around noon, after he had been brought in by Eisenhower.

"Did you smell any alcohol on his breath?" I inquired. "That will be an important issue at trial."

"No," Tollett chuckled, "and I didn't smell it anywhere else either. Otis is opposed to beer, you know."

At the trial, the courtroom was packed with city and state police officers. Hardigree was there to personally try the case, with assistance from a deputy. Mayor Holliday, obviously not understanding the role of a judge, was seated at the prosecution table with a big county records book spread out in front of him.

Twelve jurors were soon seated in the box, and Eisenhower was called as the prosecution's first witness. His testimony was the same as he had given at the mayor's court trial, but he occasionally altered a comment to make it stronger. I reminded him in my cross-examination of his previous sworn testimony, recorded in the transcript that I held in my hand at the ready.

The only other witness called by the prosecution was Tollett, who related the circumstances of placing Goacher in jail at the request of Eisenhower. But Tollett further testified that he did not notice anything odd about Goacher's appearance, such as blood-shot eyes or the smell of alcohol. From the look on Hardigree's face, I could tell that this testimony was not at all what he expected.

After the prosecution had rested, I put on my witnesses. After I had Goacher tell his story, I brought his wife and his parents up to tell their versions of the events. When our witnesses finished, I had a good feeling that the jury was on our side. From the looks on the faces of the members of the prosecution team, they felt the same way.

Suddenly, I noticed a hushed but frantic conference going on over at the prosecution table between Hardigree and Eisenhower. Hardigree then asked Judge Steel to bring Eisenhower back to the stand as a rebuttal witness. Eisenhower stunned the court by de-claring that he had just remembered finding a cold, king-sized can of beer sitting upright on the floorboard under the driver's side seat of Goacher's car.

I immediately objected on the basis that Eisenhower had never given such testimony before, and that it was not a true re-buttal. Judge Steel ruled he would let it stand. On my cross-ex-amination, I reminded Eisenhower that he had made no mention of a cold beer can under the seat in his sworn testimony at the previous trial

"No, I don't believe I did," he said peevishly.

"Do you believe that the testimony you just gave, about the cold beer can which was supposedly under the seat, is important testimony to this case?" I asked.

"Well, of course I do," he responded, somewhat indignantly.

"So it was important testimony," I said, looking at the jurors with a disgusted expression on my face, "but you did not see fit to provide it in your sworn testimony at the first trial, some two weeks after the arrest? Nor did you see fit to provide it today, to this jury in this trial, when you were questioned on direct examination by Mr. Hardigree?"

"Well, I guess I didn't think about it," he said, sheepishly.

By this time, several of the jurors were kind of rolling their eyes, and I could tell that we were making progress. I decided to bring this farce to an end. Since Goacher's car was outside in the court parking lot, a measurement was taken (with Judge Steel's permission) of the space between the seat bottom and the floorboard. The distance was three inches. The king-sized beer can that had been introduced by the prosecution was also measured. It was six and a half inches tall.

It took the jury about ten minutes to elect a foreman, deliberate, and return a verdict of not guilty. Fred's wife jumped up and down, absolutely squealing with joy, and Fred joined in. They grabbed me, hugging and slapping me on the back, all the while exclaiming how much they appreciated the wonderful job I had done. It was the best and most memorable experience of my new legal career.

Jeannie and I celebrated the win, but not for long. I had earned only $500 for many hours of work, and my law partner Don Steel was not showing any sign of recuperation. My prospects were still dismal. I had learned an important lesson, however. I had had enough of small-town life, with its parochial, ossified customs, its backward law-enforcement practices, and its complacent misuses of power.

My later encounters with criminal conspiracies in Little Rock would make all these rural activities seem tame, but, for now, Jeannie and I realized that we needed to relocate and find a better way to make a living.

17. Up to the Big Leagues

Out of the blue, I got a call from Ray Thornton, the newly elected Arkansas attorney general. After a brief exchange of pleasantries in which he thanked me for my help on his campaign, Thornton came directly to the point. He offered me a job as chief deputy of all "special projects" of the office—things that he had promised to implement in his campaign. There would be two other deputy attorneys general in the office to coordinate and manage the office's traditional functions: drafting official opinions on questions of law to assist public officials and representing the state in criminal appeals. Thornton also identified plans to simplify and streamline the state criminal code, enact legislative reapportionment, draft and lobby for legislation to create a new Consumer Protection Division, and help in creating a new computerized Criminal Justice Information System. These latter projects would be my domain.

George Fisher cartoon of Ray Thornton.

"I will need someone to coordinate and manage all of these efforts," Thornton said, "and I can't think of anyone more qualified than you."

My heart was beating fast when I heard all Thornton said. I had to remind myself to breathe as I tried to maintain a cool response and not seem too eager.

"That would be a challenging job all right, and it sounds very interesting," I said. "But I'm not sure I'm in a position to shift gears right now."

"Oh, I don't expect an answer immediately, and I know that I'm asking a lot of you," Thornton said. "How about I give you a few days to think it over, and you call me back if you have any interest?"

By that time, my hands were so clammy and shaking from the adrenaline rush that I could hardly hold the phone. But I continued in a steady voice. "I really appreciate that, Ray," I said. "I will give it some serious thought and talk it over with my wife. When do you need to know something?"

Thornton explained that his term would begin after the January 1971 swearing-in ceremony, but he was hoping I would agree to start earlier and assist with the transition from Joe Purcell's team.

"Let me think about it, and I'll get back to you next week," I said with as much control of my voice as I could manage.

So, just like that, a miracle had occurred, salvation from afar. I had an exciting new high-profile job as chief deputy attorney general for the state of Arkansas.

Two weeks later, Jeannie and I moved to Little Rock. We found a new duplex in the "lower Heights," which bordered on the most prestigious residential area of Little Rock. I joined Joe Purcell's staff and started getting acquainted with the workings of the Attorney General's Office. The first person I met upon arriving for work in Purcell's office was a large, exceedingly effusive woman named Mamie Ruth Williams. I soon learned that Mamie Ruth was Thornton's media consultant and one of his chief political strategists. She had an early job in Purcell's office as well. We took an immediate liking to each other, and she was to play a very important role in my life over the next several years.

While Mamie Ruth's size, probably in excess of 400 pounds, was startling at first, I found that I ceased to notice it after a while because her personality was even larger. Mamie Ruth greeted me with a big hug, literally squealing with delight while recounting all the wonderful things she had heard about me, as well as my family. Mamie Ruth was clearly a force of nature, probably the most remarkable person I had ever met. Along with her great girth, she had a beautiful face that beamed with twinkling black eyes and a slightly crooked, mischievous smile.

Mamie Ruth talked at a rapid-fire pace, interspersed with bursts of crackling laughter. She was exceedingly curious about everything, and she unabashedly delved into questions of a personal nature, such that she knew most of my life history after a short while.

Raised in a prosperous and aristocratic old-line Arkansas family from El Dorado, Mamie Ruth had a heritage in political activism. Her maternal grandmother had been one of H. L. Hunt's first partners during the great El Dorado oil boom in southern Arkansas in the early 1920s. She grew up in Little Rock, attending Central High School and graduating a decade or so before the 1957 Little Rock school desegregation crisis. After Faubus closed the schools, Mamie Ruth joined with a group of progressive-minded Little Rock women to found the Women's Emergency Committee to Open Our Schools. Segregationist-minded detractors derisively referred to this group as the "pushy white liberal ladies" or "PWLL." Mamie Ruth's group adopted the insult as a badge of honor. The group worked to bring national attention and public pressure to the situation, prompting a reluctant President Dwight Eisenhower to federalize the National Guard and forcibly open the school to the nine black youngsters. After the schools were reopened, segregationist forces started a campaign to fire teachers perceived to be sympathetic to integration. Mamie Ruth and other PWLLs helped to establish another progressive group known as "STOP," for Stop This Outrageous Purge, which was eventually able to soothe the roiling school situation and restore a modicum of order.

Mamie Ruth loathed Orval Faubus. The mere mention of his name would send her into spasms of disgust. The depth of her distaste, as well as the passion of her spirit, was revealed in an anecdote she told one day. Driving up to a stoplight in downtown Little Rock, Mamie Ruth noticed that the pickup immediately in front of her had a big red-and-white "Faubus for Governor" sticker on the back bumper. For some reason, she found this particularly galling. So she rammed him. Then she backed up and rammed him again.

"Why in the world would you do that?" I said incredulously.

She smiled that crooked smile of hers. "I don't know. It just made me so mad, I had to do something, so I rammed him. Overall, his bumper showed little damage, but my car had a crushed front end." By this time, she was laughing, shaking all over.

"Did the other guy ever get out of his vehicle?"

"Oh yeah," she said, waving her arms mirthfully, "he got out and came back and peered at me and my car, which by then had steam coming up from under the hood. He apparently decided I was a lunatic, got back in his truck, and drove off."

"What did you do?"

"I drove to a service station on the corner where they told me my radiator was busted. In the end, I got in two good licks on a big Faubus supporter at the cost of a busted radiator. I figured it was even," she said, still laughing.

Mamie Ruth later became one of the leaders of the young progressive group of Democrats who joined forces with Rockefeller's Republican team to defeat the segregationist Democrat, Jim Johnson, in 1966. She managed the election campaigns for many of these progressive Democrats, such as Ted Boswell, Cal Ledbetter, Tom Glaze, and Jim Guy Tucker. I knew these men from my days as president of the Young Democrats Club while at SAU and from the governor's race in the summer of 1966.

★ ★ ★

During my relatively short tenure at the Attorney General's Office, I was busy with interesting and exciting work. I felt fortunate that I did not have to labor over the traditional tasks performed by the office, churning out legal opinions and briefs. We had thirteen assistant attorneys general, most of them assigned to that traditional work. One of them was Lee Munson, a stocky man with prematurely graying black

George Wimberly, mayor of Little Rock, and a principal supporter of the author's political opponent, Lee Munson. (Courtesy of the Arkansas Democrat-Gazette)

154

hair who was a few years older than me. He had a perpetually rumpled appearance as if he usually slept in his clothes. Munson was assigned to the Opinions Division, and his office was down a side corridor from the main part of the office.

I did not know Munson very well and seldom saw him, at least at the office. However, we both joined the office staff for Friday afternoon drinks at the Whitewater Tavern. At these gatherings, Munson would often stay close to an attractive secretary, drinking beer, laughing, and joking. They were often pawing on each other and were frequently seen leaving together. As both were married to other people, this was also noticed by others and became grist for the rumor mill.

Munson had previously been a staff attorney under former Pulaski County prosecuting attorney Richard B. "Dick" Adkisson, a man with a somewhat shady reputation in the legal community. Adkisson was widely considered to have political support from some marginal businessmen suspected of having underworld connections. Adkisson was also closely associated with Little Rock mayor George Wimberly, longtime owner of Buice Drug Store on West Markham Street. Wimberly was a kind of godfather figure to some of the more unsavory elements in the Little Rock business, legal, and law-enforcement communities.

Wimberly had been instrumental in getting Gale Weeks promoted to Little Rock's chief of police. Weeks had started out as a patrolman, was promoted to detective, and finally became head of the vice squad. Wimberly wielded enough influence to swing the job to Weeks instead of to a highly qualified out-of-state candidate favored by most members of the city's board of directors.

Adkisson's chief deputy was Allan Dishongh. He and Munson were buddies and often hung out together, sometimes at the Whitewater Tavern. After two terms as prosecuting attorney, Adkisson decided to run for circuit judge, leaving the prosecuting attorney seat open. Dishongh and Jim Guy Tucker both filed for the position. The race was close, but Tucker easily won after a damning letter surfaced and was published in the *Arkansas Gazette* shortly before the election. It was written by Dishongh to a known crime figure in Hot Springs, suggesting that they had a cozy relationship.

Such was the political environment in which Munson operated before getting the job in Thornton's office. Little did I know at the time that these figures would play a prominent role in my future.

George Fisher cartoon of Gale Weeks.

18. Getting in the Race

The next general election was to be held in November 1972. The Democratic primary election was held in May and was the only one that mattered much, since Arkansas was still a one-party state. A lot of officeholders were angling for an opportunity to move up, thereby leaving vacancies in several offices. It looked like a big shakeup was in the offing, and I wanted to get into the mix.

Ray Thornton was planning to run for Congress, and Jim Guy Tucker was eyeing Thornton's soon-to-be-vacated attorney general spot. It occurred to me that I might have a shot at Tucker's empty Sixth District prosecuting attorney position. I called Tucker, and he invited me to come over and talk about it. He was living in a chic restored carriage house on the grounds of one of the large antebellum mansions in the downtown Quapaw Quarter area of Little Rock. He was a bachelor, living alone in the carriage house with his dog, a big, friendly yellow lab. I went over on a Saturday and found him there with his dog and his girl-friend, Anne Bartley, who was the stepdaughter of former governor Winthrop Rockefeller.

We went to a nearby pub for burgers and beer and to talk politics. We discussed some of the problems and challenges the Prosecuting Attorney's Office faced, including friction with Police Chief Weeks and Mayor Wimberly, plus suspected corruption in high places. All in all, however, Jim Guy and Anne encouraged me to consider getting in the race.

I was certainly giving it a hard look. On the other hand, I

George Fisher cartoon of Jim Guy Tucker.

had a great admiration for Thornton, who had opened a lot of doors for me. I owed him. Also, he had offered me an opportunity to go to Washington DC with him, assuming that he won (which I thought highly likely), to take a high-profile job as his administrative assistant for legislative affairs.

Since I had been in grade school, I had dreamed of living in Washington. My aunt, Donna Mitchell (my mother's older sister), had lived and worked in Washington since the late 1940s. She had struck out on her own after graduating from high school in Iowa. She moved to Washington shortly after the end of World War II and landed a job in the stenography pool at the Commerce Department. Somehow, by dint of determination and wolfish tenacity, she worked her way up the ladder and got a better position at the Navy Department. There, she came to the attention of Nelson Rockefeller, who had just been appointed as undersecretary of the navy.

Aunt Donna was so valuable to Rockefeller that she became his private secretary, then later, after he became vice president, his office administrator and gatekeeper, stationed just outside his office in the old Executive Office Building. I had spent two summers living with her in Washington when I was in college, working at the Smithsonian Institution. So I had already breathed the intoxicating air of Washington.

Still, I was acutely aware that a stint in Washington as a congressional aide would not offer much long-term job security. If you were a congressional aide, your position was secure only until the next election. You were dependent on the political fortunes of the politician for whom you worked. Another consideration was that serving as a congressman's administrative assistant would provide little in the way of useful knowledge and experience to someone who wanted to follow a career path as a working lawyer. Essentially, it would just be wasted time.

After much internal debate and external consultation with others, I declined Thornton's offer and struck out on my own. After all, I had a law degree and had accumulated some experience in the courtroom. Whether I won the prosecuting attorney race or not, I would be headed down a road where I could make better use of my law license.

If I won the race for prosecuting attorney, I could pick up a lot of criminal law knowledge, get in the courtroom, try some high-profile cases, and perhaps position myself to continue a political career. If I lost, I could always find work as a practicing lawyer, and at least I would have raised my public profile in a positive way.

Once the decision was made, I went in to tell Thornton. He was gracious and understanding, and did not seem particularly surprised. He said I could make my own determination as to when I would need to formally resign to announce and begin my candidacy. I began the rounds of visiting with the powers-that-be in the district for support and potential financial contributors.

One of my first visits was with Police Chief Weeks. The Little Rock Police Department headquarters on Markham Street was in a low, rambling two-story concrete building. I was escorted into Weeks's office at the back. The office was sparsely furnished with a utilitarian metal table in the middle of the room, accompanied by several drab metal chairs. The office walls were concrete-block construction, painted a dull gray and bare of any photographs or other decoration. The acoustic-tile ceiling was low, and the florescent lighting produced a spooky white halo.

Weeks sat behind an old wooden desk at the back of the room. He was a large man with black hair graying around the temples, heavy eyebrows, and a huge head, his most prominent feature. He also had a malevolent look in his dark eyes, which were staring at me from beneath the bushy black eyebrows.

When I sat down and tried to engage him in a conversation, Weeks was standoffish, saying little. He just sat there looking at me. Once I had given him my best spiel about my background (country boy from Nashville, worked my way through law school, experience as a deputy prosecuting and chief deputy attorney general, etc.), he seemed to relax and asked me a few questions. Finally, he looked at me rather quizzically and said, "Have you talked with Lee Munson about this?"

"No," I said.

"We have known Lee for a long time, and he has already indicated he is interested in this position. You two need to decide who is going to run."

"I'll talk to Lee," I said, "but I am already pretty well committed to making the race. I expect he is, too."

Chief Weeks looked at me appraisingly for what seemed like a long time, then, rather cheerfully and unexpectedly, said: "Do you know Mayor Wimberly?"

"Not personally," I replied.

"We have a little group that gets together over at the drugstore. Sometimes we sit around a table in the back and talk a little

160

politics. You might want to give the mayor a call," he said. Smiling, he got up and showed me the door.

Once I got back to the Attorney General's Office, I dropped in to see Mamie Ruth to discuss the contacts I had made throughout that day, including the rather strange session I had with Chief Weeks. She became quiet (for her) and ordered me to recount the conversation word for word.

"This is important—don't leave out a single detail," she said.

After I finished, she looked at me in wonderment. "So, you decided to go straight out and beard the lion in his den, did you?"

"No, he was on my list," I said defensively. "If I get elected, I would work more closely with him that anyone else."

"My goodness, you are a babe in the woods," she said. "Shut the door. I've got a story you need to hear."

19. Corruption in High Places

Mamie Ruth's recounting of the rudiments of the previous several years of local government—particularly as it involved crime, corruption, City Hall, the police departments in both Little Rock and North Little Rock, traffic courts, municipal and circuit judges, and the Prosecuting Attorney's Office, which was the key to it all—lasted more than an hour. Crime was big business in central Arkansas. There was money to be made if you controlled certain key elements of the criminal justice system. The most important of those were: (a) the police department, particularly the chief of police; (b) City Hall, particularly the important position of mayor, then held by George Wimberly in Little Rock and William F. "Casey" Laman in North Little Rock; (c) the local traffic and criminal division courts, where you needed to have friendly judges; and (d) most importantly, the Prosecuting Attorney's Office.

It was also helpful to have a friendly face in charge of the federal prosecution arm, the U.S. Attorney's Office. With all of these key positions tied up in a bow, there wasn't much you couldn't do and get away with, making loads of money along the way. In the past, for as long as anyone could remember, there had been a more or less constant web linking them all.

Mamie Ruth spoke of the Dixie Mafia, a group whose criminal activity included gambling, prostitution, strip clubs, money laundering, narcotics, robbery, murder, bribery, and intimidation of public officials, where necessary. Members often created small, seemingly legitimate businesses such as pawnshops and antique stores as fronts to buy and sell stolen property and to launder stolen money.[15]

The Dixie Mafia was in full swing in those days and contributed significantly to the illegal money flow. This loose-knit group of traveling criminals based mainly in the southern United States first got started in Biloxi, Mississippi, in the late 1950s. The gang did not function with a set chain of command or defined territories, nor was it connected by family or country of origin, such as the Sicilian Mafia. At any given time, the de facto "kingpin" was the one with the most money and muscle. Simply put, it was a group of vicious Southern rednecks who had decided to pursue crime for a living.

From its roots in Biloxi, the gang spread through Mississippi and into some other states in the South, including Tennessee and Arkansas. It was particularly strong during the 1970s around Clarksdale, Mississippi, and Memphis, Tennessee. In Arkansas, the Dixie Mafia's influence stretched into West Memphis, Little Rock, and Hot Springs.

I soon learned that the Dixie Mafia had extensively infiltrated the bond business in Little Rock. During the early to mid-1970s, Little Rock became a mecca for bond houses, trading companies for the sale of municipal and other government-guaranteed financial securities, as well as corporate bonds. Several of these shops operated in the city as I opened my campaign for prosecuting attorney. Big trading floors with massive telephone banks were manned by a large crew of "traders," constantly pricing these bonds and churning out buy and sell orders. Bonds were typically denominated in increments of 1/32 per dollar, and the bond "house" usually got a 3/32 commission for each bond sold. This was ordinarily shared 1/32 to the individual trader and 2/32 to the house (the owner of which was known as the "bond daddy").

Since a large trading floor could turn out transactions numbering in the millions of dollars per week, it was an enormously profitable business model for the bond daddy. The individual traders, who typically had a high school education and little training, could earn only a minimum-level commission unless they were very successful salesmen or became supervisors. One of the biggest and most successful bond houses in Little Rock at the time was Delta Securities, owned by Jim T. Hunter, who had started it in Memphis.

At the time, I had only a vague idea about what the Dixie Mafia was or how bond houses operated. Before long, I would find out more than I wanted to know. For example, for years, the flow of cash from the "shady side of the street," as Mamie Ruth termed it, had supplemented the incomes of many Little Rock Police Department detectives, particularly in the vice and intelligence divisions, as well as selected judges and other public officials. Those who were not overtly a part of the gravy train looked the other way and kept their mouths shut.

The only break in the established order came when Jim Guy Tucker, fresh out of law school, had brazenly run for prosecuting attorney two years before—and had unexpectedly won against the establishment candidate, Allan Dishongh.

For ages, the campaigns for prosecutor had been low-visibility affairs, waged by gaining quiet personal contacts among the established order, putting up yard signs, and maybe running a few radio ads. Never before had there been a sophisticated, professional television advertising campaign directed at the general public. Then Tucker came along, quietly tapping into the Rockefeller political expertise and money and running such a campaign. Dishongh and his old-guard supporters were in for a shock.

During the campaign, Dishongh fought back, pointing out that Tucker was fresh out of law school, young, and lacking in experience. The race looked tight, but about a week before election day, the *Arkansas Gazette* published the letter that Dishongh had written to a known crime figure in Hot Springs connected to the illegal gambling industry, intimating a *quid pro quo* understanding. Tucker won.

During Tucker's one term, the old-guard forces tried to smear him in every way possible. They suggested that Tucker was a drug user, and they even attempted on a couple of occasions to plant marijuana in his car, a "set up" much like the one I would experience in Mexico. Tucker had gotten a stomach full and so set his sights on the attorney general position being vacated by Thornton.

After my impromptu education at the hands of Mamie Ruth was finished, I began to appreciate the extent of my naiveté and the size of the task I had set for myself. In Nashville and southwestern Arkansas, the most serious criminal cases might involve disgruntled moonshiners, those with drunk and disorderly conduct, perpetrators of simple assault and battery, or night-stalking hunters. In Little Rock, on the other hand, you would face professional criminals who had high-up connections and long memories—and who might themselves be policemen or various other public officials. These were not the kind of people to trifle with.

But I was young, brash, and pretty much full of myself. Besides, I needed a job. So when Mamie Ruth finally asked, "Are you absolutely sure that you want to do this?" I answered with way more bravado than I was actually feeling. "Sure," I said. "Mafia hits can't hurt that much. What do you say I pay old

George Wimberly a visit and charm the pants off him. Nothing like holding your enemies close."

She gave me her trademark wicked smile and said, "Okay, big boy, but never let it be said that I didn't warn you."

I called Wimberly and tried to sound cheerful and nonchalant when I asked for a meeting.

"Well, er," he paused, clearly thinking it over. "You know Lee Munson is getting in the race. I have known him for a long time and I have to say he's got my support at this time. Of course, if there should be a runoff and Lee didn't make it, we would have to look elsewhere. Er, you know, maybe it might be good to meet, just to get to know each other better. Sure, come on by. I'm here most of the time. Just give me a ring before you come."

Trying to avoid appearing overly eager, I decided to wait a few days before making the visit. I didn't know exactly where Buice Drug Store was, except that it was on Markham Street in the Stifft Station area, so I drove by first to scout it out. It was in a row of old brick buildings near the intersection with Kavanaugh Boulevard. It had an unpretentious, rather ancient-looking sign hanging on the front. To the side was a parking lot where, it appeared, an adjoining building had been torn down in the past. I noticed that there were two "black and white" Little Rock Police Department cars parked in the lot.

"Maybe they are having a meeting around the table in the back right now," I thought.

After another day or two, I returned. I parked in the lot next to the store, noting that there were no police cars, actually no other cars at all. The store was long and narrow with a small area for customers in front. A counter running sideways across the room held the cash register, behind which was a large area with shelves for prescription drugs. Behind that was a separate area with a table and a few chairs.

As I entered, Wimberly was behind the counter waiting on a tiny, frail-looking, gray-haired woman in a very solicitous manner. "Oh, thank you, George, you are such a doll," the woman said as she picked up her small white sack and turned to leave.

"Don't forget, Marvel, two at bedtime after dinner. Remember to eat first," Wimberly said, smiling broadly and nodding as if at a baby. "And call me if you need anything, anything at all."

"Oh, I will, George," she said as she carefully made her way past me and out the door.

"That's Marvel Grimes," Wimberly said, turning to me, obviously knowing who I was. "I have been her pharmacist for over forty years. Did you ever know Dr. Grimes, her husband, a fine orthopedic surgeon? He passed away a few years ago."

"No," I demurred. "He was a little before my time."

"Well, come on back," Wimberly said, indicating the back area. "I just put on a new pot of coffee."

Wimberly was a tall, thin, rather gangly man, with drooping shoulders and a slightly shuffling gait. He appeared to be in his late fifties, with a puffy face, pug nose, sleepy black eyes, and dark graying hair swept low across his forehead, which gave him a somewhat boyish look. His eyes seemed to shift around a lot. He never held my eyes for very long but kept glancing all about the room, quite a contrast to his otherwise affable and laconic demeanor.

We got down to the business at hand quickly. I told him I appreciated that he had a lot of sway in the business and law-enforcement communities. I acknowledged his connection to Munson, but I told him that I was better qualified and would run a strong race. I said I was confident I would win, and I asked for his support.

At that, his manner became more abrupt. He thanked me for the courtesy of the visit, said he had already committed to Munson, and declared that he was good to his word. Little did I know that Wimberly and I were soon to become implacable adversaries.

20. A Field of Four

Jim Guy Tucker's decision to run for Arkansas's attorney general left the race for prosecuting attorney wide open. Three candidates quickly joined me in filing for the position: Lee Munson; John T. Harmon, North Little Rock city attorney and favorite of longtime North Little Rock mayor Casey Laman; and Robert R. Brown, Tucker's chief deputy from the Prosecuting Attorney's Office. Of the four candidates, Harmon and Brown were the odds-on favorites, starting out with the most name recognition and money.

Shortly after the filing deadline, Brown called me for a meeting. To my surprise, he proceeded to tell me that I had little support or fundraising ability and that I had no chance whatsoever. He bluntly recommended that I should withdraw from the race. Known to be a bit arrogant, Brown clumsily intimated that he might have a place for me in his new administration after he won.

Needless to say, I was unimpressed with such an over-the-top entreaty. I knew Tucker was not aware of Brown's tactics, and I later discussed the meeting with several of Brown's colleagues, deputy prosecuting attorneys on Tucker's staff who were friends and quiet supporters of mine. They all agreed that Brown could often be abrasive, although underneath he was a good guy with his heart in the right place. They also said that Brown was over-confident about his supporters' loyalty. I could pick up a good bit of that support, I was told, if I made the effort.

By mid-March 1972, I had made my decision to enter the race. The first thing to do was resign from Thornton's staff. Once the race got under way, Mamie Ruth would also resign and go on my campaign payroll. Until then, she would continue advising Thornton on media matters, but she would move her office from the Justice Building on the Arkansas State Capitol campus to the Adkins Building in downtown Little Rock. The Adkins Building was to become the focal point for my campaign.

Thornton owned the Adkins Building, which was located just across the street from the Stephens Building, headquarters of the Stephens Group, a large private securities firm owned by Ray's two uncles: Wilton R. "Witt" Stephens and Jackson T. "Jack" Stephens. Witt was the president and board chairman of Arkansas Louisiana Gas Co. (Arkla), which supplied natural gas to much of Arkansas and Louisiana. Jack ran the investment firm. The Stephens brothers were among the wealthiest and most influential men in Arkansas before Sam Walton amassed his fortune.

Thornton rented out the first floor of the Adkins Building to a couple of local businesses, but he retained the top floor as a kind of "war room." We used this room for different projects when planning sessions needed to be away from the prying eyes and ears of the regular attorney general's staff, visitors, and others in the more public space at the Justice Building.

Thornton often met there with political supporters to discuss the sensitive work of legislative reapportionment, a task which redrew legislative district lines for both the state Senate and the House of Representatives to ensure equalized population among the districts. The task was guided by the results of the ten-year federal census. Thornton was one of three members of the Board of Reapportionment, established by the Arkansas state constitution; the other two were Governor Dale Bumpers and Secretary of State Kelly Bryant.

This reapportionment was particularly tricky and chock full of political peril because of a recent U.S. Supreme Court decision requiring "one man, one vote." Among other changes, this ruling would prohibit several persons being elected from one large district. In Pulaski County, for example, a five-member House district had all five representatives living within blocks of each other. It was clear that this arrangement would no longer pass constitutional muster. Across the state, legislators who lived in the same district would either have to face each other for election or move. Much angst resulted. Worried legislators wanting to know how their district was going to be redrawn frequently contacted Thornton and me.

Many hours were spent at the Adkins Building drawing and redrawing maps of the possible legislative districts, and many more were spent explaining these maps to concerned legislators. Finally, even more time was spent in meetings with the other two board members and their representatives in an effort to reconcile our maps with theirs. Never have I been involved in a more complex, thankless task. No matter what you did, it seemed, important people were going to be disappointed and dismayed, often downright angry. It was another lesson learned about politics in its rawest stage, a process that bore little resemblance to the seamless and harmonious workings of democracy as taught in civics classes.

Thankfully, much of the work was done behind closed doors away from the view of the press and the public. The Adkins Building was a perfect refuge for that.

21. Mamie and Max

In addition to Mamie Ruth Williams, whose imposing physical presence seemed to fill a room, the other key person on my campaign team was a shady-looking character in a rumpled raincoat and faded gray fedora who was often seen shuffling down the street beneath a cloud of cigarette smoke. This was R. Max Allison, the perfect caricature of an old-time pol. But Max was not a caricature; he was the real deal, preternaturally attuned to the erratic wafting of the political winds like nobody else I'd ever met.

I had no idea how old Max was, perhaps in his fifties or sixties, but one had the distinct impression that he had looked the same way forever. Max was of medium height, somewhat stooped at the shoulders, with unruly thin white hair combed straight back, a hawk-nosed face, and watery pale blue eyes that were piercing if he was looking straight at you while emphasizing what he regarded as an important point.

Among Max Allison's peculiarities was his tendency to doze off anyplace at anytime and then awaken a while later as though nothing had happened. Strangest of all, whenever he fell asleep and awoke later, even if a considerable amount of time had passed, he seemed to have followed all the conversation that occurred in between. He had a sleeping illness, what I guessed was a type of narcolepsy, but I never questioned him about it. His disability certainly did not reduce his political effectiveness. Max had engineered the election of Representative John E. Miller to the U.S. Senate in 1937 after the death of Senator Joseph T. Robinson. Miller, an attorney, had represented Allison in a suit against Metropolitan Life Insurance Company for his sleeping sickness. As Miller, later a U.S. district judge, told it, he called Allison to the stand on a hot and windless August afternoon in the courthouse at Batesville, where the windows had been thrown open to catch a stray breeze. After Allison fell asleep in midsentence, Miller called for a brief recess. When Allison awoke, Miller rested his case. The jury awarded Max Allison a lifetime annuity for his disability. The year after Max got Miller elected to the Senate when he ran against Governor Carl Bailey, he maneuvered Wilbur D. Mills, then the county judge of White County, into Miller's old seat in the U.S. House of Representatives.

Max did not drive a car. He walked, took the bus, or had someone drive him around. I worked with Max when I was in Thornton's office and during my own campaign for prosecuting attorney, often driving him home or to other places he wanted to go. Once I drove him up to the federal courthouse in Searcy to visit with Mills, who was then chairman of the Ways and Means Committee of the U.S. House of Representatives and widely regarded as the second-most-

George Fisher cartoon of Wilbur D. Mills.

powerful man in America behind the president. Mills wanted to talk to Max about his prospects for successfully running for president in the next election. The easy familiarity the two men displayed toward each other was an obvious sign they had been friends for a long time.

★ ★ ★

My campaign officially kicked off on March 20, 1972, with a press conference in the lobby of the Sam Peck Hotel.[16] Mamie Ruth garnered a fair amount of print press coverage from the major newspapers. Even the local television stations sent crews. I made a stock speech laced with rather meaningless phrases and banalities. I said the efficient administration of justice "depended on good relationships among the prosecutor's office, law-enforcement officials, and the judiciary." I pledged to establish close working ties with these agencies. Unaware of the heinous events that would follow the election, I had no idea of the deep irony embedded in my words.

The only thing I said remotely new or original was that I would run a full-time office, and, accordingly, none of my deputies would engage in the private practice of law while serving in the prosecutor's office. At the time, deputy prosecutors were allowed to hold down a private practice. Many of them did, deputy prosecutor Lee Munson among them, and they used their positions and the prosecutor's office to recruit clients. Later, they could represent these clients in their private practice for both civil and criminal matters.

This practice was an obvious and inherent conflict of interest. It presented the possibility, even likelihood, of serious abuses. I promised that my office would pay the deputies a decent salary since private practice would be prohibited. My promise was newsworthy enough that it caused a slight stir with the working press and was featured in subsequent coverage.

Mamie Ruth worked her magic by persuading the *Arkansas Gazette* to send over a photographer and use a flattering photograph of me to highlight the next day's news article. I was off and running, quite proud of myself.

My exhilaration was destined to be short-lived. The next day, we had the first of many "state of the race" debriefings. These were usually held first thing in the morning, after I had returned from whatever daybreak handshaking/meet-and-greet event Mamie Ruth had put on my schedule. Usually, Mamie Ruth and I were the sole attendees at these debriefings, but sometimes Max joined in, as he did on this morning. The purpose was to assess, in a brutally honest way, what we had accomplished and the state of the race vis-à-vis the other candidates.

Conducted by two highly experienced political strategists, this meeting and the many others that followed provided me with a brutally honest dose of reality. Among the key issues immediately identified were: (a) I was broke and unemployed; (b) the piddling amount of money I had previously raised had already been spent on our first order of yard signs and bumper stickers; (c) although I had garnered a modest amount of press coverage from the announcement event, I still had virtually no name recognition; (d) I had just turned thirty, had lived in Pulaski County for only about two years, and had never prosecuted or defended a single criminal case in the county; (e) we desperately needed to hire a public relations firm to help us with television and radio spots; and (f) shaking hands was important, but I would never win this race on shoe leather alone.

Given this dire and frighteningly accurate assessment of my circumstances, I wondered what could be done. Apparently, Mamie Ruth and Max had been having the same thoughts.

Max summed up the dismal state of my campaign in his low, halting, gravelly voice: "Well, I can tell you for sure we ain't gonna do nothing without some money—and it's gonna take a damn sight more than we've raised so far."

Mamie Ruth and I agreed with Max's pronouncement, and we looked at him expectantly for his usual sage advice on the subject. Max sat there, seeming to doze off, but he finally rolled his eyes around to look straight at me. He reached into the inside pocket of his old suit coat and pulled out a crumpled piece of paper.

"Go call on these guys," he told me. "Do it in the order in which they are written down. It is very important that you don't skip around, understand? Do it as soon as you can and report back to me." Max looked at me for a moment longer, and perhaps satisfied that I understood his meaning, dozed off again.

Meanwhile, Mamie Ruth and I busied ourselves talking about the other candidates, particularly Robert Brown. Mamie Ruth knew Brown's wife, the former Nan Selz, and something of her history. From a prominent Jewish family, Nan Brown was well thought of among the elite of Little Rock's fifth ward, a "silk stocking" district in the Pulaski Heights–Country Club area of Little Rock where Brown had his strongest support. Further, Nan was an activist with several progressive, liberal women's groups and had worked with the schools and on other educational endeavors. Mamie Ruth agreed that Robert Brown had something of a prickly personality but suggested that we might be able to make some inroads into his support if we went about it the right way. Mamie Ruth knew a lot of people in the fifth ward, and I had a number of friends there myself.

The opportunity to gain support from this elite demographic group came through a questionnaire to candidates sent by the Political Action Committee of Arkansas Women's Rights. This was a statewide women's group headquartered in Little Rock. Its members were politically astute, and their questionnaire contained twelve probing questions. Mamie Ruth had a friend, a member of the group, who gave her an advance copy. With Mamie Ruth's help, I prepared some draft answers whose wording would most impress the group. Mamie Ruth was even able to have my draft responses reviewed by her friend to ensure their effectiveness. Here, too, was another political lesson—this one about having friends in the right places.

This particular group was influential far beyond the mere size of its membership. They were committed and were willing to work, raise money, and advocate for candidates they liked. Mamie Ruth thought that it would be a real coup to gain their early support. So I prepared my responses and sent them in.

Of the fifty candidates who responded, I was the only one who received a "perfect" rating. This generated a fair amount of publicity and won me some early, ardent supporters who stayed active on my behalf throughout the campaign.[17] Nan Brown was a member of this group. We could never figure out why her husband failed to take advantage of this opportunity.

★ ★ ★

Toward the end of our first strategy meeting, after quite a while had passed from when he had dozed off, Max stirred himself, got out of his chair, and shuffled to a hat rack to fetch his ancient, faded fedora. I never saw Max without this fedora whenever he was outdoors, no matter the weather—hot, cold, storming, snowing, or a clear day with sunny, blue skies.

When Max reached the door, he glanced back at me and paused, apparently lost in thought for a minute. Then he said, "You ain't gonna do any good in this race using kid gloves. Nobody will pay any attention. The only thing you can do is pull it all out in the open. Call a spade a spade."

With those challenging and ominous words, he turned to the door and left.

22. FUNDRAISING STRATEGY

With four candidates initially in the race, a final two-man runoff election was highly likely. Mamie Ruth, Max, and I continued to map out a plan we thought might get me in the runoff.

First and foremost, we needed to raise more money. The bulk of this we hoped would come from Max's list. Second, we wanted to generate as much free press as possible by keeping up a steady flow of press releases. In those statements, I outlined the steps and initiatives I would take when elected, and I contrasted my positions with those of my opponents. Also we would get on "free" television at every opportunity by calling press conferences whenever we had significant news.

Another idea was to publicize Munson's associations with Chief Weeks and Mayor Wimberly as presenting troublesome prospects for conflicts of interest, thus ginning up a public fight and putting Munson on the defensive. We would continue to work on chipping away at Brown's strength in the fifth ward area of Little Rock and at Harmon's strength in North Little Rock. We would push for open debates with the other candidates, especially on television. Finally, we would hire a good public relations firm to help create polished, professional advertising.

Of primary importance, of course, were my efforts to meet with the people on Max's list. The first person on the list was Witt Stephens, Thornton's uncle, who had been a major mover and shaker in Arkansas political circles since the '40s. Getting a meeting with Mr. Witt, as he was generally called, was not easy.

He had an office he used sometimes in the Stephens Building, but he had a busy schedule and was not there every day. His secretary kept putting me off, telling me she would check with him if she could ever catch him in a free moment and call me back to let me know if, and when, I could get in for a visit. This went on for a couple of weeks. Beginning to despair of ever getting a meeting, I shared my anxiety with Max.

George Fisher cartoon of Witt Stephens.

Max cautioned me to be patient. He felt sure the meeting would be arranged, and he reiterated how important it was I start with Stephens. He never mentioned to me exactly why this was, but Mamie Ruth and I pieced together his strategy: "Crack the first nut and others will follow." If we could get Stephens to financially support my campaign, word would quickly get around, and the pump would be primed. Finally—I'm sure that Max was personally behind this—I got word from Mamie Ruth that Stephens would meet with me in his office the next morning at 10 o'clock.

Excited, nervous, apprehensive—all of these emotions were churning in my stomach as I struggled to keep my outside composure as cool as possible—I stepped into the tastefully appointed office of Witt Stephens.

Stephens's father was A. J. Stephens, a Grant County farmer who had served two terms as a state representative. The story was that the elder Stephens advised his son that he would have to "get off the farm" if he wanted to make a decent living. According to legend, Stephens Sr. showed his son a pamphlet offering opportunities to travel and sell inexpensive jewelry, belt buckles, and other gadgets. Witt proved amazingly adept at this, especially at selling belt buckles. He even did well while in summer camp with the Citizen Military Training Corps at Fort Leavenworth, Kansas, convincing the commander to let him set up a table next to the paymaster to market his wares. Many of the trainees, naturally, thought that they were supposed to buy the belt buckles as part of their equipment, so Stephens earned a tidy profit.

Later, he traveled the state selling highway bonds and began acquiring interests in small banks, mostly in small towns, through which he was able to market more bonds. He got into the oil and gas business, which took off after the war, and built a small fortune.

Stephens was always interested in politics, and he gave his support to Sid McMath for governor in 1948. Not long returned from World War II, McMath was a U.S. Marine war hero, leading many battlefield campaigns as a lieutenant colonel in the Pacific Theater and earning the Silver Star and Legion of Merit awards. Arkansas had stagnated under a succession of weak governors through the 1940s, and McMath presented a young, energetic, "can do" progressive candidate. He proposed to build new schools, institute an ambitious highway construction program, and build a state medical school. He championed rural electrification. The voters, fed up with the backward policies of the old-guard politicians, elected McMath.

Of course, Stephens recognized that the proposed new building programs would entail many large public bond issues, and he would get to handle his fair share of the financing. Thus was established Stephens, Inc., which, in a couple of decades, grew to be the nation's largest privately held brokerage house off Wall Street.

Stephens's inner office had a big floor-to-ceiling bay window overlooking East Main Street and was located on the top floor of the Stephens Building. Centered in the office was an elegant antique French Empire-style table topped with a giant crystal vase filled with fragrant flowers. The flowers in the vase had translucent pink petals as delicate-looking as butterflies, surrounded by large, waxy green leaves. The flowers were the first thing I saw upon entering the room, and I was rather startled by their beauty.

Stephens was seated behind a stylishly carved mahogany desk in a tall-backed black-leather chair. Despite his formidable reputation, the man I met displayed the genteel qualities of a small-town banker or merchant. Stephens's silver-white hair was combed in a boyish style. His large frame was draped in a dark business suit, and his shoes were shined to a glossy "banker's black." He was chewing on the stub of an unlit Cuban cigar.

"Roger, come on in and have a seat," he said in a friendly tone, rising to shake my hand. I sat down on a white silk-brocade-covered chair, one of a pair arranged in front of his desk.

"It's a real pleasure to see you, Mr. Stephens," I said. "Thank you for having me over."

"We don't stand on formalities here, Roger. Please just call me Witt," he said.

Somehow, I thought, that would be awkward. I had been taught from childhood to refer to my elders as Mr. or Mrs.

"Okay," I ventured, "but mind if I meet you halfway and call you Mr. Witt? You are probably twice my age and multiple times my experience."

He leaned back and let out a deep chuckle, saying, "Well, age and experience don't mean much unless you've learned some things along the way. But I can see that you've been raised well, so 'Mr. Witt' it is."

I relaxed a bit and my stomach began settling down. "I hope that you don't mind me asking, but that wonderful fragrance I smell, does that come from the flower arrangement over there?" I inquired, indicating the crystal vase.

"Yes it does," he said. "Those are pink camellias. We used to have them at home when I was growing up. I get them from a nursery here in town. I get a fresh batch every day when they are in season. Some put out a lot of perfume and some don't. I like the ones that smell good."

"Well, you certainly hit the jackpot with those," I said.

"Didn't I hear that you are from south Arkansas—Nashville is it?"

"Yes, that's right," I answered. "Well, actually about five miles out in the County Line community toward Lockesburg. I grew up on a farm but went to school at Nashville."

"No wonder you are interested in flowers," he said. "I guess you had experience with all kinds of plants growing up on the farm."

"I did," I said, "but mostly the kind that you eat."

He chuckled again. "Sounds like my childhood. I grew up on a farm in Prattsville but went to school in Sheridan. That's smaller than Nashville." We both laughed, and I knew I had hit the right chord with Mr. Witt.

We talked some more, and the conversation turned to politics. He said he had heard good things about me from his nephew, Ray Thornton. I told him how Ray and I first got to know each other in the Constitutional Convention, and how much I admired Ray and appreciated the responsibilities and opportunities he had provided me.

The whole conversation didn't take long. I didn't even get around to asking for a campaign contribution. Stephens cut it off by saying, "We want to help out, Roger. I know you would do a good job in that position, and you have a good chance of winning. Tell you what, let me pass the hat around here and we'll see what we can do."

At that, he stood up, indicating that the meeting was over. We shook hands again as I headed out. "We'll be back in touch soon," he called as I closed the door behind me.

23. From Nothing to Something

After my meeting with Witt Stephens, I diligently followed Mamie Ruth's daily schedule, rising before dawn to go to some factory shift change to shake hands and hand out campaign cards, then returning to our office for our usual state-of-the-race meeting. We had rented the upstairs of a storefront on Third Street, about three blocks from the Adkins Building, for our official campaign headquarters. We used that space for our meetings and for logistics—assembling yard signs, directing volunteers, making and taking phone calls, preparing press releases, etc. These were the early days of the primary campaign and, quite frankly, not a lot was going on.

I had gotten some publicity from the perfect rating from the women's action group, and we were continuing to generate press releases on various mundane subjects. I put out a twelve-plank platform, pointing out that none of my three opponents had done so, whereupon they all put out platforms. Then I criticized their platforms and tried to differentiate my excellent views from their foolish ones, whereupon they all responded with criticism of my platform and offered justification for theirs.

None of this was very exciting stuff, and my campaign felt listless, stolid, and phlegmatic. I began to imagine a worst-case scenario—a horrible, devastating last-place finish. In other words, a disaster was looming. I tried desperately to boost my spirits and energy level, but it seemed that everything was slipping off into a deep and waiting abyss.

One morning, I dragged in for my meeting with Mamie Ruth, having skipped my factory shift handshake tour, feeling low indeed. Mamie Ruth gave me that crooked smile, looking coy.

"Okay, I'm listening," I said, sounding a little irritated and thinking that she was going to chide me in some back-handed manner for missing the factory meet. She said nothing but held out a white envelope, waving it in front of me.

"What's that?" I said, a little more sharply than I intended. "A bill for yard signs?"

"Nooo, it's not a bill," she said teasingly.

In no mood to play, I said, "Well, if it's not real good news, I don't want to look at it."

Mamie Ruth must have sensed that I was not in a good place mentally, for she dropped the teasing attitude and said, rather dryly: "Okay, party pooper, you did it. Mr. Witt just sent over a check. Do you have any interest in seeing it?"

"How did we do?" I asked.

Mamie Ruth handed me the envelope and I took out the check—$2,000, with a handwritten note from Witt Stephens: "Roger—I hope this helps—good luck!"

Today, $2,000 is not a lot of money, but in 1972, with the state my campaign was in, it was heaven sent. I raised the check to my lips and gave it an extravagant kiss: "Thank you, Mr. Witt," I proclaimed. "We ain't out of this thing yet!"

I realized, as did Mamie Ruth, that the most important aspect of the check was the softening effect it was sure to have on other potential contributors. The grapevine was likely already buzzing. Sure enough, the people on Max's money list—Bill Dillard, Brick Lile, Warren K. Bass, William J. Smith, Fred K. Darragh, and others—suddenly began to return my calls, and they agreed to meetings over the next few weeks. They let loose another $3,000 or so. Even the continuing smaller donations began to pick up.

We finally had enough to hire a public relations firm. We selected Ben Combs, who, although his agency was small, was an enthusiastic supporter of our campaign and had good contacts with the media. His wife at the time was an important news personality for KATV, Channel 7, the ABC network affiliate in Little Rock.

Mamie Ruth and I met with Combs to map out a general strategy for the primary campaign. They both thought that Munson was our top opponent because of his connections with Mayor Wimberly and Chief Weeks, and, through them, the extended law-enforcement community in Little Rock and their traditional old-guard supporters, plus the underworld crime syndicates Mamie Ruth had warned me about.

We decided to mount an immediate television campaign, using paid ads, plus as much television coverage as we could get. This was primarily based on the Jim Guy Tucker model. But unlike Tucker, I had no large built-in support base and little name recognition. So, Combs bought as much early television airtime as we could afford. In a four-man race, our main goal was to get into a runoff.

We were well aware of the power of the press, and Mamie Ruth was a tireless worker at the persistent cajoling, persuading, and feeding of media outlets to get what was needed. The editorial boards of the major newspapers would be making endorsements as the primary election approached. We considered how to better manage and tailor our message to favorably impress the editors.

Overall, we felt that the campaign was in reasonably good shape. We had gotten relatively good press initially after my announcement, and we had the support from the women's action group. In addition, my platform had been announced, leading to the back-and-forth with the other candidates and the early television ads.

As it turned out, I got endorsements (two of them shared with Brown) from all three of the major papers: the *Arkansas Gazette*, the *Arkansas Democrat*, and the *Times* of North Little Rock. Also, I got the full-throated endorsement of the North Little Rock Good Government Committee, an influential private group of leading citizens in North Little Rock. The committee was stoutly against two of my opponents. It opposed John Harmon because of his ties to Mayor Casey Laman of their city, and it was critical of Lee Munson because of his ties to Mayor Wimberly and Chief Weeks in Little Rock.

All the newspapers echoed this sentiment in their editorials. They stressed the importance of continuing the Tucker tradition of maintaining an independent watchdog Prosecuting Attorney's Office uninfluenced by special-interest groups, other government officials, judges, or other segments of society. The *Times*'s editorial endorsement was particularly strong:

> Roger Glasgow has been out of law school less than five years, but he has acquired a depth of experience in public life and the law that enables the Times to endorse him today for the office of Prosecuting Attorney in the upcoming Democratic primary.
>
> Taking a look at Mr. Glasgow's relatively short career in public life, we have found it to be marked not only by a variety of practical legal experience, but by an involvement in public interest causes.
>
> But qualifications aren't everything. To be effective, a prosecuting attorney must also be prepared when he goes to trial. This Mr. Glasgow promises to do by assigning two

members of his staff to each felony trial—one with primary responsibility and the other as a backup attorney. That type of approach should make the state's cases stick.

But neither are qualifications and thorough preparation enough. The prosecutor must also seek out wrongdoing, particularly when local law enforcement breaks down. By convening the county Grand Jury, he can then ask for indictments on the basis of evidence developed by his office.

This Mr. Glasgow promises to do. "I will use the Grand Jury extensively, " he said the other day, "and I will continue the practice of cracking down with the full force of the office on gambling, prostitution, and corruption in public office."

That is the kind of talk every law-abiding resident of Pulaski and Perry Counties wants to hear, particularly those of us in North Little Rock, where suspicions linger about such offenses.[18]

Mamie Ruth skillfully seized upon these editorial endorsements to create paid ads that we worked into all our campaign advertising. As the race heated up, the press, civic organizations, and the public began to pay more attention. The endorsements, together with my early television ads, were proving effective in increasing my name recognition, public awareness of the issues, and support for our campaign. Things were definitely looking up.

The primary election was to be held on May 30. As time wore on, the other three candidates did not appear to be spending a lot more money than we were. Nor did their campaigns appear to be making major headway. We thought my chances to make the runoff were so good that I might lead the ticket. But about two weeks before the election, we began to notice, particularly in the southwestern and western parts of Pulaski County, an impressive proliferation of Lee Munson yard signs.

About this same time, Munson's campaign broke out a catchy radio jingle, set to the tune of "American Pie," urging voters to cast their ballot for him. This jingle ran almost constantly through election day on virtually all of the local radio stations. In response, we ran a verbal-message radio ad, using my announcer-trained voice, but without anywhere near the saturation coverage Munson achieved. I thought that Munson's jingle was silly and amateurish, but Mamie Ruth and Max were not so sanguine.

"He's spending a lot of money," Max observed. "We're in good shape with folks in the know, but that jingle targets the ignorant people, and you would be surprised how many of them there are."

Mamie Ruth was impressed with Munson's radio ad but more so with the prolific sprouting of yard signs. "Every yard sign," she explained, "represents a committed group of voters—not just one—but the whole household and usually some friends and relatives to boot. A rule of thumb is that one yard sign represents about five votes, on average."

On election night, we had a watch party in the back room of a local bar and restaurant, with several televisions scattered about so we could follow the voting results. A cash bar served beer and wine. In the early hours, the mood was festive, with cheering breaking out occasionally when a precinct reported in with me leading or in a close second. But later in the evening, the results came in more slowly. By 10 p.m., we realized that many more hours would pass before the final results were known.

Nearly everybody had left by 11 p.m., as the next day, Wednesday, was a workday. I left about midnight. By that time, Munson had pulled to a strong—and, to me, surprising—lead of about 4,000 votes. I was in second place, holding a 1,500-vote lead over Brown. Harmon trailed the ticket.

By the next morning, most of the votes had been counted. Munson had held and extended his lead, and I was a solid second. So I was in the runoff, which was great, just what we had wanted, but Munson was ahead of me by some 8,000 votes—22,500 to

14,500. Brown had about 13,000, and Harmon had slightly under 12,000.

The runoff was scheduled for two weeks later, and a lot of ground had to be made up. Yet my campaign had spent most of what we had during the primary and was nearly broke.

Runoff opponent Lee Munson (left) and the author pose together for the press following the primary election, 1972. Munson would go on to win the race two weeks later. (Courtesy of the Arkansas Democrat-Gazette)

24. Press and Pigs

Mamie Ruth was forgiving when I dragged in at about 10 o'clock in the morning for our strategy meeting. Max Allison was there as well, dozing in an easy chair. He roused himself when I got there, and we quickly focused on the most immediate problem, a severe lack of cash in the campaign coffers. Mamie Ruth had examined our bank account and reckoned our balance at about $1,500.

That depressing news did not deter my small team, and we quickly got to work on the next phase of my campaign. Political lessons learned do not end at the polls on election day. It was time to study the numbers and the maps.

In this case, the election results were revealing, especially the pattern of voting. Munson had carried all the rural areas of Pulaski and Perry Counties. Munson also carried southwestern Little Rock, where he lived, an area home to many of the LRPD rank and file, their families, and the police auxiliaries. As well, he carried many of the precincts in western Little Rock, where the more affluent *nouveau riche* lived.

I split the vote with Brown in Little Rock's fifth ward, home of the old money, and I carried the five most affluent precincts in North Little Rock, which encompassed Lakewood, Indian Hills, and Park Hill. Brown and I had also essentially split the vote in all the predominantly black precincts.

It was clear that I had done well with minorities, as well as with the established businesspeople and professionals, those likely to be among the best informed and conversant with the issues. Munson had done well with the old guard and the police-influenced areas, plus the predominantly white rural precincts and the newer suburban areas of western Little Rock. It was also clear that my solid vote in North Little Rock, largely attributable to the efforts of the North Little Rock Good Government Committee, is what put me into the runoff.

The *Arkansas Gazette* reported on the primary race results as follows:

> Brown and Glasgow showed considerable strength in Little Rock's fifth ward, where both live. Brown and Glasgow together outpolled the other two candidates, Munson and John Harmon, in almost all of the fifth ward precincts. Glasgow and Brown were also strong in most of Central and East Little Rock, which are predominantly black precincts. Brown did not run well in northern Pulaski County, but Glasgow led in North Little Rock's five most affluent precincts. Munson led in all rural county precincts except for the Hensley, Wrightsville, and College Station precincts, all predominantly black areas that went to Brown.[19]

A news article appearing in the next day's edition of the *Arkansas Democrat* reported that "Munson's campaign peaked late with signs springing up and his radio jingle to the tune of 'American Pie' being played profusely only about the last two weeks of the campaign." The same article quoted me saying that

I "thought the primary reflected name recognition only, but the runoff would be issued-oriented."

Max, Mamie Ruth, and I agreed that my only chance to close Munson's big lead and have a decent chance of winning was to run an extensive television campaign. We needed to lock up airtime with adequate time slots, and we needed to move immediately. We decided to buy what we could with the $1,500, a pitifully meager amount.

"That's a bad predicament all right," Max rumbled. "Fifteen hundred dollars won't buy more than two or three days' worth of television time, and we need a lot of other stuff, too. Roger needs to be out campaigning, and he sure as hell won't have time to make the rounds to beg for more money."

"Is there some place we can get some kind of bridge loan, just to tide us through?" Mamie Ruth ventured.

"Not likely," Max said. "The banks won't do it. They've been burned too many times in runoffs, and most individuals with that kind of money are already tapped out. They would all be looking at that 8,000-vote difference, too, figuring it is probably insurmountable."

Meanwhile, I was thinking, *This is my campaign. It's my responsibility to find the money. I've come too far not to finish this thing.* At the same time, less-positive thoughts flickered through my mind, such as the extreme embarrassment I would face from a blowout loss.

As Max and Mamie Ruth continued to discuss the situation and mull over various ideas, none of them very good, I considered any property or possessions I owned that could be sold or offered as security for a loan. Suddenly it hit me—pigs. I still owned an interest in a bunch of pigs. They were like cash on the hoof, and a livestock sale was held every weekday down in Texarkana.

When I was practicing law with Don Steel in Nashville, my dad and I decided, as a kind of bonding experience I think, to get in the hog business. We started in the old barn out on the family farm, retrofitting a few cow stalls into farrowing crates. These are smaller enclosures for protecting baby pigs from the mother sow, who might lie down and smother them shortly after birth. We built a strong new fence enclosure from the barn to a stock pond so the pigs would have water and a place to cool off. We also bought some large metal feeding bins. Working together on the project, my dad and I did grow closer.

Hogs are very prolific. The sows can be bred again as soon as the piglets are weaned, in about two months, and they then give birth again in another six months. We bought eight sows, each one capable of birthing up to a dozen piglets at a time. We established a breeding schedule to produce several groups of market-sized pigs at three-month intervals. My dad and I had equal shares of the hog-farming operation, and though I had moved to Little Rock, I never thought about selling my share. Now contemplating the financial squeeze my campaign was in, I wondered if the hog-farming operation could be a source of some money.

A phone call home affirmed my speculation. "We've got a sizable bunch ready for market right now," my dad said. "I'll get them shipped out early next week, and we'll see what we can get. Should be $2,000 or so. Don't worry about selling your share of the operation right now. I'll send you the entire proceeds from the sale, and you can reimburse me for my share when you are able. I don't need the money at the moment."

I don't recall if someone on my campaign team made a joke at the time about this new twist on "pork barrel politics," but with the benefits of my rural background and family support, the immediate money problem was solved. We returned to the task of mapping out our strategy for the runoff. Max felt strongly that I should more directly call out Wimberly, on the theory that Munson was merely a puppet under his control. During the primary, I had talked about this only in general terms, emphasizing the importance of maintaining the independence of the Prosecuting Attorney's Office and protecting it against undue influence from special-interest groups. Max wanted me to name names. Mamie Ruth was less sure, warning of the danger in "kicking a wounded wolf."

I agreed with Max that our only chance to close the gap was to be much more aggressive. Doing so, I reasoned, would generate a good bit more public interest and publicity, perhaps goading the Munson campaign into doing something foolhardy we could capitalize on. Mamie Ruth's "wounded wolf" scenario raised a specter of unpredictable retaliation. But at the time, I thought of it only in the context of the political campaign. If my naming names made the Munson campaign angry, and we expected that it would, there undoubtedly would be some type of response.

I speculated that Munson's camp might start spending additional money for negative ads to attack me. But I believed that I would have the advantage in that kind of war. It never occurred to me that there were much more sinister ways to strike back.

25. The Fight Gets Ugly

As the runoff campaign got under way, I got an important endorsement from the third-place finisher, Robert Brown, which was widely reported in the press. Brown personally worked hard manning the phones, actively encouraging his former supporters to turn out at the polls and vote for me.

The *Arkansas Democrat* ran a nice article featuring a photo of Brown as he presented his endorsement at a news conference at the Sam Peck Hotel in downtown Little Rock. Brown spoke favorably of me and disparaged Munson: "The independence of the office of prosecuting attorney must be preserved inviolate," Brown said. "Mr. Glasgow owes no favor to any man—I cannot say the same of his opponent."[20]

Several civic clubs held invitational public-service events for the candidates, and the Little Rock Jaycees invited Munson and me to a live debate for their Challenge '72 program. Our comments would be videotaped live and then shown on KARK-TV, Channel 4, a couple of days later following the six o'clock news.

My team was ecstatic for me to have the opportunity to face Munson so early in the runoff and also get a free thirty-minute television show in prime time. I was also excited, believing my background in political stump speaking would serve me well. We prepared our strategy carefully, determined to go on the offensive immediately and stay there.

The Jaycees held their meetings in a large conference room at the Riverfront Hotel in North Little Rock. When the time for the debate came, Munson and I were directed to a raised platform in the front of the room where two straight-backed chairs were placed side by side. Questions were to come from a moderator seated to one side. The audience—composed of the Jaycees, their guests, and representatives of the press—extended out in front of us, seated in numerous rows of metal folding chairs. The room was packed.

I noticed Wimberly and Weeks sitting side by side in the middle of the front row. They were smiling confidently, beaming paternally at Munson. I saw Wimberly give him a big wink. When they glanced in my direction, their expressions changed to arrogance and aggression. But I was determined to ignore their menacing signals.

I went on the offensive on the first question, pounding Munson on his record and occasionally jabbing Wimberly by name. Munson seemed unprepared for this and looked shell-shocked. He defended himself tentatively and weakly, and was never able to mount much of an offense of his own. Wimberly and Weeks sat glaring, then got up and left in a hurry as soon as the program was over. I felt I had done quite well. The tone for the rest of the campaign had been struck.

After the Jaycee debate, Munson went underground, seemingly content to just ride it out by playing his radio jingle, running print ads, and getting out more yard signs. But we were determined not to let him rest in peace.

Through the efforts of Mamie Ruth and Ben Combs, we persuaded Robert Doubleday, president of KATV, Channel 7, the top-rated Arkansas TV station, to offer a thirty-minute prime-time live debate between the two candidates as a public service. This offer was extended via a telegram from Doubleday to both Munson and me.[21]

I immediately accepted, and we called Munson's office to get his position. We were told that Munson was out and was not expected back that day. His office did acknowledge receiving the telegram but claimed to have no idea whether or not he would accept the debate offer. Of course, we knew the answer. He was hiding out.

So we quickly got out a press release, Max Allison deeply involved in the wording, challenging Munson to accept and chiding him in advance if he declined. We again called out Wimberly by name, accusing him of controlling Munson's campaign, and, in effect, holding Munson as his captive. Among its provocative statements, the press release proclaimed:

> "…the real issue in this campaign: Whether the office of prosecuting attorney will remain independent, providing the most vigorous, responsible and effective prosecution possible, or whether it will revert to a time of case backlogs, open gambling, prostitution, and the giving of special service to special interest groups or individuals.
>
> The time has arrived to pull the ripcord and expose to everyone the controlling and dominating issue in the runoff primary for prosecuting attorney. My opponent has become a captive of the forces that support him. The present mayor of Little Rock is the chief architect of his campaign. My opponent has very little control and very little knowledge about what is going on. He has no platform and is not permitted to help prepare or correct his own false and misleading political newspaper advertisements.
>
> The question of an independent or controlled prosecuting attorney's office is of major importance to every voter

and taxpayer. I am committed to an independent policy. I do not propose to change my course. My opponent may have good intentions of independence, but he cannot escape the clutches, influence and control of those in charge of his campaign. All people in Pulaski and Perry counties are entitled to an explanation of the motives and objectives that dictate the activities of the Little Rock mayor in the present race and campaign for prosecuting attorney.[22]

Max insisted upon the blunt wording in the press release, stating his belief that we needed to "build a fire" under the campaign. He explained his firm opinion that the only way we could close Munson's large lead was to create a major controversy, putting Munson's campaign on the defensive, which would generate a lot of public interest, and, in turn, cause a huge volume of press coverage.

Max also thought we should continue to jump on Munson, making him look weak and tentative for refusing the free debates. We tried to purchase the Jaycees' Challenge '72 videotape from the previous debate, but we were told that Munson's permission was required. Predictably, he refused. So, we added a final demand to the already contentious text, challenging him to give his permission for the rebroadcast.

Thus, the gauntlet had been thrown down, clearly and unequivocally, for all to see. Munson declined the debate and its accompanying free television airtime. He also withheld permission for me to purchase the Challenge '72 video and the television airtime to show it again.

His strategy was evident: hunker down and ride out the storm. We felt that gave us an opening to close the gap. Although it was not obvious to me at the time, our strategy of vigorous attack also invigorated Wimberly, Weeks, the LRPD, the Police Officer Auxiliary Support groups, and other Munson supporters, causing them to redouble their ground game and grind on toward the finish.

Since Munson declined the KATV offer, we persuaded Doubleday to air an "empty chair" debate if Munson did not show. We knew Munson would not risk another public meeting, and we were prepared to make the most of this one-sided televised event.

Bill Henslee, a Little Rock lawyer and strong supporter of mine, acted as moderator. I sat on the television stage with an empty chair beside me. Bill asked the scripted questions we had prepared, and I slammed Munson unmercifully. The program aired as scheduled, and three major papers ran prominent news articles about it the next day.

The *Arkansas Gazette* quoted my main statements that during Munson's time as a deputy prosecuting attorney, the district had the highest rise in gambling, vice, and corruption in recent years and the largest backlog of criminal cases in its history. The article stated:

> Glasgow said the "primary issue in this campaign is the independence" of the prosecuting attorney's office. He said it was important for the voters to know who was supporting a candidate because "I believe that it has a direct bearing upon the degree of objectivity and independence that the candidate can exercise if he is elected prosecuting attorney."
>
> Glasgow said he had already pointed out that Munson was being supported by Mayor Wimberly. He said that "certainly there is nothing wrong" with a candidate being supported by a public official, but when a "public official actively campaigns for a person, raising money, planning and helping strategy in the campaign, I think it does raise a question about whether or not the candidate, if he is elected, will have such a large political debt that he won't be able to, despite his best efforts, exercise the independence and objectivity that is required, in my opinion, of a prosecuting attorney."
>
> Glasgow also noted that Munson had said he had "100 percent police support." Glasgow said there was nothing wrong with that, either, but "when that constitutes your

basic source of support, I think it again raises the issue that the prosecuting attorney should be independent, especially in cases that may involve the Police Department."[23]

In the final days of the runoff, all the newspapers renewed their endorsements of my campaign in even more emphatic terms than before. An editorial in the *Arkansas Gazette* stated:

Roger Glasgow is choice for prosecutor.

The race for Sixth District prosecuting attorney has become, during the runoff campaign, one of the most hotly contested races for the office the community has seen for some time.

Through it all our own choice favoring the candidacy of Roger Glasgow has been strengthened. He has handled himself in the runoff campaign with a strong, forthright willingness to discuss the issues. That element, alas, has not been present in the campaign of his opponent, Lee Munson, who led the ticket in the four-man field of the Democratic preferential primary and perhaps feels that his best course is to say as little as possible of substance...

The *Gazette* now does not hesitate to state its endorsement of Mr. Glasgow's runoff candidacy, recognizing the superior qualifications that he would bring to the job as well as the prospect he offers for continuing the high level of performance established in the office during the 17 month tenure of Jim Guy Tucker, who has won the Democratic nomination for state attorney general.[24]

During the runoff, Munson and I attended several on-the-ground political events around the district. We milled through the crowds, shaking hands, asking for votes, and handing out cards. I noticed a strong, visible presence of members of the LRPD at these events. In particular, a couple of plainclothes detectives often hung about. They seemed to be eyeing me suspiciously.

I learned that the two men were Lieutenant Kenneth Pearson, head of the vice division, and Lieutenant Forrest

200

Parkman, head of the intelligence division. Pearson had a chubby, slack face, a fleshy jowl, and long sideburns. He was affable and fidgety, always laughing and grinning, and he wore the worst-looking mismatched clothes imaginable. He looked more like a clown than a detective.

Parkman was the opposite. Every time I saw him, he was wearing a suit and a clean white shirt and tie. A big barrel-chested man, he had wavy, dark, slicked-back hair, a dark complexion, and a solid square jaw. He was stern, quiet, and unsmiling, with piercing, hooded black eyes. He looked like a study in evil.

Many times, these two were accompanied by Jim T. Hunter, CEO and majority owner of Delta Securities, a Little Rock bond firm that housed its operations on the fifteenth floor of the Worthen Bank Building.

Lieutenant Forrest Parkman of the LRPD Intelligence Division. A Munson supporter, he was sometimes a menacing presence at campaign events. (Courtesy of the Arkansas Democrat-Gazette)

Hunter showed up frequently at various campaign events Munson attended. Hunter always wore sunglasses, and he dressed in a suit over a dark shirt and a matching tie (usually maroon). He drove a new, white Lincoln Mark IV Continental, top of the line, with an Arkansas vanity license plate reading JTH.

During the last week of the campaign, I went to an evening event at Barton Coliseum and found the three of them standing at the entry. Pearson called out to me, and I went over.

"You are Roger Glasgow, right?"

"Yes," I said, "and who might you be?"

"I'm just a messenger," he responded. He looked me over and continued, rather menacingly, "The mayor wants to see you."

"Well, he knows where to find me," I replied casually. "I'd be glad to visit with him any time."

I could see Hunter nearby with his foot propped up on the railing leading into the coliseum, but Parkman had disappeared. Suddenly I felt a rough shove to my right shoulder, and a big figure in a dark suit pushed past. I found myself staring into the dark eyes of Lt. Forrest Parkman.

He snarled in a low sinister tone, "I'd be careful driving home if I were you. Bad things can happen on a long, winding highway at night if you are not careful."

I took this for what it was, an undisguised threat. But I managed to respond in an even voice, "To put your mind at ease about my safety, Detective, I live just a short ways from here, not way out in the country on a winding road."

A faint smile slowly crept across Parkman's mouth. He said, "We know very well where you live."

"You guys have a good night!" I shouted as I walked away.

"Oh, we will, for sure," I heard one of them say as I disappeared into the cavernous interior of Barton Coliseum.

26. LOSING AND WINNING

As the runoff campaign headed into the final week, I felt momentum swinging our way. We had knocked Munson against the ropes and never let up. He had not landed a single significant punch. When election day finally arrived, I believed my campaign had done all it could to win the vote. All that was left for me to do was to visit selected polling places around the county to check on things, encourage my poll workers, and shake hands.

At the Dunbar Community Center polling place, one of the largest election precincts in southwestern Little Rock, I noticed the familiar white Lincoln Mark IV with the JTH license plate and a couple of unmarked, but obvious, police cruisers.

I thought little about it. I had become accustomed to seeing Jim Hunter in the company of LRPD detectives as the campaign wound down. Besides, I was extremely busy and hurried, and there was little time to speculate on the opposition's activity. In the late afternoon, when the polls were closing, Mamie Ruth reported a rumor from a reliable source that Munson had been seen personally "buying off" my polling-place campaign workers.

After the polls closed that night, we joined an election watch party. A large and loud crowd had settled in for a long night of vote counting. Through the early part of the evening, as the first returns trickled in, mostly from the more affluent areas of Little Rock and North Little Rock, the count remained close. I was in good spirits. I had fought hard and done all I could. But as more precincts reported, Munson pulled ahead. By 9 p.m., he had a commanding lead.

Within a short time, it became clear that Munson was going to win. I talked to Mamie Ruth and Ben Combs about my concession speech—when I should give it and in what format. Ben said he could get me on KATV "first thing out of the box." The interview would be conducted by his wife, Judy Pryor Combs, who was the station's night anchor.

Mamie Ruth quickly realized the opportunity this would afford. "This would give you a great chance to advertise for a new job in prime time before a huge audience," she said. "Just because the final vote isn't in doesn't mean you can't concede with the qualification that if the vote should suddenly swing back your way, you could retract it."

"And I'll work on getting you an early appearance on the other two channels," Ben said. "Most people will quit watching after 10:30, so if we're going to do it, I need to get cracking."

Ben lined up my appearances: Channel 7 at 10 p.m., and the other two channels at 10:30 and 11. We rushed down to the Channel 7 studio in Ben's car, where Judy was waiting to put me on. We came in the back door. I slapped on a little makeup to cut the glare of the television lights, and then I was on a stool being interviewed, the very first candidate to appear that night.

I had no time to prepare anything formal to say, but it didn't matter. Judy knew what to ask. First, she introduced me, recounted my second-place finish in the first primary, and referred to my strong runoff campaign. Then she noted the current vote that showed Munson well ahead and said sweetly: "I understand you have an announcement?"

"Yes, at this point I would like to make a concession to my opponent, Mr. Munson," I said graciously. "It appears the vote trend has been set, and he will win the race. I offer him my hearty congratulations on a hard-fought campaign."

"But, understand," I continued, smiling somewhat mischievously, "if the vote should suddenly swing back in my favor during these last hours, which I don't expect, but if it does, would you please not consider this to be a forfeit?"

At that we both laughed, and Judy said teasingly that she would let me take it back if I won. Then she asked me in a more serious tone: "What now, Roger, assuming the trend continues as you expect? Any plans you can share with us?"

"None other than the obvious," I said. "I'll soon be an unemployed person."

"Anything in particular you would like to do?" she inquired.

"As much as I have enjoyed this long, bruising political campaign," I said, looking askance and rolling my eyes, "it would be nice to get back to a regular job practicing law again."

"You have thousands of people watching you right now," she said, closing it up. "Anything you want to say to them?"

"Sure," I said, looking straight into the camera lens, using my most sincere tone. "To my supporters, I can never thank you enough. You made it all worthwhile." Without missing a beat, I added: "To anyone watching who needs to hire a lawyer, I am available." Again I laughed, as did Judy.

27. Bribery and More

The next morning I awoke early, still full of nervous energy, and went downstairs for the newspaper. Unofficial returns showed that Munson had won by a good margin—about the same as in the first primary. That afternoon, an *Arkansas Democrat* article caught my attention, one that substantiated the rumors Mamie Ruth had shared.

Munson purchased Glasgow's cards, 2 observers say

Two persons claimed Tuesday that they saw Prosecuting Attorney–elect Lee Munson pay his opponent's campaign workers to stop passing out campaign literature at two polling places.

Glenda Johnson of Little Rock said that she was handing out campaign literature for a candidate for another race when Munson and two other men arrived at the polling place at 23rd and Wolf streets. Munson had a "big roll of money and he was handing it to these black guys," she said.

Miss Johnson said that Munson had approached a woman next to her who was working for Roger Glasgow and had said "he was tired of looking at her face and would she leave."

Miss Johnson said the woman hid behind a tree and started working again for Glasgow after Munson left although she was scared. Munson had paid the woman $10 to leave, Miss Johnson said.

Miss Johnson said that she had asked Munson and his two colleagues to identify themselves and explain what they were doing. "They just kind of brushed me off," she said. "I said again, what are you doing? It looks to me like you are bribing people." According to Miss Johnson, Munson said: "We are not bribing people, lady. We are just buying their cards."[25]

How stupid can you be, I thought, *to go out personally with a roll of cash on election day and bribe the other guy's campaign workers? We'll hear more about this for sure.*

There was more, much more, over the next couple of days. Munson was caught in a firestorm of his own making. Without a doubt, if there could have been another election, I would have won in a landslide. But there wouldn't be another election, and I resolved to let it go. But at least I could sit back and enjoy the fireworks.

When Munson was contacted about the story by multiple news outlets, he initially admitted that he paid cash to my campaign workers to stop passing out literature. But he later changed his statements and claimed the literature was "smut." Apparently not satisfied with the media response to his comments, Munson, or someone on his behalf, had some henchmen phone Glenda Johnson and threaten her. This prompted Robert Johnston, a respected political science professor at the University of Arkansas at Little Rock and candidate for the Arkansas House of Representatives (for whom Glenda Johnson was working), to come forward to corroborate her story. An article in the *Arkansas Democrat* reported:

Munson gave workers cash, Johnston says

Robert E. Johnston...said he saw Prosecuting Attorney–elect Lee Munson pay poll workers not to pass out campaign material for the prosecuting attorney candidate who was defeated, Roger Glasgow.

Johnston said he saw Munson pay four dollars or five dollars to a small black boy and an undisclosed amount to a black woman to leave the Precinct 49 polling place, Dunbar Recreation Center at 1001 W. 16th St., on June 13, the day of the runoff election. He said the two were distributing "green and yellow Glasgow material, which were signed and widely circulated before the election."

Johnston said that since he was a candidate himself with Republican opposition in November, he had preferred to stay out of the incident in-volving Munson, but that he could not stand by "when a malpractice occurred, particu-larly when it was followed by attempted intimidation."

Johnston said that Miss Glenda B. Johnson...who told reporters last week that she had seen Munson pay at least one Glasgow worker, had received a threatening telephone call.

Miss Johnson said the man's voice that called her Friday night said, "You'd better keep your big mouth shut... you're in big trouble." She said

George Fisher cartoon of Robert Johnston.

she was gone for the weekend, but received calls both Sunday and Monday nights in which the caller hung up be-fore speaking...

Munson admitted to a *Democrat* reporter Friday that he had approached several Glasgow workers and asked them to stop passing out "smut" literature at predominantly black polling places...

Prosecuting Attorney Jim Guy Tucker said Glasgow perhaps could file a complaint against Munson alleging a vi-olation of the Political Practices Act, but today Glasgow said he would take no action.

"The election is over," Glasgow said. "I don't think that his paying off my poll workers had any effect on the outcome. It's a regrettable action, and I don't condone it, but nothing could come of a complaint."[26]

A flurry of condemnations soon followed, with calls for Munson's resignation, a grand jury investigation, and prosecution. The editorial page of the *Arkansas Gazette* issued a strong condemnation:

Grand Jury Case

It is no secret that we had lingering doubts about the campaign and the candidacy of Lee Munson for Prosecuting Attorney, an office that he won…over two candidates who were demonstrably better qualified.

We were not quite prepared, however, for the charges made since the election that Mr. Munson paid campaign workers of his runoff opponent to stop distributing opposing literature at two Little Rock polling places. Munson has been quoted as saying he paid a worker for Roger Glasgow, the opponent, $10 to stop distributing "smut" literature.

The charges against Munson were made by Robert Johnston, a Democratic nominee for the legislature, and by Miss Glenda Johnson, a Hall High School history teacher. Both charges are eyewitness allegations, involving separate incidents at separate polling places. Johnston says the only things that he saw being distributed by the Glasgow workers were ordinary campaign cards.

Let us make no mistake about the issue here: These are grave allegations by responsible citizens in reference to the passing of money in the conduct of an election. We believe that the issue cannot be settled without a thorough investigation….Unfortunately, Mr. Munson himself has been closed-mouthed about the whole affair, leaving entirely too many questions unanswered.

Prosecuting Attorney Jim Guy Tucker has said that he knows of no statute prohibiting this kind of payment, as alleged against Munson, and that he (Tucker) does not plan further action. We understand Tucker's point and even appreciate that the matter has some delicacy for him, what with Munson nominated as successor to the prosecuting attorney's office. Nevertheless, if the alleged polling place payments are not necessarily a subject for Tucker to investigate strictly on his own, we are convinced that it is an appropriate subject for the Pulaski County Grand Jury.[27]

Munson avoided the press and stayed hidden for several weeks. Calls by the media to his home only resulted in his wife, Alice Ann, saying that he had "gone fishing" and that she did not know when to expect him back. In the meantime, the condemnation of his actions continued. The *North Little Rock Times* ran the following editorial:

Outrageous

Lee Munson, who has just been elected Pulaski Prosecuting Attorney, has admitted paying people not to distribute campaign literature for his opponent in the runoff on June 13.

Munson's only defense is a claim that some of the material was smut that was illegal because it was unsigned. A witness who reported the incident denies that the workers had anything but legitimate cards and bumper stickers for Roger Glasgow.

It is not clear whether Munson's actions are illegal. There are laws prohibiting payment to influence votes, but that might not apply in this case.

If it wasn't illegal, it certainly was an outrageous way for a candidate to behave. It is especially shocking that the man who did it is a man whose job will be to create respect for the law.[28]

A few days later, the *Arkansas Gazette* published a stinging George Fisher cartoon depicting Munson as a baby in a playpen wearing a headband reading "pay off charge" and smoking a big cigar *à la* "old guard politician." The caption to the cartoon said: "And not even out of the cradle yet."

After the initial furor died down, Munson slunk back into town. He continued to avoid the media, but he had another problem. He would have no job for several more months. I had the foresight to make a deal with Ray Thornton before the election that, if I lost, I could come back to my old job at the Attorney General's Office, which I did.

Fisher

—And Not Even Out of the Cradle Yet.

The runoff election was in June, and Munson would not take office until January, so he was looking at seven months of unemployment. Finally, no doubt with help from his foster father (who was a former federal judge), Munson was hired as a law clerk by one of the state associate Supreme Court justices and provided a small office in the Justice Building.

Shortly before his disappearance, Munson made a perfunctory visit to Jim Guy Tucker and got cornered by a reporter who was in Tucker's office at the time. Munson reluctantly agreed to a short interview in which he expressed bitterness over his recent misfortunes and his ire with the news media in general, mentioning in particular the editorial endorsements in favor of my campaign. A news article in the *Arkansas Gazette* reported on the encounter.

**In reluctant interview Munson
expresses his ire with the news media**

Lee Munson, who has been virtually inaccessible to reporters since the June 13 Democratic primary runoff when he won the nomination for prosecuting attorney of Pulaski and Perry counties, unexpectedly visited prosecuting attorney Jim Guy Tucker at 2:50 p.m. Thursday.

Munson spent about an hour in a private conversation with Tucker. He reluctantly agreed afterward to an interview with a reporter who happened to be in the prosecutor's office when Munson arrived....

Munson, after some coaxing, went to the courthouse pressroom for the interview. He appeared tense most of the time and finally indicated some irritability with the news media in general because of endorsements that his opponent, Roger Glasgow, had received from newspaper editorials.

Munson refused to comment on published reports that he had paid two Glasgow workers not to pass out campaign cards at a polling place on the day of the primary....

Munson's only comment Thursday about the reports was, "I'm not going to pick a fight with anybody."[29]

While Munson's fortunes were taking a sharp dive, mine started soaring. Within days of returning to my old job at the Attorney General's Office, I got calls, in rather quick succession, from three high-profile sources asking to set up job interviews. These included: (1) Governor Dale Bumpers, (2) the Smith, Friday, Eldridge & Clark law firm, and (3) the Wright, Lindsey & Jennings law firm. Governor Bumpers wanted me to be insurance commissioner for the State of Arkansas, and the two law firms (being the largest and second-largest in the state at the time) offered me the position of associate attorney, on track for partnership.

Never had I dreamed of such marvelous opportunities. I had all three of these offers open at once, any one of which would have before been considered unattainable. Jeannie and I considered each offer carefully. I conferred with my old campaign staff and decided to take the offer from the Wright firm. A few months later, that proved to have been a very wise decision.

This was the landscape after I resumed my work at the Attorney General's Office in June, leading up to the ill-fated trip to Mexico in August. The good news was that I had made some outstanding new friends during the campaign and had lifted my profile with the public and the business community across Arkansas. And I had accepted a great job with one of Arkansas's blue-chip law firms. On the other hand, I had made some implacable and bitter enemies in my opponent's camp, who were both vindictive and ruthless. I should have been more conscious of the latter; my naiveté in that regard would soon bite me hard.

As I was planning the vacation trip to Mexico, I knew Munson had landed the temporary law-clerk job and was in an office just down the hall in the Justice Building. I also realized that Munson still had good friends and ardent supporters on the attorney general's staff, including his former secretary and Jim Neal, one of his most loyal campaigners. But it never occurred to me to keep my travel plans more private. It was another lesson learned.

I should have done so, but then again, committed enemies with far-reaching resources could cause great harm at virtually any time, at any place, and in many ways. Perhaps I was lucky things happened as they did. At least I stayed alive.

28. SOUTH OF THE BORDER

In August 1972, Matamoros was hot, humid, and permeated with the acrid odor of open sewers, diesel fuel, and exhaust that gets stuck in your throat and burns your eyes. Jeannie and I were staying at the Holiday Inn just a few blocks from the international bridge. Vehicles going into Matamoros were stopped at a guard station at the middle of the bridge where sleepy-looking Mexican officials asked a few desultory questions. If the destination was only Matamoros and the stay would be short, the vehicle was casually waved through. Passports were not necessary, and driver's licenses were seldom checked.

For vehicles traveling into the United States, however, the American border guards were considerably more alert and assiduous in their questioning. They were particularly concerned with organic material by which any alien insects, bacteria, or other pathogens might get into the country. They were also on the lookout for any illegal drugs, although at that time the drug problem was not nearly as prevalent as it is today. Drug inspections were fairly rare.

I had specifically selected the Holiday Inn as our destination in Matamoros because I had been in the city two years before. Located near the bridge, the site was a modern, well-appointed chain hotel with a pool and restaurant. On that previous occasion, I had been attending a conference in Brownsville, Texas, organized by the attorneys general of several southern states. Our purpose was to study and possibly revise antiquated state drug laws. In Arkansas, the governor had appointed a commission for this purpose, consisting of a member from the Arkansas Supreme Court, the Arkansas State Legislature, and the Attorney General's Office. At that time, I was a deputy attorney general for Arkansas Attorney General Ray Thornton. Two of my colleagues, Fred Harrison and Robert Morehead, also attended the conference.

Harrison was of slight build, a taciturn, bookish lawyer about my age with unkempt, prematurely graying hair hanging down to his eyebrows, seemingly held up by a pair of heavy wire-rimmed eyeglasses. In keeping with his professorial appearance, Harrison was our ace brief writer. He later became chief counsel for the University of Arkansas System.

Moreland was the antithesis of Harrison. He was a tall, lanky, rawboned black attorney with a bushy Afro. Moreland was inordinately affable. He had a ready laugh and was quick with a joke, usually of the off-color variety. Thornton had recruited him to be in the opinions division of the office.

Also attending the conference in Brownsville was Arkansas Supreme Court justice John A. Fogleman. Fogleman was in his sixties, had a big ruddy face with a protuberant nose, and had sparkling, slightly mischievous blue eyes behind thick bifocals. He was an avuncular man, of middle height, rather rotund, with a few frayed white strands of hair combed back over an otherwise bald dome, the vestiges of a once luxuriant hairline. With a ready and hearty laugh, Fogleman was one of my favorite justices. He enjoyed a good joke, fine wine, and tasty food. He was famous in Arkansas legal circles for his interminably lengthy, often convoluted, and seemingly contradictory legal opinions. His comments always concluded with the correct result, but few readers were able to clearly follow his reasoning.

George Fisher cartoon of John Fogleman.

The conference in Brownsville lasted three days. On a couple of evenings after adjournment, the four of us walked over the bridge to Matamoros to enjoy the sights, browse the tourist shops, and have drinks and dinner. Local sources at the conference had informed us that the premier restaurant in Matamoros was called the Texas Bar. We went there one night and found it to be delightful. A wonderful aroma of richly cooked food wafted through the night air, mingled with the sounds of the strumming guitars of sombreroed Mariachi players strolling among the diners. The place was clean, tastefully decorated in an Old Mexico style, with a majestic, secluded inner courtyard surrounded by stuccoed brick arches and laced with fragrant flowering vines. The food was excellent, the beer served frosty cold, and the conversation in our Arkansas group lively. After dinner, we walked back to the bridge and Brownsville. Under a full moon and with a good buzz and full stomachs, we unanimously agreed that Mexico was a fine place indeed.

Less than two years later, I would be crossing that bridge again, but with a far less pleasant outcome.

★ ★ ★

It is fair to ask, "Who in their right mind would voluntarily go on a road trip to the interior of Mexico in the blistering heat of August?" Most would agree that only a complete fool would do such a thing. In retrospect I agree, but, fools we were that summer of 1972.

I blame the trip to Mexico on a reporter for the *Arkansas Gazette*, Bill Lewis, who occasionally wrote travelogues for the Sunday edition of the paper. In one article, Lewis chronicled a several-day automobile trip he had taken down to Mexico City. According to Lewis, it was fabulous, not to be missed by anyone who had the time and nerve to take the drive. He fairly rhapsodized about it.

Jeannie and I had less than a week to fit in our vacation trip before my start-date at the Wright, Lindsey & Jennings law firm. We decided to drive to Corpus Christi, Texas, stay a night or two with Jeannie's relatives there, then head farther south into Mexico before returning to Little Rock. I wanted to get a feel for the country so vividly described by Lewis. I figured a two-day drive into the interior would be adequate.

Actually, I was beginning to think that losing the prosecuting attorney race might not have been such a bad thing. It fulfilled what my old law professor, Dr. Robert A. Leflar, had proclaimed in torts class one day as the best way to jump-start a law practice. "What you should do," he said, "is get yourself known in a favorable way to as many people as you can as quickly as possible. A good method for doing this is to run for a local high-profile political office, and then lose—but barely."

George Fisher cartoon
of Dr. Robert Leflar.

During my last week at the Attorney General's Office, the only remaining work was to prepare for the transition by the new staff, not a very demanding task. This gave me ample time to visit the local AAA (American Automobile Association) office and obtain a travel kit. I took the guides and maps to my office at the Justice Building and spread them out on my desk. Several friends around the office came in to see what I was planning and offer suggestions. A few who had been Munson supporters also wandered in.

In particular, I remember Munson's secretary, Sue, pretending to be exceptionally interested in our trip, inquiring about the places we intended to go and studying my travel materials. By this time, I had decided on the specific route. We would enter Mexico at Laredo, drive to Monterrey, spend the night, then drive back up to Matamoros. The whole trip would last from August 20 to the 26th, including the stop in Corpus Christi. I made reservations at the Holiday Inn at Monterrey for one night and the Holiday Inn at Matamoros for two nights. In addition I purchased Mexico automobile insurance for the time we would be there and applied for a Mexican driver's permit.

My detailed planning did not prepare us for the extremely unpleasant conditions that greeted us once we crossed the border. I don't know what Lewis saw on his trip to Mexico City that enthralled him so, but there was nothing of any scenic value on the road to Monterrey—just a narrow, crumbling, blacktopped pavement filled with potholes, dusty bushes hugging the sides of the road, and dead, rotting armadillos, the hapless victims of passing vehicles.

Add the stagnant and stifling heat, and the whole place seemed just a step short of hell. It was so hot and miserable that the vultures, going about their grisly business of gorging themselves on the putrefying flesh of the dead armadillos and other decaying detritus along the roadside, did not even rouse themselves to take flight as we drove by; they simply lazily hopped aside to avoid the spinning tires.

"Pretty country," Jeannie finally commented sarcastically, breaking the silence.

"Yeah, if you're a rattlesnake," I retorted dryly.

The city of Monterrey offered no scenic improvement. Primarily an industrial town, Monterrey had smokestacks that jutted into the air everywhere you looked, belching out thick smoke that no doubt contained plenty of noxious chemicals. The next day's drive to Matamoros was worse: a two-lane, potholed road crowded with large Mexican trucks, extravagantly decorated but caked with dust and mud and blowing out copious amounts of black exhaust.

My second visit to Matamoros was very different from the first. I had an uneasy feeling that things had changed for the worse, although there was nothing obvious one could point to.

It just seemed gloomy, not as many people on the streets, even on the central plaza, and those who were there seemed downcast, unsmiling and rarely meeting your eyes. The tourist curio stalls were still there, but they were without the upbeat friendly banter with the local salespeople I had previously found so agreeable.

At that time, the narcotics trade by Mexican drug cartels had not yet escalated into open street warfare, and Matamoros still had a semblance of a tourist industry. It had a population of about 20,000, a few decent retail stores in the downtown business district, a clean and attractive central plaza, and a well-maintained Spanish-style cathedral. Yet, the atmosphere had definitely changed.

Jeannie and I arrived in the late afternoon on Wednesday, August 23, 1972, following a hard drive from Monterrey. The Holiday Inn was a brick structure near the international bridge, laid out in typical motel fashion—a central courtyard containing an outside swimming pool, lobby and registration area at the front of the building, and two stories of guest rooms framing the other three sides. When we arrived, the hotel parking lot was nearly empty, suggesting that few other travelers shared our interest for excursions in the summer heat.

Since we had made advance reservations, I expected an easy, quick check-in. Instead, we were put through a thorough inquisition. The clerk at the registration counter wanted an unusually detailed amount of personal information: full names; personal and business addresses and phone numbers; make, model, and color of our vehicle; and license tag number. He also asked all the places that we had previously been in Mexico, when we expected to leave, and what would be our final destination in the United States.

Exasperated, I asked, "Don't you already have most of this information? We preregistered here several weeks ago."

"Oh, *señor*," he explained, not very convincingly, "it is for your own protection. Now, *por favor*, may I see your driver's license?"

I had no clue why he needed so much more information than we had produced at the Holiday Inn in Monterrey. But we were hot and tired from the miserable drive, so I decided not to push it. I grudgingly handed him my driver's license, which he took to a back office, photocopied, and returned to me. Finally, he produced a set of keys, accompanied by a room number, and scribbled the directions to the room on a crude map.

Our room was at the very back of the motel, adjacent to a big, graveled, unlighted parking lot. Ours was the only vehicle back there. I thought this strange because the motel was not even half full. Why would they put us all the way in the back? But, it was quiet and we would not be disturbed by all the street noise. An ice machine was nearby, which was always handy, so we decided to stay where we were.

We had planned to have dinner that evening at the Texas Bar, but after the long drive from Monterrey and the hassle of the check-in, we decided to eat at the hotel restaurant and turn in early. We would have a full fun day tomorrow, we figured, with pool time in the morning, sightseeing and shopping in the afternoon, and dinner at the Texas Bar.

29. THE NOOSE TIGHTENS

We began our second day at the Matamoros Holiday Inn looking forward to a relaxed tourist's schedule. Breakfast at the hotel restaurant was to be followed by a couple of hours poolside, lying in the sun. We would clean up and drive downtown to the central plaza area for lunch. The afternoon would be filled with sightseeing and shopping. The day would end with dinner at the Texas Bar.

The hotel restaurant overlooked the pool, where a few of our fellow tourists were beginning to gather as we finished our breakfast, spreading their towels over the reclining plastic pool lounges and breaking out the sunscreen lotion. We went back to our room, changed into our swimsuits, and joined the people at the pool. After spreading our towels on a couple of lounge chairs as well, we lay back to soak in some sun. The weather was very warm, and the air was still and stagnant, but we were determined to make the best of it.

A rather unattractive pool attendant taking drink orders made the rounds among the guests and deck chairs. He was tall and skinny, with a bad complexion, dark shifty eyes, and yellow stained teeth. He seemed to be perpetually puffing cigarettes. He was a young man, in his early twenties, I'd guess, and he wore a green shirt with a Holiday Inn insignia.

When he came our way, Jeannie and I each ordered a margarita on the rocks—after all, we were on vacation. The sun rose higher, and the morning got hotter We sipped from our watery drinks as the ice quickly melted. Before long, the air grew distinctly stuffier, and soon sharp odors of sewage and rotting vegetables could be detected, perhaps from the river nearby. By that time, most of our fellow tourists had fled inside to their air-conditioned rooms. Jeannie and I decided to do the same.

We looked for our strolling waiter so we could sign our tab. We spotted him standing in the shade by the entry to the front office, smoking a cigarette and talking to another Mexican man, a big, paunchy guy in jeans, a black T-shirt, and cowboy boots. The big guy had a heavy, black handlebar mustache, and on his belt was a big, bright silver buckle. He looked out of place, we thought, and certainly did not seem to be associated with the hotel. The waiter pointed in our direction, and the big man peered at us intently. We waved at the attendant, and he walked slowly to our chairs.

"Bring us our ticket, please," I said. "We're going in."

"Certainly, *señor*," he said. "Was everything good?" He smiled, showing his yellowed teeth, then walked to the front office and disappeared inside. Quite unexpectedly, the second guy wandered over.

"*Buenos días, señor e' señora*," he said, smiling broadly and showing off a missing front tooth beneath the bushy mustache. He continued in English, "Beautiful morning, eh?"

"Yes, it is," I said cautiously, my suspicions already raised.

"You enjoy yourselves?" he inquired. "Nice hotel, eh?"

"Sure," I replied, curtly, making a distinct effort not to prompt any further conversation.

But he persisted, "How long you stay?"

"We're leaving tomorrow," I said, adding, "Need to get back to work." I immediately regretted it, for it gave him an excuse to inquire further.

"Ah, work," he said, grinning again. "What kind of work you do, *señor?*"

Again, against my better judgment, but not wanting to seem rude, I said, "I am a lawyer."

"Oh, *sí,*" he exclaimed. *"Abogado—muy buena profesión."*

"Yes, good profession," I said dismissively, and started gathering up our belongings, hoping he would get the message and leave.

But he didn't. "*Señor,*" he said, "you and *señora,* perhaps you like to have good time before you go home?"

"No, we already have plans," I said.

"You go to dinner?" he persisted. "I know very good place. Maybe you want *compañero?*"

"What?" I said, not sure that I understood his meaning.

"*Compañero,* companion. I can arrange very nice companion for you both," he said with a salacious grin.

"No!" I said emphatically. "We are not interested in anything like that."

"Perhaps you like drugs, pills. I can get them," he said, "whatever you want."

"No!" I said sharply. "I told you we are not interested."

About that time, our waiter came back with the ticket for our drinks. I signed it, and we abruptly left, leaving them both standing there.

"What in the world was he talking about?" asked Jeannie, concern and fear on her face.

"Oh, he was just talking crazy," I said, trying to calm my own nerves as well as hers. "A Mexican scam of some sort. Don't worry about it."

Jeannie and I went back to our room and decided we would follow the local siesta custom and stay indoors through the midday heat. We ventured out later in the afternoon, heading to the central square about four o'clock. The air was still hot but not as bad as in the morning. We parked on the square, cracked the windows slightly to vent some of the heat, locked the doors, and started exploring the shops and curio stalls. The downtown area was busy, with food carts scattered about dispensing hot peanuts, tortillas rolled with spicy beef and chicken, and cold beer and soft drinks.

The stores were opening after the afternoon siesta, and merchants were setting up racks filled with fabric goods and clothing, which spilled out onto the sidewalks. A few solo pedestrians were hawking silver jewelry and trinkets, and a couple of freelance photographers were looking to take photos of tourists to sell. Business was not nearly as brisk as when I had been to Matamoros the first time, but a decent number of shoppers and sightseers were milling about.

Jeannie and I strolled casually, shopping a bit here and there, and occasionally rummaging through the racks of clothing and other cloth goods displayed on the sidewalks. Jeannie bought a nice bolt of colorful fabric she thought would make a pretty tablecloth.

At one point, as we were crossing the street back toward the central square, I noticed a yellow taxicab with a white top parked on the corner with the motor running. The cabbie was a big guy and had a heavy black handlebar mustache. Peering closer, I realized it was the same man who had accosted us out by the pool that morning.

We skirted past the cab driver and walked to the lovely Spanish-style cathedral that graced the center of the square. The front doors were open, and we went in. A service was in progress, and we quietly stood at the back, enjoying the majestic view of the colonnaded nave, the ornate altar bedecked in silver, and the tall, colorful, intricate stained-glass windows.

It was getting close to dinner time, so we left the cathedral and walked back across the square toward the Texas Bar, which was nearby. On the way, we walked past our car parked near the corner. As we walked in front of the car, I noticed a small rectangular slip of paper under the windshield wiper.

"Oh, crap," I thought, "I bet we got a parking ticket." I removed it, and sure enough, we had: "Parking *prohibido*," the ticket read. I could not make out the rest of it, which was in Spanish, so I stuck it in my pocket, thinking that I would ask about it when we got to the Texas Bar.

We crossed the street and went inside, where it was refreshingly cool and dark. The restaurant was mostly empty, as it was around 6 o'clock, a good bit earlier than most locals go out to dinner. We were greeted by the waiter, who bowed slightly, offered a smooth "*Buenas tardes*," and seated us.

"*Carta Blanca—dos*," I said, holding up two fingers.

"*Claro*," he said, walking away.

As we were studying the menu and drinking our beers, one of the *turista* photographers we had seen outside working the town square walked up to our table.

"*Foto, señor*? You and *señora*, cheap price, very good," he implored.

"How much?" I asked.

"Only *cuatro dólares*," he replied.

I bargained him down to three dollars, and he snapped his Polaroid. I tucked the image of Jeannie and me at our table into my jacket pocket, totally unmindful that it would later prove quite useful.

After dinner, which was decent but not nearly as tasty as I remembered from the previous trip, we drove back to the Holiday

Inn. I parked in the back lot, and we were in our room by 8:30. By 10:00, we had turned in for the night. Jeannie was able to go to sleep at the drop of a hat, but I usually needed more time to wind down. I had just dozed off when the room phone rang.

"*Buenas noches, señor. ¿Está todo bien?*" a male voice said.

My Spanish was rudimentary at best, and I was still half asleep, so I responded, "*No habla Español.*"

"Oh, I beg your pardon, *señor*," the voice said. "This is the reception desk. I was just calling to see if you needed anything. Is everything good?"

"Yes," I said, sounding irritated, "we don't need anything. We have turned in for the night."

"Okay, *gracias.* Sleep well," the voice said and hung up.

Part III

30. The Trial—Day 1

As Jeannie and I flew to Brownsville for our first face-to-face meeting with our attorney Tom Sharp in early October, my mind replayed the detailed memories of my lost election campaign and our subsequent trip to Mexico. But now I had additional layers of complex thoughts to add to those recollections. The first of those sub-plots was all the nefarious scheming and conspiratorial subterfuge that had taken place in Little Rock and Mexico by then-unknown parties who crafted the "set up." Even more pressing were my concerns about how our new attorney would guide us though a biased local judicial system seemingly determined to do us wrong.

Meeting Sharp quickly assuaged many of those concerns. He was some ten years older than me and was already an accomplished trial lawyer with many felony jury trials under his belt. He had a ready smile, although when in "legal mode," he was calm, with his face revealing little emotion. We immediately dove right into the central question: Should we try the case as we had originally envisioned before the informant's revelations, or should we plunge in headfirst with the testimony from Little Rock cab driver John Patterson and his account of a conspiracy by my political enemies in Little Rock to frame me and destroy my chances of ever running for political office again?

I went first: "Tom, it looks to me like we've been handed a gift from heaven. This cab driver guy just fell into our lap. Won't his testimony explain everything?"

"It's true that the cab driver's testimony will provide evidence of who put the drugs in your car, and why," Tom replied, "but we don't have the burden of explaining how and why the drugs got there. That's the government's burden."

"I understand that," I protested, "but wouldn't the actual fact of showing that someone else did it improve our chances?"

The level-headed Sharp brought me back to the most pressing issues. "The government has charged you with possession with intent to distribute," he said. "The prosecution has the burden of proving beyond a reasonable doubt that you were the one who did it. The prosecution must prove, first, that you acquired the drugs from some source—bought it, actually, because nobody just gives away pounds of marijuana, second, that you hid it in your car and knowingly possessed it, and, third, that you intended to sell it to others after you returned to the United States. Right now, they don't have a shred of evidence for any of that."

"I agree with everything you said," I ventured, feeling less confident in my argument already, "but based on the sole fact that there was marijuana hidden in my car, might the jury just leap to conclusions that I must be guilty through sheer speculation?"

"As you know, juries are strongly instructed about speculation," Sharp answered. "I'm confident that Judge Garza will read them those instructions in such a way that there will be no misunderstanding."

"But what if the jury had direct evidence of another scenario?" I asked. "Would that make it easier?"

"That would bring up the whole political situation in Little Rock," Sharp said, "and the cab driver's credibility, and just dump a lot of stuff into the trial that we don't need. That could be confusing to the jury. I can almost guarantee you that none of the jurors have ever been to Little Rock, and probably couldn't even find it on a map. It would be counterproductive to get the case all sullied up with evidence of crooked politicians and various other bad people from Little Rock. You and Jeannie are a nice-looking and clean-cut young couple. I'm confident the jury will like you. We don't need that other stuff. Let's keep it clean and simple."

"Okay, Tom, you've convinced me," I said, and, looking over Jeannie's way, added: "What do you think?"

She said simply, "I think Tom knows what he's talking about."

I feel confident that very few readers of this book have ever stood in the dock before a jury in the austere, high-ceilinged, marble and mahogany confines of a federal courthouse in an unfamiliar Texas border city. Finding oneself in such circumstances and facing charges for a drug-related felony is a terrifying experience.

The courtroom process itself is meticulous and slow, allowing one ample time to helplessly watch the erosion of one's every defensive position as an aggressive and diligent U.S. attorney builds his case point by point. As each component of the prosecutor's strategy is revealed, as witnesses testify and evidence is brought forth, one can feel the ground underfoot giving way. At the conclusion of these venerable proceedings, the accused party may stand on the brink of an unfathomable precipice, knowing that the next words he hears will provide the final thrust to send him plunging into the abyss.

These were my feelings as I stood beside Tom Sharp at counsel table and the jurors were ushered into the courtroom. It was 9 a.m., Monday, October 16, 1972, in Brownsville, Texas. Outside, warm fall sunshine filled the sky with a bright and cheerful glow. In the cavernous courtroom where I stood, the air conditioning was cranked down low. Despite the chilled and sterile atmosphere of the courtroom, I was sweating profusely beneath my suit jacket. Jeannie was seated nearby on a bench that ran just inside the rail. While she certainly shared my concerns, her calm and composed demeanor offered no clue to her thoughts.

About fifty potential jurors had been seated behind the rail in the high-ceilinged courtroom. As I looked out over the group, my heart sank. Most of them looked to be working-class Hispanics. Few whites ("Anglos" in the local parlance) were in attendance and, of those I saw, only a small number appeared to be professionals or businesspeople, jurors I presumed would be more sympathetic to my case. I whispered to Sharp: "Not that many Anglos." He replied quietly without looking at me, "We'll discuss it later."

After the roll was called of the jurors present, Judge Garza announced a fifteen-minute recess so the parties could consider their selections. Back out in the courtroom, he proceeded with the first part of the *voir dire* procedure by reading to the jury panel a synopsis of the facts of the case, agreed to by counsel for both sides.

"Members of the jury panel, I will now read to you a short statement of the case. Remember what I have already said: This is not evidence for you to consider but only to help you understand what this case is about. First, the United States has charged the defendant, Roger Glasgow, (he points at me) with transporting illegal drugs across the border from Mexico into the United States with the intent to distribute or sell it to others. It is alleged that the illegal substance was marijuana (and here he improvised)—twenty-four pounds hidden under the back seat of his car, as I understand it…"

Reminding myself not to stare at the jury panel, I glanced at the group as the judge spoke. I saw several panel members blanch and stiffen, looking my way in apparent disgust. I sat unmoving as a queasy feeling grew in the pit of my stomach. Judge Garza continued reading the short summary that outlined our defense contentions: I didn't buy the marijuana, didn't load it, didn't know it was there, and had no intention of selling it. But I had been so shocked by the jurors' reactions to the first part that I did not dare glance their way again. My fears were reconfirmed—this was going to be a long and perilous trial.

The jury selection process occupied most of the morning. Six women and six men were eventually selected. The group seemed evenly divided between Anglo and Hispanic, with diversity in age and background, making me feel a little better. Sharp said he was pleased with the jury, pointing out a couple of the men who were well-regarded businessmen in the community. Under the circumstances, he felt the selection had gone about as well as it possibly could have.

We had subpoenaed the following witnesses, intending to present them during our part of the case: Arkansas Attorney General Ray Thornton, U.S. District Judge G. Thomas Eisele, Circuit Judge Bobby Steel of Nashville, lawyer Edward L. Wright of Little Rock, and Rev. A. D. Stuckey, a minister from Nashville.

Out of an abundance of caution, and to confuse Gonzales about our trial strategy, we had also subpoenaed witnesses who could testify about the alternate scenario, the Hunter marijuana "plant." These included John T. Patterson, who was the cab driver informant, and attorney Robert J. Brown, who was the former chief deputy for Prosecuting Attorney Jim Guy Tucker, who could establish that Patterson was a reliable paid informant.

Brown, my former opponent in the prosecutor's primary race, had since become a friend and supporter. He agreed to fly down for the trial with Patterson, so he could "ride herd" on him. In addition, we subpoenaed the two U.S. Customs Service investigators, Simmons and Edwards, who had come up to Little Rock to obtain witness statements.

The prosecution also subpoenaed several customs agents, those who were involved in the detention and arrest at the bridge: Ms. Medley, Mr. Meharg, and Owen Crockett, another agent. They also subpoenaed a person from the U.S. Agriculture Department who could verify that the material in the packages was, indeed, marijuana. In addition, Gonzales subpoenaed Little Rock bond trader Jim T. Hunter and Lieutenant Kenneth Pearson of the Little Rock vice squad.

The first day of the trial went as planned, with the testimony developing much as we had expected. The most exciting moment came when Gonzales, with great drama, had two federal court deputies bring the entire back seat of my car into the courtroom. The seat was turned upside down and placed on a table directly in front of the jury box. Of course, it was still crammed with the newspaper-wrapped packages of marijuana. Most of the jurors gaped wide-eyed. I'm sure that they had never seen that much marijuana before. I tried to look unconcerned, but I cringed inside.

Gonzales then called his first witness to the stand, and the trial was under way. The *Arkansas Gazette* summarized the testimony of the government witnesses in the next day's edition. The article described the search of my car and the discovery of seven packages of marijuana stuffed into the springs of the seat. Most significantly, the *Gazette* stated that in the subsequent collection of sweepings for chemical analysis from the car, our clothing, and Jeannie's purse, "A customs agent and a chemist testified that no trace of marijuana was found in any of the sweepings material."

The article further stated that "no attempt was made to prove that Glasgow had purchased the marijuana or that he intended to sell it after his return to the United States."[30]

Sharp had told me previously that the lack of marijuana trace material in the car was very significant. This incriminating tidbit was almost always found in drug cases, he said, because the smugglers are users themselves, and traces of marijuana are inevitably found in the floorboard of the car, the ashtrays, and the fabric of the seats, as well as on the clothing of those in the car. If a female passenger was involved, her purse would likely also contain traces.

On cross-examination of the government witnesses, Sharp maintained a strong focus on these facts, repeatedly pointing out how rare it was to find no such traces in the sweepings. One witness even agreed that he did not recall ever encountering such a case except ones in which innocent tourists were used as mules by smugglers to get drugs over the border. Sharp got him to acknowledge that this was a fairly frequent occurrence.

Some of the testimony of the government witnesses also demonstrated shoddy police work. For example, the *Gazette* reported as follows on the testimony of the chief customs inspector, John Vandiver:

> John Vandiver of Brownsville, the special customs agent who was placed in charge of the investigation, testified that his first act after arriving at the customs office was to read the Glasgows' constitutional rights to them. In his inspection of the Glasgow car, Vandiver testified that he found a map of southern Texas and Mexico, which had the same route marked which Glasgow told him he had taken.
>
> Under cross-examination, Vandiver testified that he had not attempted to confirm Glasgow's account of his trip to Mexico until after the indictment was returned. Since then, he said, he had checked out the account and confirmed it.

Asked by Sharp if there were any investigations between the time of Glasgow's arrest and the time of his indictment, Vandiver said he did not believe so. Vandiver said that Glasgow "adamantly" requested that the agents refrain from handling the packages until fingerprints were taken. Vandiver said he told the agents not to "over handle" the packages and then called Francisco Ortiz of the Brownsville Police Department to check for fingerprints.

He said he did not ask Ortiz to check for prints on the plastic wrapping because he did not believe it would be possible to find prints on the flimsy material. He said he did not know if attempts were made to get fingerprints from the seat or the interior of the car.

He testified that Glasgow offered to cooperate in the investigation and asked to be allowed to take a lie-detector test.

Ortiz testified that he was unable to get any fingerprints from the newspapers used to wrap the marijuana. However, he said that he could have taken prints from the plastic wrapper if he had been asked to do so.[31]

Listening to Vandiver's floundering testimony, I was struck by the inept work he described and the flimsy excuses he offered. Vandiver was an experienced law-enforcement officer who was certainly aware that the best place to look for fingerprints is on a slick surface, such as plastic wrappings. He would also know that fingerprints cannot be lifted off newspapers. Ortiz's statement that he didn't check the plastic wrappers simply because he wasn't asked to do so was highly suspect. One would think they didn't want to find anything that would help me.

Other testimony by government witnesses was simply ludicrous. Miriam Medley, the eagle-eyed, redheaded customs inspector, whom we first encountered when we crossed the border, was the government's first witness. She did not disappoint. Sitting stiff backed in the witness chair and wearing her brown customs garb (still tightly stretched around her plump frame), she glanced my way with a contemptuous expression.

Medley stated that her suspicions were aroused immediately when she saw the strange ice chest on our back seat. Her statement that the ice chest was "unusual in a nice car like that" directly contradicted the comments of Inspector Owen Crockett, who said he saw "40 to 50 of those ice chests every day." Medley also mentioned the "McGovern for President" bumper sticker on my car, suggesting its political message was a sure sign of evil intent. No questions were put to Medley regarding any informant's tip-off to her office to be looking out for my car.

The jurors listened attentively, but they displayed no facial expressions or body language that hinted at their thoughts. In fact, during the whole trial, the jury remained stone faced, which did nothing to ease my anxiety level.

Midway through the afternoon, we learned that the statements of key government witnesses—the informant John Patterson and the bond daddy Jim Hunter—had been only partially recorded and transcribed. We also discovered that the two special U.S. Customs Service agents, Earl Simmons and Edward Walker, had spent ten days in Arkansas conducting the interviews, and they had been assisted in that work by Lieutenant Kenneth Pearson of the Little Rock Police Department.

Pearson had been subpoenaed as a witness, but he was not allowed to be in the courtroom during the proceedings. This is a fundamental rule of judicial procedures. Witness are prohibited from being in the courtroom while others are testifying. Nor may they receive information about others' testimony. These restrictions are meant to prohibit a waiting witness from changing his testimony based on what those before him had said. Serious penalties can be imposed for violation of this rule if the court finds out about it. Pearson, however, kept up with the testimony by having an LRPD detective, Fred Hensley of the intelligence unit, sit in the courtroom while the testimony was being given, taking notes and then conferring with Pearson during recesses. This was both unethical and illegal under court rules, as Pearson undoubtedly knew. Though he was caught red-handed by reporters, Pearson's actions were apparently never reported to the judge. The *Gazette* article stated: "Pearson was kept outside the courtroom with the other witnesses Monday. A man, apparently accompanying him, sat in the courtroom taking copious notes and joined Pearson during the recesses. The man refused

Lieutenant Kenneth Pearson of the LRPD vice squad. A Munson supporter and a government-subpoenaed witness at the author's trial, he was excluded from the courtroom but kept up with the testimony through an informant in violation of court rules. (Courtesy of the Arkansas Democrat-Gazette*)*

to give his name to reporters and would say only that he was associated with Pearson, and 'from time to time,' with the Little Rock Police Department. Gonzales said he knew the man, but refused to identify him."[32]

I had seen Pearson in the corridors outside the courtroom and occasionally noticed him conferring with various people. I certainly suspected that he was up to no good, but I had no idea he was being fed the testimony of all witnesses. The account in the paper did not come out until the next day, and only in the Arkansas markets, so I didn't see it until after the trial. Obviously

Pearson thought he would be called as a witness, and he wanted to have an advantage.

I started my testimony around four o'clock in the afternoon and finished direct examination (answering Sharp's softball questions) about 5:30 p.m. The exchange was quite straightforward, and rather mundane, consisting mostly of a detailed description of our trip to Mexico and introducing documenting papers such as receipts, hotel bills, and travelers cheque stubs. The *Gazette* accurately reported that my account of the events at the border was almost identical to the accounts given by the customs officers.

When we left the courtroom after that first day, most of my anxieties had abated. I felt I had done well taking the stand to testify on my own behalf. By outlining and documenting the trip, I believed we showed rather convincingly that we were not drug smugglers. Jeannie's testimony had come just before mine and was also good. She appeared earnest and a little shy, which gave her an endearing quality. Her description of the trip was particularly effective, I thought. Gonzales did not even cross-examine her.

After court, we gathered in Sharp's office for debriefing. On the way, he commented favorably on our testimony, but he then added a cautionary note. "Remember, Roger, today was only the first part of your testimony. Tomorrow you will have to face Raul's cross, and I guarantee he will be ready. Raul is a skilled trial attorney and probably has some surprises in store. When I have faced him in the past, he has tried to make most of his hay during the cross-examination of the defendant. He's very good at it."

We had sandwiches brought in for dinner, and Sharp continued preparing for my cross-examination.

"As you know, Raul will be permitted to ask leading questions. He can state just about any proposition he wants, and then ask if you agree. Most of his questions will end with 'that's true, isn't it?' or 'correct?' The questions can be real tricky. You have to listen very carefully and keep your head in the game. Don't let him wear you down so you get careless with your answers. Do not agree with him if there is anything at all that is incorrect or misleading in what he says. Just say 'no.' Also keep in mind that you are entitled to explain your answers, but try to avoid getting in an argument with him."

Sharp grilled me with sample cross-examination questions of the kind he expected from Raul Gonzales. As a lawyer, I was familiar with this type of witness preparation. I had done the same thing with witnesses myself, but I had never before been on the receiving end. Answering these questions took intense concentration to avoid getting boxed in. After about an hour of pounding from Sharp, I felt better prepared, but I was exhausted and still worried. Sharp's warnings had raised concerns about tomorrow—and justifiably so, as it turned out.

31. THE TRIAL-DAY 2

At the very beginning of the second day of the trial, things began to heat up. Before the jury came in to be seated, Judge Garza was reviewing with the attorneys the witnesses they expected to call that day. I had already taken my seat in the witness box, waiting for cross-examination. I was close enough to hear Judge Garza mention that he had been informed about new testimony to be introduced that day. The comments, Garza said, were to come from a Little Rock taxi driver, a police informant whose testimony would essentially affirm that the marijuana had been planted in my car. I almost fell out of my chair.

Our defense strategy had been crafted to show that the government couldn't prove I had the opportunity, intent, or funds to buy that amount of marijuana and stash it in my car. We were not going to build a case on how the marijuana might have gotten there, only that I did not do it. The introduction of the cab driver, John Patterson, was a total surprise. I knew Tom Sharp would not have changed our plans without letting me know. But someone had identified Patterson and the testimony he would give. Was the prosecution planning to call him as a hostile witness?

My mind was racing. I had not prepared for Raul Gonzales to question me on this subject. Concerned and confused, I quickly looked around to see if any jurors were in the room. If a juror overheard the comments, the careless mistake on the part of the judge might be grounds for a mistrial. We would have to start all over again, and I desperately wanted to get this ordeal over with. I saw no jurors, but I did notice some reporters in the room busily jotting in their notepads.

Now Gonzales was on his feet objecting, rather vociferously, to the judge's statement, pointing out the reporters in the room and stating that he could introduce evidence discrediting the cab driver's testimony. Even if this new information was not going to be presented to the jury as evidence, it had certainly gotten the attention of the press. The *Arkansas Democrat* reported the dialogue as follows: "An exchange between Federal Judge Reynaldo Garza and attorneys here today indicated that the government had encountered a witness whose testimony might indicate that marijuana allegedly found August 25 in a car belonging to Roger Glasgow of Little Rock, Arkansas, might have been planted there....Garza said he understood that there was a taxi driver who could testify that he had overheard the comment: 'How do you like the way we fixed up old Glasgow?'"[33]

As it turned out, Sharp never called Patterson, and Gonzales, apparently fearful that we would, never called Jim Hunter or Lieutenant Pearson. But Gonzales did make a very zealous, concerted effort to destroy my credibility.

He began with questions about the *Law Review* article I had written criticizing existing marijuana laws. Having identified the topic of my law school article, Gonzales then revealed his real purpose.

"Have you ever smoked marijuana?" he asked.

Sharp immediately blocked my answer with an objection. Judge Garza then asked Gonzales if he had an independent witness who would testify to such, and, if not, he would not allow that line of questioning. Gonzales said he intended to prove it by re-calling Ed Wright to the stand. As this was going on, I sat in the witness stand, my mind racing. I recalled my conversation with Wright, telling him about smoking marijuana following the publication of the *Law Review* article. The only other person in the room at that time was senior partner Dick Williams. Neither Williams nor Wright would have revealed that conversation to Gonzales. So, how did he know about it?

There was no time to speculate, as Gonzales quickly resumed his cross-examination.

"Is it true you have written an article advocating the abolition of marijuana laws," he asked.

"Absolutely not," I replied.

Gonzales made certain the jury could see the disbelief on his face as he pulled out a copy of the *Law Review* article and waved it in front of them, shouting: "Really, Mr. Glasgow? I've got the article right here in my hand. Do you want to look at it?"

"No," I said calmly. "I'm well aware of what's in the article. If you have read it, you have seen that it does not advocate the abolition of marijuana laws. It only criticizes laws that treat the penalties for the use or possession of marijuana in the same way as the hard narcotics, such as opium or heroin. I just don't think that possession or use of a small amount of marijuana should get you thirty years in prison."

Gonzales then asked if I was a fan of marijuana use, to which I said no. That returned us to the question of if I had ever smoked it. Gonzales started by asking me if I had ever told Ed Wright I had used marijuana. By then I knew he would be calling Wright to the stand, so I calmly told him about the meeting I had had with Wright upon returning from Brownsville after the arrest.

"I just told Mr. Wright the truth," I said, looking Gonzales directly in the eyes. "I had never smoked marijuana before I wrote the *Law Review* article. After that, when I was in the Attorney General's Office and we were considering revisions to the Arkansas drug laws, I decided to try it. I knew that medical research indicated that marijuana was not a particularly dangerous drug, but I wanted to find out the effects myself. Call it 'academic curiosity.'"

Out of the corner of my eye, I watched the jury's reaction. Most showed no response, but I did see a couple of the men smile. I recognized that Gonzales's question had fallen flat. The disappointed look on his face confirmed my impression.

Since Gonzales had stated in open court the intention to recall Wright to the stand, he had no choice but to do so. Wright was prepared and had no trouble further deflating the issue. He said that he and another partner had met with me in advance of a general partners' meeting to consider my employment, and he had asked me the question. Wright said I conceded that I had tried marijuana and had explained the circumstances. At the meeting, the partners were told about it, and they voted unanimously to continue the offer of employment. Again I watched the jury's reaction, and the same two men smiled slightly and nodded. The attempt to impugn my credibility seemed to have failed. The exchange was reported in the next day's *Arkansas Gazette* in what I thought was a favorable way:

> "I simply wanted to find out for myself," Glasgow said. He said he told Wright and Dick Williams, another partner in the Wright law firm, about the marijuana cigarettes in a conversation the three of them had August 27.
>
> Wright corroborated Glasgow's testimony and said that 12 of the firm's 14 senior partners, who met the afternoon of August 27, were aware of this when they voted unanimously to continue their offer of employment to Glasgow.

The source that had allegedly overheard the conversation of Glasgow, Wright and Williams wasn't revealed in the trial.[34]

As I sat at counsel table during Wright's testimony, I puzzled over how the private conversation I had had with him and Williams somehow got leaked to Gonzales. Wright testified that it had been mentioned at the partners' meeting before the vote was taken, so obviously some partner at the meeting had "talked out of school." Partners' meetings were supposed to be top secret. Mentioning anything discussed there, even to one's spouse, was considered a serious breach of protocol. But someone had spilled the beans. Who and why, I had no idea.

Again, Gonzales left me little time to speculate. Though it seemed to me that he had fallen flat on his face with this line of questioning, Gonzales continued to pursue it with vigor. Seated by Gonzales's side at counsel table was Earl Simmons, the chief customs investigator. Simmons frequently whispered in Gonzales's ear and exchanged notes.

Somebody has decided to go all out to get me, I thought. I quickly recalled the other people identified in Hunter's and Patterson's interview transcripts. While in Little Rock for those interviews, Simmons and his cohort had also spoken with LRPD vice squad detective Kenneth Pearson and Lee Munson. Strangely, no transcript of those conversations had been prepared. Gonzales explained that Simmons did not have the time to do it. It definitely looked like shenanigans had occurred and were continuing.

I was right. Gonzales bore in hard on my marijuana-use concession, as reported in the *Arkansas Democrat*'s story the following day:

> Glasgow testified that he had smoked "what was represented to me as marijuana" to satisfy an "academic curiosity" about

the effects of marijuana. At the time, Glasgow said, he was heading the attorney general's special project division, which was studying the state's drug-control laws and making recommendations on how they might be improved.

Glasgow said he was aware of two radically differing schools of thought on the effects of marijuana and that he had decided to smoke marijuana himself "rather than rely on the medical evidence and differing schools of thought."

After Gonzales had asked Glasgow whether he had smoked marijuana, and Glasgow had replied in the affirmative and had explained his reasons, Gonzales vigorously pursued the line of questioning.

Gonzales said there also were two schools of thought on the dangers of LSD and asked Glasgow whether he would be willing to experiment with LSD on that basis.

"There are not two schools of thought on LSD," Glasgow said.

"Well, let's assume that there are," Gonzales said.

Glasgow replied: "I am not willing to make that assumption."

Glasgow later added that the "great preponderance of medical opinion" indicated that marijuana was a different category of drug and not nearly as dangerous as others such as heroin and morphine.[35]

Not getting as far with me on the marijuana questions as he had probably hoped, Gonzales switched to another tactic for attacking my credibility. He called two men, Mexican nationals, as additional "rebuttal" witnesses. The identify of these men had not been previously disclosed. Ordinarily, witnesses expected to testify at trial are required to be listed and their names furnished to the other side before the trial begins. An exception to this procedure exists for witnesses called solely to rebut the testimony of a witness who has already testified. The two rebuttal witnesses, it appeared, had been recruited and prepared by customs agent John Vandiver the night before. The tactic turned out to be a disaster for the prosecution and served as a key element in influencing the jury in my favor.

The two Mexican witnesses were employees of the Holiday Inn in Matamoros, Mexico. One was the innkeeper, Felipe Mayorquin, and the other was Juan Cortez, supervisor of the hotel's busboys. Both men testified that on one of the nights we were at the hotel, Jeannie and I had gotten drunk in the Holiday Inn bar. They said that Jeannie was so drunk they had had to physically carry her back to the room. This testimony was supposedly relevant because we had previously testified that we had not frequented the bar.

Fortunately for us, Vandiver had not prepared them very well, and the men's outright false testimony was glaringly inconsistent on two key points. They disagreed on the clothing Jeannie was wearing. They also contradicted each other on how they came to be witnesses. The *Arkansas Gazette* reported on their testimony as follows:

> In rebuttal, U.S. Attorney Raul Gonzales surprised the defense with two witnesses, employees of the Holiday Inn in Matamoros, Mexico, who told the jury that both Glasgow and his wife had become intoxicated at the Holiday Inn bar on either August 23 or 24.
>
> "They were drunk," said Felipe Mayorquin, the Holiday Inn innkeeper.
>
> Juan Cortez, who said he was in charge of the Inn's busboys, waitresses and maids, testified that he was summoned to the bar where he picked Mrs. Glasgow up and carried her to the motel room with her husband accompanying him....
>
> However, there were several major discrepancies between the testimony of the innkeeper and his employee.
>
> Mayorquin said he believed the incident occurred the night of August 24 and that he remembered it because he recalled the white dress Mrs. Glasgow was wearing.
>
> Cortez was rather certain that Mrs. Glasgow was wearing long black pants....
>
> The two men also gave contradictory testimony about their reasons for appearing as witnesses.

Before either was called to the witness stand, John Vandiver of Brownsville, the special customs agent in charge of the case, testified that he had talked to both Mayorquin and Cortez and had shown them pictures of the Glasgows and had reported orally to the U.S. attorney concerning their stories.

Mayorquin insisted that he had not discussed the incident with any federal agent and that he had come to court Tuesday, bringing with him the records of the Glasgows' stay at the Holiday Inn, because he had read about the trial in the newspapers and wanted to help.

Asked by Glasgow's attorney if he had ever told his recollections of the alleged incident in the bar before, Mayorquin replied that he was telling it for the first time.

Cortez, on the other hand, testified that he had talked with Vandiver, the special agent, about the last week in September after he was told by Mayorquin that the agent wanted to talk to him.[36]

The two obviously bogus witnesses would have provided a comic interlude if the circumstances were less serious. One man spoke of a white dress; the other identified black pants. One man said he came forward on his own and brought hotel records because he wanted to help; the other said both of them had been recruited by a federal agent.

I was stunned, wondering how the government could stoop so low as to put on such clearly false testimony. I tried to make sense of what was unfolding in the courtroom before me.

The hotel employee witnesses, it had become clearly apparent, had been recruited by Customs Agent Vandiver. Customs Agent Simmons, who had been sitting at counsel table with Gonzales and whispering in his ear for much of the time, likely had some hand in this. And it was Simmons who went to Little Rock several weeks earlier to "investigate" the charges made by the undercover taxi driver Patterson that a drunken Jim Hunter had revealed the "setup."

Something was seriously amiss. My suspicions were further heightened by the presence of Lieutenant Kenneth Pearson, head of the LRPD vice division and a big Munson supporter, sitting in the hallway outside the courtroom at that very moment. Pearson had been subpoenaed as a witness and was not allowed to be in the courtroom according to court rules. But during recesses, in flagrant violation of those very rules, Pearson was getting continuous updates on the testimony from LRPD officer Fred Hensley, who was sitting in the public section of the courtroom.

I reached over and tugged at Sharp's sleeve, impatient to share my sudden revelations with him.

"Don't worry," he said. "I've got this covered."

Indeed he did. The *Gazette's* article concluded the day's proceedings as follows:

> Both Glasgow and his wife returned to the witness stand to deny the charges. They referred to previous testimony indicating that they had been at the Texas Bar, which is several blocks away from the Holiday Inn, for dinner on the evening of August 24. Sharp introduced a photograph of the Glasgows seated at a table purportedly taken at the Texas Bar, which is also a popular eating place, sometime between 6 and 9 p.m. August 24.
>
> The defense also introduced a parking ticket, which Glasgow said he found on his car that day near the Texas Bar. The parking ticket showed the time of issuance as 17:25 hours, which would have been 5:25 p.m.[37]

Who would have imagined that the photo of us at the Texas Bar taken by the Mexican tourist photographer and the parking ticket I had miraculously kept among our travel papers could have come in so handy at such a critical time? When the photograph was introduced and passed around the jury box, several of the jurors nodded in recognition.

The credibility of the government's case had been strained to the breaking point. But I still feared that the jury might think these were but minor discrepancies in the big picture. I had no doubt that the vigorous cross-examination of me by Gonzales had done some damage. Had we done enough to prevail? After all, we were in Brownsville, Texas, on the banks of the Rio Grande River just a stone's throw from Mexico, before a jury of strangers, including several Hispanic members.

What do they think of a young white attorney, with his attractive, stylishly dressed wife, from another state, accused of smuggling marijuana out of Mexico? I wondered. *Do they even care?*

Jeannie and I stood as the jury filed out to deliberate on my fate. We continued to sit there as they cloistered themselves inside the jury room. My stomach was in knots with a nagging feeling that it would all go wrong.

I can guarantee there is absolutely nothing worse than waiting on a jury—a group of twelve people whom you do not know and who do not know you, but who will decide your future. You are helpless. You have no earthly idea what they are thinking. Dread is your constant companion.

Two agonizing hours crept by before the court bailiff announced, "The jury has reached a verdict." Time seemed suspended for another few minutes until the jurors filed in and took their places in the jury box.

"Would the foreperson please stand?" intoned Judge Garza. The foreman did, holding a sheet of paper in his hand.

"Has the jury reached a verdict?"

"Yes, we have, your honor."

"Was it unanimous?"

"Yes, it was, your honor."

"Would the bailiff please hand the verdict form to the clerk?"

He did, and the clerk read it, slowly, painstakingly counting the names signed thereon, and noted something in his record. He handed the slip of paper to Judge Garza, who also read it, slowly and painstakingly. Garza also counted the signatures, again!

Garza laid the paper on his desk and stated, "Would the defendant please rise and face the jury?" I did, barely able to keep my knees from buckling.

Garza then gravely announced, "In the aforesaid styled and numbered case, the jury has reached a verdict, signed by all twelve jurors. The verdict of the jury is, **NOT GUILTY.**"

My knees finally buckled. I had to sit. The federal judge gazed down and gave me a grandfatherly smile. He said, "Mr. Glasgow, you are a free man!

32. Furor Over Injustice

Jeannie and I flew home to Little Rock the next day, too exhausted to go through the process of getting my car released from the U.S. Customs Service impound lot. I figured I would fly back to Brownsville and drive it home in a few days. For the immediate future, however, we were thrilled to be among friends and family again. Telephone calls from well wishers were received daily, our friends saying mostly the same things: they had been extremely worried about us and were glad the ordeal was over. Several callers, their confidence in the criminal justice system unchanged, said they were thankful the jury did the right thing. Others more naïve said they had known the whole time that the jury would enter a finding of innocent. And more than a few expressed grave doubts about the integrity of the system in general, and the government's conduct in particular.

My parents were highly vocal in their criticism. My mother was so riled up about the injustice of the whole affair, she sent a letter to the editor of the *Arkansas Gazette*, which the newspaper printed. Her direct condemnations and strong language reveal her disappointment in a system of justice that she had unquestioningly believed in.

To the Editor of the *Gazette*:

I make no bones about it. I am angry, very angry, at the extreme injustice of this whole deal. I have no ill feelings toward Mexico or Mexican-American people. They had precious little to do with this. These were our own federal agents and our own customs agents. It was the United States of America Department of Justice that investigated this case for two weeks.

Even when they found no evidence, none, that Roger was connected with this in any way, other than being a victim, they refused to dismiss the case and resorted to every dirty, scummy trick they could think of to try to nail his hide to the wall.

My dad was equally angry and disillusioned. He and his peers had fought in World War II to preserve the American values of freedom and justice. He was one of the most ardent law-and-order men anywhere, and he had served on many criminal case juries. But after attending my trial, he wrote a letter to Judge Garza severely castigating the government and the manner in which it had presented the case. To my knowledge, my dad had never before written a letter to the editor of any newspaper on any subject, much less a letter to a federal judge questioning the conduct of a government prosecution. In the letter, he outlined the government's underhanded tactics, lack of adequate investigation, and production of obvious perjured testimony. His letter to Garza concluded with:

In short, the Justice Department had no case and they knew that they had no case. Mr. Gonzales told me personally that he wanted to drop this case but was not allowed to do so. So they attempted to make a case and, fortunately, failed. But, not before an innocent man and woman, to say nothing of family and friends, were put through weeks of mental anguish and worry and were forced to spend several thousand dollars in defense. I believe that the prosecuting and investigating officers were at least reasonably certain that Roger was innocent.

Can it be that the United States Department of Justice was more interested in getting a conviction than they were in the right or wrong of the case?

Both Little Rock newspapers carried the story of my acquittal, and both offered editorial commentary. The *Arkansas Democrat* published a cartoon deriding the weakness of the government's case, showing me standing defiantly in front of a large, just-fired cannon, labeled: "Gov't case against Roger Glasgow."

Out of the cannon billowed a large plume of smoke, but it managed to eject only a tiny cork hanging on a small, limp string. Staff cartoonist Jon Kennedy effectively ridiculed the prosecution, but his clever drawing diminished the experience into a brief and seemingly painless circus-like moment.

The *Arkansas Gazette* was more serious and articulate in its response. The newspaper ran an excoriating editorial condemning in the strongest terms the government's vigorous pursuit of such a flimsy case:

Triumph and Travesty in the Glasgow Case

The trial of Roger Glasgow is now finished and the conventional rules against comment during a trial are thus dissolved. Let us declare for the forthwith that the acquittal of Glasgow in U.S. District Court at Brownsville, Texas, is a triumph of justice but that bringing the case to trial in the first place was a travesty....

It is plain that Glasgow was either framed by unknown enemies or he was used as the innocent carrier for smugglers who planned to track his car and regain the marijuana after the Glasgows had crossed the border. The latter is reported to be common practice on the border.

What is outrageous is that the Justice Department officers in the federal district in South Texas took such a flimsy case to prosecution. Glasgow was indicted by a grand jury that he was not permitted to appear before, just as he was not allowed at the time of his arrest to take a lie-detector test on the spot. Mr. and Mrs. Glasgow were forced to endure long weeks of anguish, not to mention several thousand dollars in expense, in an ordeal that a decent-minded U.S. attorney would not have allowed.

In the end, Glasgow stood trial. The government had nothing to support its case to suggest that Glasgow had had the time, money or desire to import marijuana from Mexico. Glasgow, a young Little Rock lawyer of the finest reputation, brought in character witnesses ranging from the attorney general of Arkansas to the immediate past president of the American Bar Association, the former having employed Glasgow as a principal assistant and the latter having recently brought Glasgow into his own firm. All that the government was able to attempt, finally, was a minor exercise in character assassination.[38]

Perhaps the most thought-provoking comments came in a letter from Robert A. Leflar, a former dean of the University of

Arkansas Law School and professor emeritus at that time, who was teaching as a visiting professor at the Vanderbilt University School of Law. Leflar was a nationally known lecturer and author of leading law textbooks, and he was one of the most loved and celebrated law professors in Arkansas history. Stating his view of the trial, Leflar suggested a loss of confidence in the criminal justice system, a paradoxical position for a man whose life was dedicated to that exact process. He wrote to me, "Your comment that you had confidence in the system of criminal justice was good, but I am not so sure. The contradictory testimony, the inadequate investigation by the government, and the obviously mistaken evidence from witnesses, all as reported in the *Gazette* news story, make one wonder."

Personally, I was infuriated to a level I had never before experienced, literally consumed with deep and abiding outrage, especially following the cheap, sleazy fabricated testimony from the two Mexican men put on at the end of the government's case. It would take me years to calm down.

The whole experience created an effect in me that, I am sure, was akin to severe posttraumatic stress, now known as PTSD. In the early stages, I had frequent vivid and disturbing nightmares; lost interest in almost everything, including my work; felt depressed and anxious much of the time; and found it hard to be around other people, even Jeannie.

In addition to all that, I wanted to kill the bastards who did it. Call it my country background and the core rules of survival country people follow, but I became devoured with "malice aforethought," which, in legal parlance, is the first element in the crime of first-degree murder. Fortunately, the second element is the actual killing, which I managed to resist. But the urge persisted for a long time.

Strangely, at that moment, I was as angry at Gonzales and his customs cohorts as I was at the actual coterie of malefactors who had planned and executed the planting of the marijuana in my car. After all, Hunter, Wimberly, Weeks, Pearson, et al., were just a group of lowlife hooligans from whom such was not unusual. Agents of the people's government were expected to act more honorably, however.

I thought back to the episodes of my youth when other lowlife hooligans, also people in public employment, inadvertently taught me lessons in human failings and the misuse of power—the trip to Little Rock with my high school buddy Royce Tallant, for instance, that had included an unpleasant encounter with the Arkansas State Police. They roughed us up, cuffed us while we were spread-eagled on the ground, and took us to headquarters in Little Rock, where we were separated and grilled for several hours while sitting under a hot, blinding light. We had broken no law, were not charged, and never even got an accurate explanation of why we had been picked up. Being the victim of such injustice at the hands of law enforcement is a terrible thing. It creates scars that last for a lifetime.

The state police arrest was in 1960, a time when police excesses were common. I also thought back to 1963 when I rode with the city policeman in Magnolia and watched him brutalize an old black man on the highway. Another scar. And as I recalled that one of my reasons for going to law school was to get equipped to defend myself and others against such injustice, I remembered the Fred Goacher case in Nashville in 1970 in which I had successfully defended a man unfairly charged with DWI by the town marshal.

And here I was in 1972, with political enemies, enthusiastically supported by the federal government, trying to get me convicted of a felony so as to ruin my chances of ever again pursuing a political career, and, in the process, lose my law license. The deepest scar.

I didn't know it at the time, but I was destined to have a very successful forty-three-year career as a trial lawyer at the Wright, Lindsey & Jennings firm. I would become a member of some of the most prestigious legal organizations for trial lawyers in the world, and I was fortunate enough to earn several awards over the years in recognition of my legal abilities. Maybe the accumulated scars provided the impetus for this success, I don't know. I do know that the scars are still there.

33. The Strange Case of the 1970 Ford

I was free, but the U.S. Customs Service was by no means through with me. They had not been able to put me in prison, but they had my car impounded and were determined to keep it. To secure its return, I took the steps necessary, filing a lawsuit against John P. Shultz, secretary of the U.S. Treasury.

Seeking justice from one of the highest-ranking members of the federal government, a member of the president's cabinet no less, might seem a bit excessive for the simple act of getting back a used car. But I had been pushed to my limits by the repeated refusals of the customs office in Texas to do what was right.

This last chapter of my ordeal began when I called Tom Sharp a few days after returning home. I told him of my intention to return to Brownsville to pick up my car from the customs impoundment lot. I asked if he would go to the lot before I arrived, check for any damage done by the customs inspectors, and perhaps have the repairs made.

Sharp called back a little later with this shocking news: "Customs will not release your car."

"Why the hell not?" I shouted.

"The car had been confiscated by the government," Sharp continued. "The customs office here said you can't get it back."

"What is this all about?" I asked, my mind reeling from this latest outrage.

"It happens down here all the time," Sharp answered. "The government position is that any vehicle carrying illegal drugs or other contraband is subject to seizure and confiscation. It doesn't matter if the owner or driver is innocent or guilty. They consider the vehicle itself to be guilty."

"But we were found innocent," I protested. "The car is just an inanimate object. How can a car be guilty?"

Sharp explained that the protocol was based on an ancient English common law which held that the means of conveyance of contraband material, from a horse to a vehicle, known in law as the res, is itself considered guilty.

"If you're thinking of challenging the law as unconstitutional," Sharp said, as if reading my mind, "a lot of cases have been filed based on that premise. I'm not aware of one that outright found the practice unconstitutional."

The phone went silent for a moment as Sharp let the information he had just conveyed sink in. I was silent, too, nearly dumbstruck trying to understand how such a situation could exist.

"What is this really all about?" I asked, although I already had a good idea of the answer.

"Customs down here confiscates a hell of a lot of drug-carrying vehicles," Sharp continued. "They sell them at auction; it's a huge source of revenue."

So there it was again, I thought, the same small-time graft, where a few empowered people abuse their power and influence to advance their personal agenda. Only this time, it was performed by an agency of the federal government.

Sharp then informed me of a possible administrative remedy. The District Customs Office in Laredo could be petitioned to release the car. But he quickly added that he had never seen such a petition granted. My petition, if I filed one, would be virtually hopeless, since the local customs people had already declined. The only value a petition would have, he explained, would be to show I had exhausted all administrative remedies in the event I decided to file suit at a higher level.

"What about getting to the federal court by filing a motion with Judge Garza?" I asked.

"You'll have to go higher and sue the U.S. Department of the Treasury, Customs Service." Sharp said. "Once they decide to confiscate, it's very hard to get a vehicle back."

"Okay," I said dejectedly.

I thanked Sharp again and ended the call. I stewed over this development for a few hours before thinking to myself: *By God, the bastards have gone too far this time. I'm not going to take it lying down. It's time to go on offense.*

Meanwhile, news about the car had already been broken by the *Gazette* in an article by staff reporter Tucker Steinmetz:

Glasgow Has More Trouble: He Can't Get His Car Back

Although a federal court jury acquitted him Tuesday on charges of illegally importing marijuana, Roger A. Glasgow...may not be able to reclaim the 1970 Ford LTD he was driving at the time of his arrest.

Federal law provides that any vehicle in which contraband is found is subject to immediate forfeiture. Assistant United States Attorney Raul Gonzales Wednesday said Glasgow's car was forfeited August 25 when he was arrested at the Mexican border.

Glasgow may petition the district customs director, Wallace Sewall of Laredo, Texas, for the return of his car, Gonzales said, but Sewall has the sole authority to decide whether the car should be returned.[39]

I was determined to do something about this outrage, even though I was out of funds again. I had no illusions that Sewall would release the car. His strings were being pulled from elsewhere. So it would take another exhausting legal effort from me to get anything done. Paying for that effort would be a tremendous barrier.

Over a hundred individual contributors from all walks of life had raised some $2,500 for the Glasgow Defense Fund through small donations ranging from $5 to $150. My dad had come through again, selling the remainder of the pig operation and presenting me with a check for $3,000 to help defray defense expenses. But all of the money had been spent, and I had nothing left with which to gear up for another legal battle with the Customs Bureau.

The cost of waging a long legal battle with the government would undoubtedly be more than the car was worth. I'm sure the customs people knew that, which was one reason the agency decided to exercise its administrative discretion against me and declare the vehicle to be forfeited. "Kick a man when he's down" seemed to be their motto.

I might not be able to afford an extended legal fight, but I could kick back. I decided to call a press conference for the following Sunday afternoon, confident the paper would give the story extensive coverage. The *Gazette* came through as I expected, assigning two of its best reporters, Ernest Dumas and Tucker Steinmetz, to cover the story. I planned to stir up a hornet's nest and pop the bureau with some sharp stings, so I held nothing back at the press conference. The *Gazette*'s story accurately recorded my bitter feelings toward the government's handling of my case, and the subsequent truculent and disgusting attitude of the Customs Bureau:

Glasgow Plans to Fight for Car

Roger A. Glasgow received word Saturday that the Federal Bureau of Customs would not return his car, which the government had confiscated August 25 after finding marijuana in it at the Mexican border. He said Sunday that the government had handled the whole case in an "outrageous" manner, the loss of his car being "the final indignity."

He had been silent since a federal jury acquitted him of responsibility for the marijuana on October 17, but Sunday he angrily denounced the government for its part in the case while discussing the loss of his car.

He said he intended to go back to court to get his car back and, hopefully, to strike down federal laws authorizing forfeiture of the property of innocent persons.

He said he had intended to immerse himself in his work after the trial and be content with the verdict until he received a copy of a letter from the Customs Bureau, saying that the agency had "investigated" his petition to have his car returned and that "this office fails to find the existence of any circumstances to justify the extension of relief."

"The audacity of the government to say it's been investigated," Glasgow said. "They have done the most outrageous job of investigating this case from its inception that I have ever seen."[40]

A few days later, the *Gazette* came out with a withering editorial severely castigating the Customs Bureau:

Bureaucrat's Hide Fit for the Wall

The final outrage, or what Roger Glasgow calls the "final indignity," has been perpetrated now by the federal government in the case of Glasgow's arrest, trial and acquittal. Both the Justice Department and the Customs Bureau are culpable in this travesty, in precise degrees that we are not prepared to define.

What has happened now is that Customs, with insufferable bureaucratic effrontery, has declined to return Glasgow's automobile after the jury found him innocent of the charges. There is a federal statute (itself of dubious constitutionality) that gives the bureau some discretion in such matters, and the bureau has elected to proceed as if Glasgow had been found guilty.

The prosecution's handling of the case...was disgraceful. At one point, two Mexican motel employees were brought in to give contradicting testimony, which was either incompetent or perjured, and turned out to be what we have previously described as a minor exercise in character assassination.

The confiscation of the Glasgow automobile is simply too much. Glasgow says that he will take the case to court, as he certainly should. But he shouldn't have to, and we would hope that the Arkansas powers in Congress would swiftly demand that the car be released. We think that Senators John McClellan and J. W. Fulbright, and Congressman Wilbur Mills should proceed to nail the offending bureaucrat's hide to the wall. It is, for the record, an administrative matter, one in which the voice of Congress can and should be heard.[41]

I was in my office at Wright, Lindsey & Jennings the afternoon the editorial appeared, glad for the *Gazette*'s strong voice but pondering how I could manage to file a lawsuit without any funds. Suddenly, Winslow "Win" Drummond, one of my favorite partners at the firm, burst into my office.

"Roger," he boomed in that trademark baritone of his, "we've got to make those insufferable sons of bitches pay. What were you thinking in terms of a lawsuit?"

"I would love to sue them," I said, "but I don't have much left in the way of funds, and I can't think of anyone who would want to take it on pro bono."

"I'm your man," he bellowed majestically. "You do the legal research and I'll do the rest. Let's sue the bastards," he proclaimed, slamming the palm of his hand on my desktop.

The suit was soon filed in federal court in Little Rock. Jeannie and I were the plaintiffs (inclusion of her name was necessary since the car title listed us as joint owners), and we were suing John P. Shultz, Secretary of the Treasury of the United States of America, case # LR-72-C-272. We wanted my 1970 Ford LTD retuned forthwith, plus $1,500 for all the damage they had done to it while it was in their custody. In addition, we wanted the statute they had operated under to be declared unconstitutional.

The case was assigned to U.S. District Judge J. Smith Henley and, at our request, it was soon transferred to a three-judge panel in the Eighth Circuit Court of Appeals in St. Louis. This prompt assignment by Judge Henley to the Eighth Circuit was a good omen for us and did not portend well for the government.

At the same time, tremendous political pressure was being applied to the Customs Bureau by the Arkansas congressional delegation in Washington DC. Arkansas senators John L. McClellan and J. William Fulbright, as well as Congressmen Wilbur D. Mills and David Pryor, wrote forceful letters to the customs commissioner, Vernon W. Acree. These Arkansans had some of the most powerful committee chairmanships in Congress—Mills at Ways and Means, McClellan at Senate Appropriations, and Fulbright at Foreign Relations. Their word carried prodigious force among government agencies.

An immense public outcry also began over the government's arrogance. Numerous calls and letters were sent to the Customs Bureau, to newspapers, and to the congressional delegation. While all this was going on, the *Gazette* ran another editorial that added even more fuel to the fire. The editorial first noted a recent case decision in Tennessee that declared unconstitutional the seizure and sale of a vehicle containing marijuana belonging to an innocent college student. The editorial then brought the hammer down on the actions of the Customs Bureau in my case:

On the Glasgow Case

The state law in Tennessee was similar, at least, to a federal statute under which the Customs Bureau, with insufferable bureaucratic arrogance, is still holding Mr. Glasgow's car after he was tried and acquitted. The prosecution's case was so flimsy, and its malice so apparent, that the case had become an outrage even before Customs advised Glasgow of the retention of his vehicle.

In Tennessee the court held unanimously that due process of law under the Fourteenth Amendment had been violated. Certainly the same kind of violation has been committed by the Customs Bureau in its decision to hold Glasgow's car.

It is a pity that Glasgow has to go to court to find remedy against such flagrant injustice. The decision to keep his car was made administratively and it seems to us to be clearly within the purview of the Arkansas congressional delegation, which is supposed to look after its constituents and help protect them against such high-handed abuses by the executive branch.

We do not know if Glasgow has asked for any congressional assistance in his grievance against the Customs Bureau, but we think that Congressman Wilbur Mills, Senator John McClellan and Senator J. W. Fulbright should address themselves to this last miscarriage of justice.[42]

The public opprobrium was so great that even people not likely to give me support weighed in on my behalf. For example, Farrell Faubus, son of the former governor (whom I had frequently opposed), wrote a letter to the *Gazette* stating: "To the Editor of the *Gazette*: For once I agree with an editorial in your newspaper and this is indeed a very rare occasion. However, your editorial asking our congressional delegation to take action to free Mr. Glasgow's car is commendable. Since Mr. Glasgow has been found innocent, there is no possible reason for the Customs Bureau to keep his car impounded."[43]

Within days, customs folded under the pressure. Commissioner Acree reversed the decision and notified Laredo District Customs Director Walter Sewell to set a time for releasing the car. When called by reporters on the same day of the decision, Sewell said he had not heard anything about a change in the status of the case, but he added, "It may be true. I hope not."

A reporter for the *Brownsville Herald* contacted Tom Sharp. He credited the vast outpouring of public outrage as the deciding factor in the sudden release of the vehicle:

> Sharp said he feels the public furor arising in the state of Arkansas was enough in itself to secure the release of the auto even without intervention by the senators and congressmen.
>
> "All I can say," said Sharp about possible political influence, "is that political influence was not originated by the politicians themselves."
>
> Sharp said the Glasgow story, even though it unfolded in Brownsville, was one of the top ten news stories in Arkansas during 1972. "It was the great hue and cry by the public in the state of Arkansas," commented Sharp, noting newspapers in that state, and particularly in Little Rock, had taken up Glasgow's cause.[44]

The newspapers and the public had rallied to my case, I believe, because they were fed up with the endemic corruption and crime at all levels of government in Arkansas (and America) during that time. The situations existing at lower levels were encouraged and abetted by the corruption and crime existing at higher levels. When Orval Faubus served as governor, his administration was awash with corruption and criminal conduct. Officials at the lower levels were not stupid—if such was happening under the aegis of the state house, they felt encouraged to get on the gravy train, too.

Corruption and unethical conduct abounded at the federal level as well. Richard Nixon's well-chronicled Watergate scandal occurred during the timeframe of 1972 to 1974. If Nixon and his law-enforcement officer, Attorney General John Mitchell, were not concerned about the crimes they, and others under their direction, were committing, why should lower-level federal law-enforcement officials, such as those with the U.S. Customs Bureau and the U.S. Attorney's office, be more honorable? Corruption itself is endemic—like a virus, it spreads and infects everything it touches.

I was encouraged by the outrage my story engendered in so many people and news agencies at the time in Arkansas. The callousness and disregard for personal rights demonstrated by the U.S. Attorney's Office and Customs Bureau officials, both in Brownsville, Texas, and Washington DC, were obvious. People in Arkansas saw my case as a chance to vent the residual disgust at the shenanigans that occurred during the Faubus years, and the resulting world-wide opprobrium. Arkansans responded by vigorously expressing their disdain and contempt. My story became one of the top news items in Arkansas in 1972.

34. Return to the Scene of the Crime

Customs had released my car with no strings attached. All I had to do was go down to Brownsville and pick it up. Also, I needed to decide what to do about the remaining counts in my lawsuit, seeking payment for damages done to the car and requesting a declaration that the forfeiture statute was unconstitutional.

Tom Sharp had looked at the car and reported to me that there was little actual damage. To continue to pursue the lawsuit under these circumstances would amount to no more than tilting at windmills, I reasoned. I talked with Win Drummond about it, and he agreed. So we dismissed the lawsuit and put an end to that particular unpleasant episode.

In the interim, I had been contacted by Tucker Steinmetz, who had been covering my story, including all of the tomfoolery associated with the car forfeiture. He let me know that the *Gazette* remained very interested in my case and wanted to help in any way it could to expose those who were guilty. He said he had received the go-ahead to travel down to Matamoros and nose around to see if he could dig up any intelligence about the shady marijuana shenanigans.

I told him that I expected to be flying down to retrieve my car soon and invited him to go along. As Steinmetz and I got along well, we decided he would join me on the ride back home. So we flew down to Brownsville and spent one night in a motel, giving him time to cross over the border and investigate any leads that looked promising. He managed to interview the two Holiday Inn employees who had given the bizarre and conflicting testimony at trial.

From what Steinmetz told me about his conversations with Cortez and Mayorquin, and reflecting back on their physical appearances when they came to the trial to testify, I realized these were the same two men that Jeannie and I had encountered around the Holiday Inn pool. Cortez was the chain-smoking pool waiter and Mayorquin was the big gap-toothed guy with the cowboy boots and drooping mustache (which had been shaved off when he came to trial).

Steinmetz said their stories continued to be bizarre, even more so than at trial, and that they both tried to "shake him down"—in other words, trade information for money. The most interesting tidbit was that a couple of men, "rich-looking Anglos," had shown up at the Holiday Inn the day we arrived, or perhaps the next day, inquiring about us: what room we were in, what kind of car we were driving, etc.

Mayorquin claimed that they said they were "good friends" of ours, had heard we were staying there, and just wanted to stop by and say hello, as they were staying there, too. The men, he said, were driving a big, shiny new white automobile, maybe a Cadillac. Steinmetz said Mayorquin told him the names the men used for their hotel registration. Suspecting the names were fictitious, Steinmetz asked to see the hotel registry and vehicle license number. I immediately thought of Jim Hunter's new white Continental with the JTH license plate, but we had no proof.

At this point, Steinmetz said that he had been with Mayorquin in his taxicab somewhere along the dark alleys of downtown Matamoros. Mayorquin promised he could get the information by the next morning, but he would "require a small fee" for his trouble. They agreed to meet at a certain place and time the next day. Steinmetz showed up, but Mayorquin was nowhere to be found and did not answer his phone.

While Steinmetz was in Mexico, I had regained possession of my car. He and I left Brownsville that afternoon with a fascinating story but no hard evidence to back it up. We began the long drive back to Little Rock in my repatriated Ford LTD. I had long suspected that one or both of the two Mexican men had somehow participated in the marijuana setup. Perhaps that is why Mayorquin decided to skip the appointment.

A few days after we got back to Little Rock, I got another call from Tucker Steinmetz relaying an intriguing proposition. The *Gazette* would love to develop an "investigative exposé" about my case, assuming I gave my approval and would cooperate. This would be a comprehensive story, Steinmetz assured me, perhaps a two-part series that would name names, times, and places. The only thing the *Gazette* would require of me before it started work on the story was that both Jeannie and I agree to take polygraph examinations, which the *Gazette* would arrange.

I was eager to do it. *Why not?* I thought. *What better way to expose the perpetrators and further burnish my own reputation? I could come out of this smelling like a rose, maybe even to the point of positioning myself for another run at some high political office.*

Jeannie was also willing, although a bit apprehensive about being wired up to a polygraph machine, which was something she knew absolutely nothing about. I explained the whole process to her, and assured her it would be safe and accurate. I called Steinmetz back and told him to have it set up.

The tests were conducted by Powell Security Services, a Little Rock firm I had never heard of but was assured was completely impartial and independent. The polygraph report concluded as follows:

Special Instructions
Above listed subject was examined to ascertain if he was being completely truthful in his allegation that he had no knowledge of narcotics in his vehicle and to his possible involvement in the purchase and attempted smuggling of said narcotics into the United States from Mexico....

Conclusion.
It is the opinion of this examiner that the subject was in no way connected with the smuggling of "pot," nor does he have any knowledge concerning the smuggling.[45]

Steinmetz said the *Gazette* was eager to get started with developing the story and just needed the green light from me. The first step was to invite both Jim T. Hunter and taxi driver/informant John Patterson to voluntarily submit to polygraph tests as well. The newspaper had gotten word that Patterson would agree, but it was sure Hunter would not. Hunter was still being represented by counsel, Jack L. Lessenberry of Little Rock, whom he hired after being subpoenaed to the trial in Brownsville.

Next, the *Gazette* reporters would seek to interview the other witnesses who were subpoenaed but did not testify: Kenneth Pearson and the other LRPD officers who showed up at the trial, Forrest Parkman and Fred Hensley. The *Arkansas Democrat* had previously run an article shortly after the trial posing questions about the appearance of these men. The *Democrat's* article, by staff writer Arlin Fields, read in part:

274

Familiar Faces at Glasgow Trial...But Why?

When Federal Judge G. Thomas Eisele walked into the courtroom at Brownsville, Texas, in which Roger A. Glasgow was being tried this week on a charge of marijuana smuggling, he looked around at all the familiar faces and said: "You would think we were in Little Rock."

In Brownsville for the trial were a number of persons from Little Rock, including three members from the Little Rock Police Department; Jack L. Lessenberry, a lawyer; Robert L. Brown, a former deputy prosecuting attorney now in the mortgage banking business; and John T. Patterson, a driver for Dixie Company of Little Rock.

George Fisher cartoon of G. Thomas Eisele.

Eisele had appeared as a character witness for Glasgow, as did Edward L. Wright, senior partner in the law firm of Wright, Lindsey and Jennings.

Patrolman Fred Hensley, of the Police Department's intelligence squad, who was not subpoenaed to testify, sat in the courtroom and took copious notes on the testimony of all witnesses.

During recesses Hensley would consult outside the courtroom with Lt. Kenneth Pearson, head of the Police Department vice squad. Pearson was under subpoena and was excluded from the courtroom under a judicial rule that prevents witnesses from listening to the testimony of other witnesses.

Hensley declined to identify himself to reporters. When asked whether he was a policeman, he replied: "I work with them from time to time."

Also in Brownsville was Sgt. Forrest Parkman, also of the intelligence detail.

None of the men from the LRPD would agree to explain their role in the trial.

Lessenberry, a criminal lawyer, declined to say why he was in Brownsville. He said that to explain his presence would "not be in the best interest of my client. I had better leave it at that."

Contacted Friday, Gonzales [the federal district attorney] said he knew why Lessenberry was in Brownsville, then answered "no comment" when asked to explain.[46]

The *Democrat*'s article, though factual, was full of intimations and suggestions of foul play. The *Gazette* planned to inquire further. Concluding the phone conversation with Steinmetz, I asked him to give me another day or two to think it over before giving my assent to go forward with the story.

I felt that I had to confide the whole plan to Ed Wright before making a decision. My gut instinct was to go forward, but recent experience had taught me that there could be a considerable amount of unpredictability and danger lurking just around the corner. I went by Wright's office the next day and told him what I knew of the *Gazette*'s plan and about the polygraph results.

"They won't go forward with it without my consent," I said. "I need to let them know something by tomorrow."

Wright sat quietly, rubbing his chin for a while, before saying, "First, to quote an old proverb, 'Don't sleep with mangy dogs, if you don't want to get fleas.' You were completely exonerated at trial. I am confident that by far the majority in this community accepts that and is convinced of your innocence. You also gained a lot of support around here after the trial with that ridiculous fiasco over the seizure of your car. The point is, I don't think you have anything to prove. Stirring the pot again can only cause you more grief."

I stood there silently for a minute, digesting what he had said.

"What you said makes a lot of sense," I conceded, "and I have been thinking along the same lines. But, I did want to do the polygraph test, if for no other reason than to banish for good any doubts that anyone at the *Gazette* might have harbored about my innocence, not that I had any reason to think there were any. And I really appreciated their willingness to go to bat for me."

"I agree completely," Wright said. "You did the right thing there. Here's my thought. The public has a short memory. This whole thing will fade away in a couple of years. You can enjoy a long and satisfying legal career here at this firm, or anywhere else you might choose to go in the future. You needn't worry at all that this thing will impede your progress in any way."

"Thank you," I said. "That's very kind and reassuring. I think I know what to do."

I went to my office and called Steinmetz. "I have decided to pull out of this, Tucker," I said. "I don't want to rake the coals any further."

At that, the story ended.

I have since pursued a successful career as a trial lawyer with Wright, Lindsey & Jennings, now spanning some forty-three years. Reflecting on it, there is no doubt in my mind I had made the right choice. To that end, I consider the whole affair to be a blessing, though, to be sure, it was in disguise for a rather long while.

Although the blessing was disguised, the criminal activity of my erstwhile nemeses was not. If fact, it seemed to blossom, as if the ending of the two-year reign of Jim Guy Tucker, who was a responsible prosecuting attorney they did not control, had un-corked a vacuum of pent-up demand. I could do nothing about it but sit back and watch. It soon would become apparent that my case was by no means unique, simply an example of the modus operandi these thugs employed on a regular basis.

Part IV

35. No Honor Among Thieves

Over the next few years, the most significant of the villains, those holding official positions in Arkansas, disappeared from the scene. The Little Rock Police Department's Kenneth Pearson, Forrest Parkman, John Terry, and Gale Weeks, along with Mayor George Wimberly, had all been toppled by the end of 1977. The downfall of these individuals was caused by many actions, but the most significant chain of events began with a jewel heist in St. Louis, Missouri, just a few weeks before my trial in Brownsville. The robbery was followed by two murders, a drugstore robbery, and three grand-jury investigations.

This story began on September 7, 1972, when a small-time hoodlum named Leon "Pete" Pettry, accompanied by another small-time crook Ray Emery, robbed the Four Seasons Antique Shop, a St. Louis store that specialized in antique home furnishings and jewelry. The armed robbery provided the thieves with two briefcases full of over $250,000 of jewelry (valued at over $1 million today). Though the heist went off smoothly, Pettry and Emery's luck would soon run out.

Jewelry is notoriously difficult to fence, especially antique jewelry, because it is easily traceable by law-enforcement authorities. Most of the pieces, reportedly nearly 500 in all, taken in the St. Louis heist were distinctive-looking, so trying to move the stolen goods in the St. Louis area would be risky. The thieves enlisted the help of a St. Louis bar owner, Norman Journey, in selling the stolen goods.

Journey contacted a longtime friend, Bill Smith in Little Rock, who worked as the manager of the bar and restaurant at the Little Rock Sheraton Hotel, reputed to be a safe haven for underworld figures. In a couple of days, all three of them had checked into the Sheraton.

Unfortunately for them, because of the Sheraton's notorious reputation, an informant for the Little Rock Police Department had just been assigned to infiltrate the organized-crime elements at the hotel. The informant was named Manfred "Big Man" Barron, and he reported to the LRPD Organized Crime Intelligence Unit, an elite group of plainclothes detectives under Chief Gale Weeks and Captain John Terry. The intelligence unit itself was headed by Lieutenant Forrest Parkman and included several detectives, including James Vandiver and Fred Hensley. On September 11, 1972, two days after the robbery, Barron informed the intelligence unit that a large amount of jewelry was being offered for sale by men staying at the Sheraton. Two of the names mentioned were Pettry and Emery, known to be convicted felons.

On September 16, 1972, the hotel bar manager Bill Smith contacted Metro Flight Service, a private charter company, to arrange a charter flight to take Pettry and Journey to Lafayette, Louisiana, where they hoped to sell some of the jewelry. Once again, the thieves' luck turned bad. Unknown to them, the charter flight service was owned by Lieutenant Kenneth Pearson, chief of the LRPD vice squad.

Once Pettry returned from the unproductive trip to Lafayette, he decided he would be better off without his accomplice, Emery, hanging around to share in the proceeds. Pettry told the police informant Barron that he wanted to kill Emery, and he asked for help in planning the murder. Barron passed this information along to detectives in the intelligence unit, who suggested a wooded area off Rebsamen Park Road in Little Rock as a good spot for the hit.

Detective Vandiver drove Barron to the murder site to "case it." Barron then drove Pettry out to the area to look it over, and he agreed to let Pettry use his car to drive the unsuspecting Emery out to meet his fate. Vandiver and another intelligence unit detective enlisted Captain Terry to be near the scene when the murder occurred. With the three police officers in close proximity, Pettry brought an unsuspecting Emery to the preselected site and shot him three times in the back of the head, execution style, killing him instantly. After Pettry left, Vandiver and Terry returned and found Emery's body. The officers decided the body should be left where it lay, and no attempt was made to arrest Pettry that night. Emery's body was found on October 21, nearly a month after the murder, by a man and his son walking in the woods. A grand jury investigation looked into the affair in 1973, but no testimony, interviews, or official records made mention of the three officers or their awareness of the crime.

Shortly after the murder, Pettry returned to St. Louis, where he was apprehended and charged with the jewelry robbery. Pettry was jailed and then released on bond. He called on his presumed friend Barron to come up and drive him back to Little Rock, where much of the stolen jewelry was hidden. Barron obliged, but he alerted the LRPD intelligence unit detectives, who arranged a room for Pettry at the Downtowner Motel. The detectives rented an adjacent room and set up surveillance. Believing he was safe in his Little Rock motel hideout, Pettry asked Barron for advice on his next caper, robbing a drugstore for narcotics and cash.

Barron faithfully reported the plan to Lieutenant Parkman, who suggested Dawson's Drug Store at 15th and Main. Parkman instructed Barron to drive Pettry to the store area in the afternoon to show him the site. While Barron and Pettry were out, Parkman had his officers enter Pettry's room and disable his gun. The officers first tried to substitute bullets with the gunpowder removed, but the replacement bullets they brought were the wrong size. Undaunted, the officers then bent the firing pin of Pettry's gun, making it inoperable. The two police officers later joined other intelligence officers who were planning the stakeout of Dawson's Drug Store, under the direction of Parkman. The proprietor of Dawson's Drug Store was not told the store was to be robbed.

At 8 p.m., Dawson's Drug Store was occupied by only two workers: storeowner Mr. Allen Monroe and an employee. Pettry entered, and, brandishing his tampered gun, ordered Monroe to fill a sack with prescription drugs and all the money in the store's cash registers. Monroe obliged, but as Pettry was leaving the store, the druggist pulled out a .38 caliber pistol and fired at Pettry. Pettry attempted to shoot back, but his weapon was useless. He ran out the store's front door, whereupon a cadre of detectives opened fire on him with shotguns. The south brick wall of the building along 15th Street was peppered with pockmarks from the shotgun pellets. Pettry's body and the bag of drugs were found lying almost exactly in the middle of the pockmarked section of the wall.

In the initial police department report, Captain John Terry said that "a police car was driving by the store on Main and the officers heard shots from inside. They stopped and told the man fleeing to drop his gun. When he didn't stop, they shot him."[47]

That was quite a lot of shooting from two officers in a patrol car who just happened to be passing by. Patrol officers are not normally armed with shotguns. It was clear that this genie was not going to stay in the bottle, despite the best efforts of all in the detective cabal.

The bulk of the stolen jewelry was never recovered. A few pieces purchased by the owner of the Little Rock Sheraton for some $8,000 in the early stages were turned in to police (and announced at a press conference with great fanfare by Chief Weeks), but most of it simply disappeared.

Chief Weeks later issued a press release that cleared the detectives of any wrongdoing after "a thorough investigation." Prosecuting Attorney–elect Lee Munson even got in on the act,

The outside wall of Dawson Drug Store in Little Rock was marked by bullets following the shooting of a burglary suspect. (Courtesy of the Arkansas Democrat-Gazette)

saying that there was "a cloud over the police department that ought to be removed." Munson did his best to remove the cloud after he took office in January 1972, issuing a report stating that he had found no evidence of any wrongdoing in connection with the matter.

Five years later, in 1977, the Pulaski County Grand Jury reviewed the involvement of the LRPD in the extensive Pettry affair. While providing considerable testimony regarding the drugstore and Rebsamen Park Road shootings, the grand jury report issued no indictments (the statute of limitations had run out on many of the crimes committed except first-degree murder). The report did, however, contain a scathing report of police involvement in Emery's death, concluding:

> Three Little Rock police officers were aware a murder was planned. They knew where, approximately when and knew which car would be used to transport the victim to the murder scene....In addition to the three officers involved, the head of the Intelligence Unit, Parkman, and the Chief of Police, Gale Weeks, both of whom were out of town, were made aware that the body was left where it fell. Both of these officers agreed that the body should be left where it was.[48]

Despite the conspiracy of the LRPD officers—and their hired informant, Barron—in the planning of the murder, and despite their knowledge of the dead body and the identity of the triggerman, they declined to make an arrest or even recover the body. Quite obviously, they did not want the murder to become public knowledge. For reasons unknown, while issuing an alarming report, the grand jury did not issue any indictments or recommend any other official actions. But the story had assumed a life of its own and was not going away.

36. WAGES OF SIN

Notwithstanding the best efforts of Chief Gale Weeks, Mayor George Wimberly, and their minions to squelch it, the news story stubbornly refused to die. Suspicions were rife in the business community that there was something seriously rotten in the Little Rock Police Department. The situation began to produce a lot of stress on Weeks, Wimberly, and the upper echelons of the LRPD. The tenuous threads that held them together began to fray as a series of peculiar events unfolded.

1. DENIAL OF INVOLVEMENT

Local press learned that Mayor Wimberly and Chief Weeks were apparently involved in the 1972 Metro charter flight that took the jewel robbers to Lafayette, Louisiana, and that both men may have known at the time that Leon Pettry was a participant in the St. Louis robbery. Both Wimberly and Weeks stoutly denied any involvement in the firm or knowledge that Pettry was a suspect. However, the press continued to dig, soon locating a loan application the flight firm had submitted to a local bank, listing Weeks as president and Wimberly as vice president of Metro Flight

Service, with Pearson serving as secretary. Weeks and Wimberly were also listed as guarantors on loans to the firm totaling some $30,000. These facts made their connection to the flight firm hard to deny, although both continued to offer various excuses.[49]

After a while, this particular issue died down, but it never completely went away. Five years later, the 1977 Pulaski County Grand Jury investigation determined that the Little Rock police officials had indeed known of Pettry's involvement in the jewel heist at the time of the flight because they had been told about it by their paid informant, Manfred "Big Man" Barron.

2. Payoffs to Police

In the closing weeks of 1972, near the end of his term, Prosecuting Attorney Jim Guy Tucker had launched an independent investigation into corruption within the LRPD. Tucker instituted the investigation after his office had received incriminating information from three former and three current Little Rock police officers. These officers gave sworn statements indicating that a large illegal "payoff" operation was being conducted by upper-echelon detectives in the vice squad whereby they received payoffs in the form of money and drugs by several nightclubs located in the 9th Street area of Little Rock. These payoffs were in return for a "hands-off" policy by the vice squad.

Tucker hired a private investigative agency that was free of police influence and appointed his chief deputy, Sandy McMath, to head the effort. They were assisted by a reporter for the *Arkansas Gazette*, who had first been tipped off about the illegal activity. The investigation focused on Pete's Club at 610 W. 9th Street in Little Rock, owned by a man named David "Pete" Mack Jr.

Tucker's investigation laid bare some fascinating facts. The statements given by the officers pointed to Pete's Place as "the focal point for collections from several other vice establishments, covering drugs, prostitution, and gambling." The officers claimed that Pete's "received weekly payments from the other establishments for subsequent distribution to the police" in return for the hands-off policy.[50]

The *Democrat* reported on the contents of Tucker's written report, stating that a confidential informant had been placed inside Pete's and was there for about nine nights in December 1972. He observed that the club stayed open at least until 4 a.m. amid open gambling. The report contained eyewitness observations concerning the pickup of the payoff, stating that "a late model Ford pickup truck left the vice squad parking area [at LRPD headquarters] driven by a man in plain clothes. At 10:45 p.m. the truck was photographed parking in the rear of Pete's Place. The driver did not leave the truck but sounded his horn and a woman appeared in the door of Pete's Place, disappeared and returned within moments carrying a small package, which she handed to the driver through the truck window. The truck left."[51] The report and photographs were shown to Chief Weeks, who claimed that the package contained only ducks left off for cleaning by his detectives after a hunting trip.

A copy of Tucker's report was filed with the Pulaski County Grand Jury, which took up the matter in early 1973 after Tucker left office. Pete Mack was subpoenaed to testify, but before he could appear, he was murdered. The slaying occurred in the back lot of Pete's Place. Lee Berry—an undercover agent for the office of the new prosecuting attorney, Lee Munson—was charged with the murder. It was widely suspected that it had been a contract killing. Berry pled guilty but claimed self-defense. He was given a light sentence and was back on the streets in a few months.

3. Additional Marijuana Setups

A story broke in the *Arkansas Times* that Detective Kenneth Pearson, chief of the vice squad and co-owner of Metro Flight Service, had attempted to plant marijuana on Jim Guy Tucker's vehicle on two separate occasions, once in 1971 when Tucker was prosecuting attorney, and again in 1974 when he was attorney general.[52]

Pearson tried to work this frame-up through a police informant, Larry Case, who had the foresight to put a wire on himself and tape the conversation related to the 1971 attempt. The *Times* printed a transcript of the tape, on which the following exchange between Case and Pearson ("Voice" on the transcript) can be heard:

> **Voice:** I know of your connections with Jim Guy and I know you know somebody that will do this, so if you do this for me, I can promise you that anything you need in any of your investigations for years to come I will see that you receive no heat from us; and you will get all the help from this department you need in any matter.
>
> **Case:** Just exactly what do you want? You know if it can be done, I can get it done.
>
> **Voice:** Here's what you do. Get some pot and get it planted on Jim Guy's cars. Call me. I'll get him pulled over for some reason and find the drugs and I hope that he tries to raise hell or resist, because I just need one reason and I'll see that he doesn't get out of it without being harmed in one way or the other, no matter if I have to use force in any way, he will be harmed to his disadvantage.
>
> **Case:** I'll check around and see what can be done about this and how they can handle it and what they would expect for doing it. One other thing, who all will know of this?
>
> **Voice:** Just myself and my superior [apparently Chief Weeks].

Kenneth Pearson suddenly retired in May 1975 from the police department at an early age, never giving a public explanation of why he had decided to end his police career so soon. Speculation at the time was that he was forced out because he had been in the news too much in an unflattering way and was becoming a liability to the upper echelons of the department.

4. RAPE AND SLANDER

Serious friction developed between Lieutenant Forrest Parkman, who was chief of the LRPD Intelligence Unit, and Harry Hastings Sr. (reputedly the "crime czar" of central Arkansas) for unknown reasons, but resulting in Hastings and some of his associates accusing Parkman of raping two women. Parkman responded by filing a civil suit against Hastings and his cohorts for defamation, seeking over $1 million in damages. The 1975 case ended up getting dismissed, as it was barred by the one-year statute of limitations for slander. It was appealed by Parkman but upheld by the Arkansas Supreme Court.[53]

5. STOLEN PROPERTY

Forrest Parkman's feud with Harry Hastings Sr. and his confederates continued, finally resulting in a federal court proceeding.[54] The facts showed that Parkman suckered the Hastings group into receiving stolen property, which he hoped would get them charged and convicted of felony crimes. The items were a truckload of tires stolen in Mississippi and a large air compressor stolen in Texarkana, Texas. These items were offered to Hastings and his associates for a steeply discounted cash price. Hastings and crew bought the items, knowing they were stolen, then were charged with the crime of "receiving."

The charges were filed in federal court, but once the government learned of the police involvement in what had happened, which was regarded as "entrapment," it filed a motion to dismiss the charges. Thus, Parkman's efforts to cause damage to the Hastings group had now failed on at least two occasions, and his tactics had been spread upon the public record in the subsequent lawsuits. Parkman was quickly becoming radioactive.

6. MAFIA "HIT" CONTRACTS

Chief Gale Weeks and Lieutenant Forrest Parkman evidently got crossways with the New Orleans mafia. As reported by the *Arkansas Times*, they took a secret trip to New Orleans on February 24, 1975, to meet with underworld boss Carlos Marcello and convince him to withdraw "hit" contracts that had been put out on them. The contracts were for $100,000 in the case of Parkman and $50,000 for Weeks, to be carried out by a Mafiosi hit man.

The *Times* reported the following exchange with Parkman explaining the situation:

> "I knew the hit man, the man who was going to kill me, and he was good," Parkman said. "Yes I had seen him; I looked him in the eyeballs once. The contract went down in early 1975, and, well, it was like this; there were local yokels running around telling people they had $50,000 in a suitcase saying it was for killing Parkman and Weeks, but that was just for show. The real hit was coming from out of town. Those others (the "local yokels") didn't even know and never would have known who the killer was.[55]

The *Times* didn't say why the hit contract was put out on Weeks and Parkman by the New Orleans mafia bosses, but, historically, such contracts stem from a few reasons, such as someone didn't pay money owed, someone was trying to muscle in on the mob's territory and thus take its money, or there was a leadership struggle. The New Orleans meeting apparently paid off. Shortly afterward, in 1976, Parkman had a heart attack and left the LRPD on medical disability. Weeks retired as LRPD chief in 1977 under pressure from the City Board of Directors.

7. Racial Discrimination and Harassment

The final blow came in 1977 and again involved a federal lawsuit. This time Police Chief Gale Weeks suspected that his public information officer, Sonny Simpson, had provided inside information to the attorneys representing some black police officers. These officers had filed a federal discrimination lawsuit against the police department and Chief Weeks, Assistant Chief John Terry, and Lieutenant Forrest Parkman, claiming that intentional racial discriminatory practices existed within the department, and that the three men actively pursued and facilitated such practices.[56]

Weeks was determined to take punitive action against Simpson for supposedly being a turncoat. He started a chain of demotions (even though Simpson had a sterling record), first demoting him to residential foot patrol and finally to night jailer. The case was closely followed by the press and generated a lot of adverse publicity for the police and the three individual defendants: Weeks, Parkman, and Terry. By that time, George Wimberly's term as mayor had ended, and a new, much more independent mayor, Don Mehlburger, had been elected. Also, the makeup of the City Board of Directors had changed. Mayor Mehlburger called for a major shift in personnel at the police department, beginning at the top.[57]

In the end, Sonny Simpson won the case and was awarded punitive damages from each of the three defendants. Gale Weeks was forced to resign, and the intelligence unit was dissolved, its detectives fired or reassigned to other duties. Forrest Parkman retired and John Terry resigned, going to work for the Sheriff's Office. Simpson was selected by the City Board of Directors as the new police chief. George Wimberly ran for county judge and was defeated.

So ended 1977, and I was pleased. The wages of sin were clearly being paid.

37. Postscript

Watching the changing fortunes of those who sought to do me harm, I certainly felt that justice had been served, if only in a back-handed manner. But mostly I was greatly relieved that the destinies of these men were no longer linked with mine. Of this broad group, Jim Hunter was the only member with whom I had a follow-up encounter.

Hunter, presumably the organizer and financier of the plant of the marijuana under the back seat of my car in Mexico, rented office space for his bond agency in the Worthen Bank Building, the same building as my law firm. One day in December 1972, shortly before Christmas, I found myself in his holiday office party.

I had been invited to the party by an old law school room-mate, Mike Horn, who had flown in from Dallas and was meeting with Hunter to explore some venture financing. Horn and I had visited earlier in the day, and I had given him a little snippet of how and why I came to know Hunter. He laughed at the strangeness of the coincidence and went on to his meeting. Just before my firm's closing time, Horn called from the Delta Securities office

Christmas party. He had mentioned his friendship with me to Hunter, and Hunter insisted he invite me down, if I "felt up to it."

What the hell, I thought, *might as well go ahead and poke the bear.*

Surprisingly, I had an agreeable conversation with Hunter, finding out that he was from Arkadelphia originally, my neck of the woods. We exchanged a few other insignificant trifles but avoided any mention of the recent unpleasantness.

I had no further contact with Jim Hunter until five years later, in the fall of 1977. I was photographing the scene of an accident involving a car wreck case I was handling when a white Lincoln Mark IV pulled up and stopped. The driver rolled down his window and motioned me over. I did not know the man, but curious, I walked to the side of the car. The man was very skinny, bald, and frail looking.

"You don't recognize me, do you?" he asked.

"No," I admitted, "you look familiar but..."

"I'm Jim Hunter. I look a lot different from when you last saw me. I've got cancer, Roger, terminal I'm told, and have been taking a lot of chemo."

"I'm so sorry," I said, then could think of nothing further to say.

Hunter looked up at me, appearing to be very small in the driver's seat of his enormous car. The expression on his pale face suggested that he was troubled about something.

"Look, you got a really raw deal out of that Mexico business, and I feel real bad about it," he finally said. "I have some things that I would like to tell you about the whole affair."

"I'm listening," I said.

"No, not here," Hunter said. "Call me in the next few days, and we can find some place to meet in private."

"I'll do that," I said. "And, Jim, I appreciate it."

When I called Hunter's home, I was told he was back in the hospital. I reached him at the hospital, St. Vincent's, if I remember correctly, and asked how he was feeling.

"Not too good," he said, his voice heavy with weariness.

I asked if he was up to continuing our discussion. Hunter sighed, was quiet for a few seconds, then responded, "Roger, I'm sorry, but I can't do it. I've thought it over and too many innocent people are likely to get hurt. I would really like to help you out, but I just can't."

Disappointed, I managed to say, "Jim, I understand. If you change your mind, I would love to hear about it. Take care of yourself." At that, I hung up.

A couple of months later, at my office just before Christmas, I received a small envelope with "personal" marked on it. Inside was a Christmas card from Hunter. Not very long afterward, he died.

Never directly associated with any wrongdoings, except by innuendo, Lee Munson went on to serve in various judgeship positions, from municipal judge to chancery/circuit judge, retiring in 2008.

Afterword: Then and Now

As a young man starting out in life, I quickly learned that the justice system was tilted heavily in favor of the wealthy and powerful, and that racial bigotry was widespread. My experience with the police, state politics, and the justice system impressed upon me that the average citizen faced a significant disadvantage.

As I write this in 2015, all of the progressive statesmen listed in this memoir (Fulbright, Rockefeller, Thornton, Bumpers, Pryor, Tucker, Clinton) have retired from office or died. For the most part, they have not been followed by office holders of the same caliber. In fact, theirs was a rare era of public spiritedness, cooperation, and progress.

It seems that the state of Arkansas, and indeed the nation, has regressed since the time of those statesmen. Washington lurches from one crisis to another, rigid partisanship results in government shut-downs and gridlock, and politicians seem much more interested in getting themselves elected than in serving the public interests. The politics of ill will, confrontation, and vindictiveness abound, particularly at the national level.

But, to be fair, substantial improvements have been made in Arkansas's courts and law enforcement. For example, a completely new judicial department, largely patterned after the judicial article proposed by the 1969 Constitutional Convention, was established by Amendment 80, approved by the voters in 2001. All the limited-jurisdiction local courts (justice of the peace, mayor, police, city, and common pleas) were replaced by "district courts" established in each county. Circuit courts were combined with the former chancery courts, and they were kept as the trial courts of general jurisdiction. The Arkansas Supreme Court was vested with "superintending control" of the lower courts and circuit courts. All judges were required to be licensed attorneys and elected in nonpartisan elections. These changes amounted to a great improvement over the old hodge-podge system in effect when I started practicing law.

In the field of law enforcement, the qualifications and training of officers have also been improved, as well as the tools and systems available to them. In 1975, the legislature created the Commission on Law Enforcement Standards and Training for the purpose of "establishing minimum selection and training standards for admission to employment as a law enforcement officer in Arkansas." Rules were established that required all officers (state, county, city, and otherwise) to have at least a high school education and to receive training and certification from the Arkansas Law Enforcement Training Academy.

Also in 1975, the legislature established the Arkansas Crime Information Center (ACIC), which set up computerized information technology services for law enforcement and other criminal justice agencies in Arkansas. The ACIC collected and computerized records from the various state and local law enforcement departments and interfaced with the FBI National Crime Information Center, as well as with similar systems in the other forty-nine states.

These changes have ameliorated the abuses and conflicts of interest I had experienced during my early years of practice. Of course, although sensible laws, rules, and regulations can and do help, official abuse and corruption continue to exist.

Nationally, a spate of killings of unarmed black men by white police officers bears witness to residual racism, while the murder of nine black worshipers inside their church by an avowed white supremacist, and the subsequent burning of several black churches, indicates that racial bigotry remains on the loose.

The corrosive influence of "big money" in our politics, both at the state and federal levels, poses a great danger to the achievement of justice by the ordinary citizen. In a series of U.S. Supreme Court decisions, culminating in the *Citizens United* case in 2009, the doors were opened wide for special interest groups, such as large corporations and labor unions, to pour massive amounts of money into the electoral process. There are now no limits on the amounts of money that may be donated for electioneering. In the case of the "Super PACs," there is not even a requirement that the donors be identified. *Citizens United* held, in effect, that artificial legal entities, such as corporations, were "persons" protected by the Bill of Rights of the U.S. Constitution, and that money donated by them for electioneering was "free speech" protected by the First Amendment.

Equating these entities with the flesh-and-blood people our founding fathers sought to protect by the Bill of Rights means that voices of ordinary people have been drowned out. As Justice John Paul Stevens wrote in the minority opinion to *Citizens United*, "the unique qualities of corporations and other artificial legal entities make them dangerous to democratic elections. These legal entities have perpetual life, the ability to amass large sums of money, limited liability, no ability to vote, no morality, no purpose outside of profit-making, and no loyalty."

The distorted views of the majority in *Citizens United* and other related decisions, and the deleterious effects that flow from them, are, in my opinion, largely responsible for corruption of the political processes across the nation. Among other ills, these decisions contribute to the shrinking middle class, the "red state–blue state" divide, polarization of political ideology among the people and their representatives, paralysis in Congress and many state legislatures, and widespread disillusionment by ordinary people in elected officials' ability to govern justly.

An election paid for by special interests is not a fair election, and a bought government is not a just government. But there are some promising signs—the new generation now coming of age seems to be more open and accepting. Hopefully, they are also wiser and can steer our state and the whole republic to a better and brighter future, a future in which the transparency of vindictive and corrupt retribution will prevent a "setup" such as I experienced from happening to others.

Notes

1. "Official Seized on 'Pot' Count." *Arkansas Gazette*, August 26, 1972.

2. "Agents Arrest Glasgow." *Arkansas Democrat*, August 26, 1972.

3. Bob Stover, "'Almost Fainted,' Glasgow Says of Marijuana." *Arkansas Gazette*, August 27, 1972.

4. Roger Allan Glasgow, "Marijuana Laws: A Need for Reform." *Arkansas Law Review* 359 (1969).

5. Transcript, Interview of John Patterson, September 26, 1972. A copy is retained by the author; Transcript, Interview with Jim T. Hunter, October 4, 1972. A copy is retained by the author.

6. Sondra Gordy, "The Lost Year." *Encyclopedia of Arkansas History & Culture*, http://www.encyclopediaofarkansas.net/encyclopedia/entry-detail.aspx?entryID=737 (accessed November 4, 2015).

7. Gordy, "The Lost Year."

8. Maxine Jones, *Maxine "Call Me Madam": The Life and Times of a Hot Springs Madam*. Hot Springs, AR: Hot Air Publishing, 2008.

9. Michael Hodge, "Vapors." *Encyclopedia of Arkansas History & Culture*, http://www.encyclopediaofarkansas.net/encyclopedia/entry-detail.aspx?entryID=3998 (accessed November 4, 2015); Shirley Tomkievicz, "Owen Vincent Madden." *Encyclopedia of Arkansas*

History & Culture, http://www.encyclopediaofarkansas.net/encyclope-dia/entry-detail.aspx?entryID=1702 (accessed November 4, 2015).

10. Roy Reed, *Faubus: The Life and Times of an American Prodigal* (Fayetteville: University of Arkansas Press, 1977), 316–17.

11. Reed, *Faubus*, 319.

12. Reed, *Faubus*, 320.

13. Tom Glaze, with Ernie Dumas. *Waiting for the Cemetery Vote: The Fight to Stop Election Fraud in Arkansas* (Fayetteville: University of Arkansas Press, 2011), 59.

14. Ernest Dumas, "Arkansas Loan and Thrift." *Encyclopedia of Arkansas History & Culture*, http://www.encyclopediaofarkansas.net/ency-clopedia/entrydetail.aspx?entryID=7477 (accessed November 4, 2015).

15. John Caylor, "Inside the Dixie Mafia: Politics of Death," 2004. Insider-Magazine.com, http://insider-magazine.com/inside_the_dixie_mafia.htm (accessed November 4, 2015).

16. "Thornton Aide Resigns to Run for Prosecutor." *Arkansas Gazette*, March 20, 1972.

17. "Women's Rights Committee Polls, Rates Candidates, Roger Glasgow Gets 'Perfect' Score on Questionnaire." *Arkansas Democrat*, May 12, 1972.

18. "Glasgow Is Best for Prosecutor." Editorial, *North Little Rock Times*, May 18, 1972.

19. "Munson, Glasgow in Runoff." *Arkansas Gazette*, June 1, 1972.

20. "Brown Endorses Glasgow in Race for Prosecutor." *Arkansas Democrat*, June 4, 1972.

21. Western Union telegram, June 7, 1972, from Robert Doubleday, President of KATV to Roger Glasgow and Lee Munson. A copy is retained by the author.

22. Press release, June 8, 1972. A copy is retained by the author.

23. Dianne Gage, "Glasgow Disputes Munson's Record." *Arkansas Gazette*, June 11, 1972.

24. "Roger Glasgow Is Choice for Prosecutor." Editorial, *Arkansas Gazette*, June 12, 1972.

25. "Munson Purchased Glasgow's Cards, 2 Observers Say," *Arkansas Democrat*, June 14, 1972.

26. "Munson Gave Workers Cash, Johnston Says." *Arkansas Democrat*, June 20, 1972.

27. "Grand Jury Case." Editorial, *Arkansas Gazette*, June 24, 1972.

28. "Outrageous." Editorial, *North Little Rock Times*, June 24, 1972.

29. George Bentley, "In Reluctant Interview Munson Expresses His Ire with the News Media." *Arkansas Gazette*, August 26, 1972.

30. Tucker Steinmetz, "Unaware Marijuana in Car, Glasgow Testifies at Trial." *Arkansas Gazette*, October 17, 1972.

31. Steinmetz, "Unaware."

32. Tucker Steinmetz, "Glasgow Found Not Guilty." *Arkansas Gazette*, October 18, 1972.

33. Arlin Fields, "New Witness for Glasgow May Be Called." *Arkansas Democrat*, October 16, 1972.

34. Steinmetz, "Glasgow Found Not Guilty."

35. Arlin Fields, "Illegal Experiment." *Arkansas Democrat*, October 18, 1972.

36. Steinmetz, "Glasgow Found Not Guilty."

37. Steinmetz, "Glasgow Found Not Guilty."

38. "Triumph and Travesty in the Glasgow Case." Editorial, *Arkansas Gazette*, October 19, 1972.

39. Tucker Steinmetz, "Glasgow Has More Trouble. He Can't Get His Car Back." November 18, 1972.

40. Tucker Steinmetz and Ernest Dumas, "Glasgow Plans Fight for Car." *Arkansas Gazette*, November 20, 1972.

41. "A Bureaucrat's Hide Fit for the Wall." Editorial, *Arkansas Gazette*, October 24, 1972.

42. "On the Glasgow Case." Editorial, *Arkansas Gazette*.

43. "A Faubus Liked Our Editorial." From the People, *Arkansas Gazette*, December 3, 1972.

44. "Glasgow Seized Car Released." *Brownsville Herald*, December 29, 1972.

45. Confidential Report, Polygraph, November 30, 1972, by Powell Security Services. A copy is retained by the author.

46. "Familiar Faces at Glasgow Trial, LR policemen, Cab Driver There, But Why?" *Arkansas Democrat*, October 20, 1972.

47. George Bentley, "Little Rock Hotel Owner Witness at Trial in Jewel Robbery." *Arkansas Gazette*, June 5, 1972.

48. "Grand Jury Criticizes Role of LR Police in 1972 Killings"; "Text of Grand Jury's Report." *Arkansas Gazette*, December 13, 1977.

49. Joe Farmer, "Weeks Listed as President of Plane Flight." *Arkansas Gazette*, December 28, 1972.

50. Joe Farmer, "Tucker Delivers Report of Probe of Club, Police." *Arkansas Gazette*, December 31, 1972.

51. "Little Rock Police Chief Disputes Photos." *Arkansas Democrat*, January 4, 1973.

52. Arlin Fields, "Drug Plot Against Tucker Subject of Inquiry." *Arkansas Times*, May 2, 1975.

53. *Parkman v. Hastings, Sr., et al.*, Supreme Court of Arkansas, 259 Ark 59, 531 SW 2d 481 (1976).

54. *United States v. Hastings, et al.*, U.S. District Court, ED, WD, 447 Fed Supp 534 (1977).

55. Bill Terry, "Officials were Marked for Death," *Arkansas Times*, December 1977; September 2004, "Family Values—Mob Plan to Kill Cop Came to Light in the *Times*."

56. *Simpson v. Weeks, et al.*, 530 Fed Supp. 196 (1977).

57. Margaret Arnold, "Mayor Calls for Shift in Police Personnel." *Arkansas Democrat*, February 22, 1977.

About the Author

Roger Glasgow was raised on a small farm near Nashville, Arkansas. He attended what is now Southern Arkansas University in Magnolia and the University of Arkansas School of Law in Fayetteville. He entered private law practice in Nashville for a few years and also served as deputy prosecutor. Glasgow was elected as a delegate to the Arkansas Constitutional Convention of 1969. He then moved to Little Rock, where he was a deputy attorney general. He ran for prosecuting attorney, finishing second in a field of four. He re-entered private law practice with the Little Rock firm of Wright, Lindsey & Jennings, where he has enjoyed a successful career for more than forty years.